AUG 1 7 2016

CAPITAL OFFENSES

CAPITAL OFFENSES

Business Crime and Punishment in America's Corporate Age

Samuel W. Buell

W. W. NORTON & COMPANY

Independent Publishers Since 1923

NEW YORK • LONDON

For information about permission to reproduce selections from
this book, write to Permissions, W. W. Norton & Company, Inc.,
500 Fifth Avenue, New York, NY 10110

For information about special discounts for bulk
purchases, please contact W. W. Norton Special Sales at
specialsales@wwnorton.com or 800-233-4830

Manufacturing by RR Donnelley, North Harrisonburg
Book design by Brooke Koven
Production manager: Louise Mattarelliano

ISBN 978-0-393-24783-1

W. W. Norton & Company, Inc.
500 Fifth Avenue, New York, N.Y. 10110
www.wwnorton.com

W. W. Norton & Company Ltd.
Castle House, 75/76 Wells Street, London W1T 3QT

1 2 3 4 5 6 7 8 9 0

For George and Janet

CONTENTS

Corporation, *n.* An ingenious device for securing individual profit without individual responsibility.

—AMBROSE BIERCE,
The Devil's Dictionary (1911)

INTRODUCTION

Candice Anderson of Van Zandt County, Texas, suffered a too common modern tragedy. At the age of twenty-one, on a clear November mid-morning outside Dallas, she lost her fiancé Gene Erikson to a car crash.[1]

The grief dealt to Candice that day was compounded several times over. Candice had been at the wheel when her new 2004 Saturn Ion left the road and smashed into a tree, seriously injuring her and killing Gene, who had been riding next to her in the front passenger seat. Then the state of Texas told Candice that she was to blame for Gene's death. Prosecutors charged her with vehicular manslaughter and she was briefly jailed. Candice later agreed to plead guilty to manslaughter. A judge sentenced her to five years of probation, with hundreds of hours of required service. Candice was marked for life as the felon who killed Gene.

For ten years, Candice Anderson had to do the grueling work of accepting this as her and the state's agreed version of Gene Erikson's death. Then, in 2014, though she thought she knew all there was to know about the crash, Candice learned that the story of that November morning that her prosecution and guilty plea had told was not true.

Texas police and prosecutors, like their colleagues across America, must make discretionary judgments about which of thousands of fatal car accidents each year will produce criminal charges. In Candice's case, an officer thought Candice was acting erratically after the accident. (No wonder.) He arranged a blood test, which showed that Candice had a low amount of Xanax in her body, a medication she had taken the night before. (Research does not establish that this medicine, at ordinary levels, impairs driving without ingestion of other intoxicants.[2]) There were no skid marks at the scene, where driving conditions had been excellent that day. Therefore, the state concluded, Candice's intoxication caused the accident that killed Gene.

The truth was that Candice's car killed Gene. Not only at the moment of impact but in nearly all respects. General Motors had manufactured the 2004 Ion with a mechanical starter that engineers at the company designed to be cheap. The starter was prone to malfunction. A driver's leg knocking the key chain in the ignition could cause the starter to rotate out of the run position, which meant, for this design of car, deactivation of power steering, power brakes, and—most importantly—airbags.

Candice lost control of the car and Gene did not survive the crash because General Motors sold her a car with a dangerously bad part. Ten years after the accident, once the truth about the car was revealed, the state of Texas corrected its understanding of Gene's death and expunged Candice's criminal conviction. Candice could now start another process of healing.

It seems we should say that General Motors killed Gene Erikson. It's perfectly sensible to summarize things that way. But what happens if we try to take a next logical step and say that, to correct matters fully, the government should replace the *prosecution* of Candice for homicide with a homicide prosecution of GM? GM is a corporation. It doesn't think, it can't drive a car, and it can't even really be seen. It's an amalgam of people, factories, vehicles, images, and offices spread across the globe. GM is an idea as much as it is a thing.

Under American law, a corporation such as GM can be prosecuted. But pursuing this remedy for the crash of that Saturn Ion would raise a host of difficult, not to say interesting, questions that nobody needed to wrestle with in an ordinary criminal prosecution like the State of Texas versus Candice Anderson.

Replacing Candice with GM is replacing apples with oranges, not a small apple with a larger one. Moving from prosecution of the corporation to prosecution of its managers and employees, it turns out, does not clarify the problem of corporate responsibility for Gene Erikson's death. Everyone in a position of senior management responsibility at GM appears to have been ignorant of the engineering decisions involved in that starter switch—much less of any connection between those decisions and what ended up to be a total of over one hundred road deaths.

Even lower-level employees handling lawsuits against the company for some of the related crashes failed, for nearly nine years, to connect the accidents to the starter switch and raise the alarm with their supervisors about a systemic problem. The engineer who designed the bad switch understood, at some point, his mistake. But, even as he corrected the switch design, he covered up his error.

GM is responsible, but who within GM could be prosecuted in this fiasco, and for what crimes? There is no crime in American law of managing a corporation badly, no matter how serious the harm that results. Under regulations governing the auto industry, there isn't even a crime of manufacturing an unsafe starter switch. Maybe the engineer should be charged with killing Gene. But, as he toiled within the bowels of GM, did he realize his neglect might endanger lives?

Suppose he did. Would a prosecution of this midlevel salaried worker, even for homicide, really be a way of saying GM killed Gene and punishing the company for that? It seems as though GM's managers, with their cost-cutting strategies and their failure to make sure the left hand in the company knew what the right was doing, are most responsible as a matter of fact—whether or not by the letter of the law.

Even if the problem of the crime could be worked out—who committed it and what law he or she violated—what about the question of punishment? GM can't be put in a prison, so it's not clear what a prosecution of GM could add to the civil lawsuits for each of the driver deaths that the company will have to settle with the survivors, no doubt at steep cost. Criminal fines could increase GM's total bill for its transgressions. But how big a fine would it take to get the GMs of the world not to make these kinds of mistakes again? Would such a penalty be so large that it could put GM in dire straits, eliminating those manufacturing jobs that the government tried so hard to save when it rescued the huge auto company from the financial crisis of 2008 to 2009?

A court could place GM, like Candice Anderson, on probation. But what does that mean for a corporation? It can't physically report to the probation office, it can't be made to pee into a cup, and its required "community service" would amount to writing another check (this one to charity, I suppose). Indeed, if GM were convicted of a felony, how could the company possibly feel anything like the stigma and remorse that Candice lived with for a decade?

Could the government round up GM's senior managers and imprison them for their serious business failures? Not in the American legal system, which strictly prohibits prosecuting a person without a clear law on the books at the time of his offensive conduct. There is no crime of "bad management of a big company," not to mention no good argument for legislating such a sweeping and amorphous power to revoke liberty. The only conceivable criminal case against managers, even in theory, would be a prosecution for negligent homicide based on the long and attenuated chain running from their unawareness at GM's headquarters all the way down to the road outside Dallas that morning in November 2004.

As it turned out, GM *was* prosecuted. Not for the death of Gene Erikson but for white collar crimes related to the bad starter switch. In September 2015, federal prosecutors in New York filed charges against the company for defrauding buyers of GM cars and making false statements to federal highway safety officials. In a now common move, the prosecutors then agreed with GM to defer those charges for some years, and ultimately dismiss them if GM complies with extensive requirements, including paying a nearly $1 billion penalty and reforming its safety processes.

In making this deal, called a "deferred prosecution agreement," prosecutors likely wanted to limit unnecessary damage to GM investors and workers who bore no responsibility for the company's misconduct. Prosecutors probably also recognized vulnerability in their legal theories, given the diffusion of responsibility within the giant corporation and the absence of specific criminal offenses relating to the auto manufacturing process.

No state prosecutor has charged GM with homicide in any of the deaths attributable to the faulty design. (Federal prosecutors lack access to comprehensive statutes on homicide, a crime generally left for state jurisdiction.) It remains to be seen whether a prosecutor might seek criminal punishment for the GM engineer who covered up the design mistake. As grave as the consequences were, GM's executives assuredly will not go to prison in this case for the wrong of running the company badly.

The story of Candice Anderson, Gene Erikson, and General Motors typifies the puzzles of corporate crime. It might seem easiest to dismiss those puzzles with a simplistic comeback: this is the usual story in American criminal justice. Working people suffer the injustices while corporations and their executives get away with everything up to and including homicide. The only reason any of these questions are difficult is that the law is not what it should be. It's the job of legislators and lawyers to fix that. Go figure it out.

There is another comeback, less often heard but equally simplistic: this kind of discussion shows why criminal law has little or no place meddling in the ordinary and vital machinery of economic growth and competition. That process necessarily involves risks that sometimes produce costs and harms. But it benefits us all immeasurably and therefore, even when it sometimes goes awry, it does not deserve the special moral condemnation and often devastating consequences of criminal sanctions.

THIS BOOK IS an effort to show why these facile responses to the puzzles of crime in corporate America are wrong, in ways that should persuade all Americans that corporate crime—and its treatment under law—is our own difficult but no less urgent business.

Law is an instrument, not an ideology. Americans don't need to understand the nuances of law for its own sake, any more than one needs to know the particulars of how the surgeon will go about taking out one's inflamed appendix. If it hurts, take it out; if he's the bad guy, put him in prison.

One can certainly write about business crime without writing about the law. The many recent books about the subject, at least those written for general audiences, have been stories about people, companies, and industries. I like reading the work of Michael Lewis, Kurt Eichenwald, Andrew Ross Sorkin, Bethany McLean, and their peers as much as, probably more than, the next person. I even enjoy the gonzo business journalism of *Rolling Stone*'s Matt Taibbi.

But this work has left a deficit. In the case of business crime, law provides a window into a subject of great social and economic import. Failing to examine closely what law is doing in this field has limited Americans' understanding of the place business crime occupies in the American relationship with corporations and capitalism. That gap isn't just a problem for how prosecutors and courts deal with cases of white collar crime. I believe, and will endeavor to convince you, that the gap has become a barrier to making progress on the project of managing our affairs in what is, like it or not, our corporate age.

For the last twenty years or so (really since the Gordon Gecko, hostile takeover, junk bond days of the 1980s) Americans have been deeply troubled and increasingly angry about the problem of crime in big business. Of course, our worries about bad behavior in the big corporation go back to the late nineteenth century, when the American story first became dominated by the "lives" of the nonhuman entities that are giant firms.[3] We have those worries to thank for (among other things) food and drug safety laws, antitrust regulation, worker rights, environmental protection laws, Teddy and Franklin Roosevelt, securities laws, secure bank deposits, and a novelty the French felt compelled to call *le weekend*.

But only in the last couple of decades has criminal law taken center stage in the drama of the American corporation. We've now spent over twenty years careening from scandal to outrage to scandal—many of them entertaining stories that have produced delightful books and movies—without deep thought about what's really going on in this drama.

This book hopes to fill that need. It's principally a book of ideas. It is also a study of a distinctive and gripping genre of American narrative. That means we'll have plenty of good stories to prevent any intellectual mustiness from gathering in the pages that follow.

INTEREST IN THIS subject, as often happens with professional lives, came to me both accidentally and inevitably. Belonging to the generation of gappers between Boom and X, I count as a first TV memory seeing Neil Armstrong step onto the moon. A precocious interest in public affairs was sparked a few years later when I was transfixed by that long summer of the Watergate hearings, looking at John Dean's glasses and those felt tables as I sat in our living room next to my Nixon-despising father. Something about those events sparked in me a fascination with the grand project of American governance and the idea of holding powerful people accountable.

Eventually I carried that fixation with public life, like a lot of Americans, to law school. After gaining admission to the bar, I learned to use the federal RICO law to prosecute gang homicides in New York City at a time when murders were epidemic there—seven times New York's more recent rates. That experience paid dividends when I moved to Boston and found myself charged with reinvigorating the investigation of James "Whitey" Bulger's criminal gang—work that led us to a marsh under an MBTA bridge in Quincy, where I watched state police and forensic anthropologists (who knew such a thing existed?) literally dig up the bodies.

Then one evening in January 2002, in a freezing commuter parking lot, I took a call from an old mentor in New York. The Justice Department, she told me, had handed her the investigation into Houston's Enron Corporation. Come do this with me, she said. I was aware there was some sort of accounting scandal around the company's collapse. The lawyer on the phone was the one I most admired and could least easily turn down. My luck included having an exceptionally strong spouse who said go, this is the opportunity of a lifetime. So off I went, into the Enron case.

I had long hoped to go from prosecution to academia, not to corporate and defense practice. But it was my time working on Enron, the business crime case of the century and maybe of all time, that showed me clearly what to teach and write about. In the subject of corporate crime, I found a great American story—at the intersection of politics, law, and economics—that was full of challenging intellectual problems.

This story has never been more pressing or more in need of deep, sustained study. It's a great fortune to have reached the point in my own work and thinking where I can hope to put this story together for the general reader.

A QUICK NOTE about terminology is necessary, in spite of the tedium of such notes. This book is about a field that consists of several categories of crime that overlap but are not coterminous.

"White collar crime" is, by the most common and least precise of several possible definitions, all crime committed for financial purposes and by financial means. "Business crime" is white collar crime committed in the operation of otherwise lawful commercial enterprises. "Corporate crime" is, by one definition, crime *by* corporations themselves. I prefer using the term "corporate crime" to designate the category of all business crimes committed *within the context* of corporations and other large firms. That, after all, is the thing that has so troubled Americans of late. And, as we'll see, corporations can only commit crimes through their people.

This book is mostly about corporate crime. But common understandings, as well as avoidance of deadly prose, counsel me to use all the definitional terms in their overlapping meanings. The reader will have no extra work to do if I'm clear, regardless of my choice of terminology, about the kind of crime—committed where and by whom—I'm describing. The expert literature debates these terms and the definitional problem in general. I have no ambition to solve that problem here.

LAST, FOR READERS who like to know where they are going, here is a rough map. The first chapter states the questions of American public life raised by the subject of corporate crime and argues why those questions matter. The next two chapters deal with how American law defines white collar crimes—that is, where and why the law draws lines between business as usual and conduct that deserves prison. Chapter four explores the perennially interesting and challenging question of why we make criminals of corporations themselves and whether we accomplish anything in doing so.

Chapters five and six deal with the work of the investigators, prosecutors, and defense lawyers who toil in the institutions of justice charged with policing corporate behavior—the machinery of criminal enforcement in the business world. Chapter seven discusses the problem of how to punish convicted business criminals and also, therefore, how the work of American judges relates to corporate crime.

Chapter eight concludes the book with two matters of wider context. The first is whether the territory this book charts is just a realm of politics—specifically Washington politics—all the way down. It's not, but the claim is an important one. The second matter is how American law and public discourse might more deeply, and with lasting success, engage with the problem of our relationship to the modern business firm.

THE JOURNEY THAT follows will, I hope, position the reader to think and talk more productively about corporate and business crime in America today. I hope it also helps readers to see more clearly and concretely what they want to argue for in the way of change in American law and the private and public institutions that make up our markets and economy.

American public life is, in large part, lived through law. That's why I became a lawyer, like so many of my contemporaries including most of the men and women who have staffed the government since I graduated from college. And that's why a nonfiction story about law like the one this book tells should get and keep the attention of all Americans. Or so I hope.

CAPITAL
OFFENSES

1

America and
Business Crime

T HE STORY OF Candice Anderson, Gene Erikson, and General
Motors led to two simple questions. What was the crime? And who
should be punished? As in many cases of crime in corporations, these
elemental questions proved hard to answer.

On a first pass, the difficulty in the questions comes from legal
rules. There wasn't a crime on the books to deal with the sloppy manu-
facture of an important auto part, nor was there a crime of dangerously
managing a consumer products corporation. The crime of negligent
homicide, at least under normal theories of prosecution, didn't fit well
as analysis traveled up the chain of responsibility and away from the
time and place of the victim's death. Corporate criminal liability—
prosecution of the company—is, as we'll see, derivative of individual
criminal guilt. And it has unsatisfying features, not least that it cannot
lead to imprisonment.

These, and the other big problems of law in corporate crime, will
merit close examination. For the most part, though, law is not the reason that the elemental questions in a case like Candice Anderson's are

perplexing. Law is a reflection of reasons we must find and consider in realms outside of law. With American business, deciding just what constitutes a crime, who (or what) might have committed that crime, and what the consequences should be is hard because of the position we have given corporations and their activities in our social and economic order.

As harnessing corporations and capital markets has become a more complex and difficult task, criminal law has not become less important in that sphere. Corporate crime is booming—many believe in its prevalence; all would agree in its prominence in public discourse and the practice of law. But while the field of business crime has come of age, criminal law seems capable of delivering less in the economic sector (not to mention other quarters of American life) at the same time it is being asked to deliver more.

The leading topic of popular conversation in America about the financial crisis of 2008 to 2009—the most serious economic calamity since the 1930s—has been a paucity of criminal prosecutions. The primary public complaint, or at least question, has been why the criminal law and its government agents have not done more for the American people.[1] Law and legal institutions, on this line of thinking, have suffered from a failure of at least ambition and perhaps also competence.

The ambition deficit is deeper than believed. The focus on criminal law has diverted our gaze, leaving larger and more pressing questions unaddressed. The alleged shortcomings of criminal law and criminal justice in the realm of American corporations and markets are symptoms of a struggle to understand problems increasingly out of our control. They are not the problem itself but evidence for it.

Most criminal law is built around concerns that transcend diverse contexts, like our rights to bodily integrity and the security of our possessions. The field of business crime is mostly about a single social institution: the business firm, most often the publicly traded corporation, and the markets built around that institution. The firm is the sine qua non of modern capital enterprise. It is, along with constitutional government, the defining institution of American society as it has developed over the last two centuries.[2]

Perhaps more than ever, Americans are ambivalent about capital enterprise and the modern company. Our lives are organized around a conflict between needing to make a living and care for ourselves—for which almost all of us depend directly or indirectly on large businesses—and encountering the constraints and harms that are the products of capital enterprise, from real estate crashes to global warming to unaffordable health care to, not least of course, deep and persistent inequality.[3] Almost none of us lives off of the corporate grid.

The aftermath of the recent financial crisis was a bitter reminder of this resented American dependence on the large corporation. The overriding imperative was to avoid outright depression by saving the vital markets placed at risk by habits and practices of the corporate sector—which required saving the corporations themselves, or at least many of them. The arsonists were pulled from the flaming wreckage and rushed straight to the best hospitals. Government officials, the press, and the public quickly turned back to watching the Dow and the S&P 500 as indicators of recovery—of the U.S. economy and, almost as importantly, the retirement and college accounts that prudent savers now must maintain. The unemployment rate remained the most urgent number. But that too depended on the readiness of large companies to start hiring again.

The sources of ambivalence about the large corporation, and the people who manage it, are more deeply rooted than even the fundamentals of macroeconomics. Americans, to put it mildly, have long given wealth a leading place in the national psychology. In *America in Our Time*, his sweeping account of American society from World War II to Nixon, the English writer Godfrey Hodgson said, "Working-class Americans don't hate the rich; they envy them. They don't want to take their money away from them; they just want to have as much themselves. . . . Looking at a Rockefeller or a Sinatra, the ordinary American is looking at a big winner in the lottery in which he also believes he owns a ticket."[4] Today, perhaps we would substitute Gates and Adele (or, alas, Trump and Britney) for Hodgson's Rockefeller and Sinatra.

Nothing provokes Americans' mixed emotions about wealth more than the subject of corporate crime. There will be much more to say about this, especially when we get to the topic of prison sentences. Consider for the moment one recurring event in American business crime: the "perp walk." In white collar crime cases, federal agents and prosecutors often insist that the accused be handcuffed and led into the FBI's offices or the courthouse in public view, even though there is rarely serious risk of flight and the arrested person usually has been in regular contact with the authorities through counsel, including about the timing of his own arrest.

It's staged. People want to see the business criminal treated the same as the street offender. And probably there is an ample dose of raw schadenfreude. Western Europeans consider the practice of parading shackled people in front of cameras to be offensive. Many will recall the white sheets held up by hotel personnel in Zurich in May 2015, as the defendants in the FIFA prosecutions were led to waiting police vehicles. Americans have a very different sort of view. We venerate great financial success and we also need, it seems, to see those on high brought low.

To begin to see how the material and psychological connections between Americans and corporate America explain the difficulties of corporate crime, let's take a first pass at those two seemingly simple problems: identifying the crime and the person (or thing) to be punished.

What Was the Crime?

FOR CENTURIES, judges and scholars writing about criminal law have used an idea to distinguish crimes that are basic moral wrongs—no matter what the law has to say about them—from crimes that would not be considered wrongs if the law did not make them so. Crimes like murder and arson would be examples of the former. A crime like catching and keeping undersized fish would be an example of the latter. As with many old ideas in Anglo-American law, this one comes from a pair of Latin terms that law students are made to learn: *malum in se* (wrong in itself) and *malum prohibitum* (wrong because prohibited).[5]

The standard picture of American criminal law is that it is both broad and deep.[6] It criminalizes all of the *in se* stuff, often in many different ways, and then it goes on to criminalize lots more things on a *prohibitum* basis. The usual question that critics pose these days is whether American law ought to criminalize a great deal less in the *prohibitum* category, especially when it comes to business activity and the thousands of rules of the federal "regulatory state."[7]

This picture of American criminal law does not neatly align with the problem of crime in corporations. Lots of things that look, in hindsight, to have been wrong in a really serious way—greedy, selfish, callous, dangerous, and harmful things—are not illegal at all. With white collar crime, one could say, not all the *in se* stuff is even *prohibitum*. While it might be true that the modern state criminalizes a lot of things that aren't seriously wrongful, it's also true that modern law *does not* permit prosecution of some things that *are* quite wrong.

This gap in the law of white collar crime is explained by the context in which this part of law operates: capital markets and corporations. Over the past two centuries, we've constructed that context for reasons of economics and politics that are more fundamental than the question of what behaviors criminal law should control. How do we want this or that market to function, like the market for securities or the market for health care services? Those are the sorts of big, hard questions that have to be answered before we can ask which securities deals or hospital billing practices should be treated as criminal fraud.

Far more often than we might want to think, criminality in America's corporations and financial industries turns on fine and difficult-to-specify lines between legitimate business and the wrongs of cheating, deception, and falsehood—in all their diverse and evolving forms. Policing these activities, and these sectors of our collective social enterprise, involves an agenda of profound conflict: to guarantee, at once, both the flourishing and the control of risk taking, aggression, creative destruction, and growth in the most evolved capitalist economic system in history.

Consider a hypothetical example, one with familiar features. Think about two sales jobs that many people in America would want to call frauds—the serious kind, for which businesspeople can go to federal prison. In the first, the seller—let's call him Lloyd— is a trader for a big New York bank, circa 2006. Lloyd has the job of selling those "mortgage-backed securities" (MBS) that became widely known only after the economic crisis that shortly followed.

These securities are called "derivatives" in the trade because, through complex financing that doesn't much matter for our purposes, their value is linked to (derives from) mortgage loans made to American homebuyers. For several years, Lloyd has been selling lots of derivatives that place the purchasers of them "long" (meaning betting that the price will go up) on other securities consisting of pools of home loans. It's in the nature of these derivative securities that if American housing prices don't fall substantially on a nationwide basis, the buyer who is long will earn a steady positive return on his investment.

Throughout 2006, Lloyd keeps selling these long positions to Angela, a trader at a big German bank. Lloyd is only too happy to feed Angela's appetite for these deals. He encourages her every day by telling her what a great price he's able to offer her and reminding her how much her bank has earned from these products over the last several years. Lloyd knows that the pools to which these derivative securities are linked are full of aggressive subprime loans: mortgages extended to buyers who are stretched to, or beyond, their financial limits and who will be forced into default if the market values of their homes decline or even flatten. Angela knows that too, or at least would see it if she examined the documents she's entitled to inspect.

Lloyd also knows that, on a different floor of its Manhattan office tower, his bank has begun to take large and growing "short" positions (bets that prices will go down) on the American housing market, by purchasing "credit default swaps." These securities act like insurance policies against large drops in the value of those mortgage-backed securities that contain the pools of risky home loans. Economists and managers at Lloyd's and Angela's banks—not to mention lay observers of the American economy—know that the American housing market is in a bubble. Prices are inflated and are at risk of a precipitous fall, sooner or later. The brains at Lloyd's bank think sooner, those at Angela's are betting a bit later.

Lloyd's bank is right. Throughout 2007 and into 2008, housing prices drop fast nationally, leading to massive homeowner defaults, especially on subprime loans. These defaults, of course, cause the prices of securities long on home loans to tumble. Lloyd's bank makes out okay because, while it owns lots of mortgage-backed securities that drop in value, it also purchased lots of those swaps (insurance) that pay off when those securities fall in price. Angela's bank did not similarly hedge its exposure to the American housing market. Angela's trading book is virtually wiped out and her bank suffers dearly. So do huge numbers of individual investors in Europe and the United States who have retirement and other portfolios that include equities in Angela's bank and other European financial institutions.

Those investors quickly make a lengthy list of targets for their plentiful anger. Lloyd's bank, for escaping from a conflagration of its own making. Lloyd, for continuing to spread all that derivative fuel around when he knew others at his bank expected the lit match of a housing crash to be thrown at any moment. Angela, for funding Lloyd's dangerous behavior without bothering to smell the gasoline. Angela's bank, for not stopping her, or at least buying its own fire insurance when other smart people were. The managers of the investors' own accounts, for investing in Angela's imprudent bank. The insurance companies, for making it easier for Lloyd to throw gas around by selling fire policies. The credit rating agencies, for giving Lloyd's securities AAA ratings without carefully inspecting them. And the United States government for, well, letting it all happen.

Almost as soon as the investors who were burned by the financial crisis, and the millions of others injured from their proximity to the fire and its offshoots, had parceled out their anger, they started asking a question that Americans haven't stopped asking since: why are none of these people in jail?

We'll come back to that in a moment. First consider a second kind of deal. This one was described in the following article as having produced some major arrests:

SAN FRANCISCO—In coordinated raids Monday at locations in Delaware, South Dakota, and California, federal agents apprehended dozens of executives at Visa Inc., a sham corporation accused of perpetrating the largest credit card scam in U.S. history.

According to indictments filed in U.S. District Court, Visa posed as a reputable lender, working through banks to peddle a variety of convincing-looking credit cards carefully designed to dupe consumers into spending far more money than they had. The criminal group would then impose a succession of escalating fees on unpaid balances, allegedly bilking some $300 billion from victims in the past year alone.

"This is criminal behavior of the most vile sort," Attorney General Eric Holder said in a press conference following the arrests, estimating that one in three Americans have fallen for the scam since its inception in the 1970s. "By masquerading as a legitimate business, this illicit syndicate was able to prey on helpless citizens for decades, charging unfathomable interest rates on the order of 15, 20, even 30 percent or more. It's staggering. Nobody could afford that."

Calling the scam's breadth and sophistication "unparalleled," Holder said the ringleaders of the plot carefully portrayed themselves as top-level financial executives, spent untold sums of victims' money on a luxurious high-rise headquarters in San Francisco, and employed scores of graduates from elite business schools—all as a means to perpetuate an elaborate confidence game.

Investigators said Visa often targeted vulnerable individuals, such as those with limited financial resources, students, and even the elderly. The group's typical con involved direct solicitation through letters supposedly written by the CEO himself, which often praised the recipients by name and stated that they had been hand-selected for favored treatment.[8]

The punch line, of course, is that this article appeared several years ago at the *Onion*, the satirical news site. No prosecutor has charged that Visa is a fraud. But why not? Satire, after all, only works when it closely approximates the truth.

While one is total fiction and the other is close to true history, the cases of the Visa joke and the failed market in mortgage-backed securities are not as different as they might seem. In both cases, ravenous big business screwed the little guy, and damaged the American economy along the way. Both involve deception, at least in broad terms. Lloyd's bank knew that Angela's bank, and its many small investors, would suffer when the bubble burst. Visa knew that uninformed card applicants could not understand the consequences of the escalating, practically usurious interest rates that they would not be able to resist triggering.

An easy response here is to say that the sellers in both cases *should* be in prison. Making them pay with their personal liberty, as America does for the workaday drug dealer, is the only way to get the people who run the powerful institutions of business to stop playing roulette with Main Street's money and the American economy. If these people are not in prison it can only be because the American criminal justice system—and the politics that govern it—are rigged to protect the wealthy and punish the poor.

For the *Onion*'s satire to be funny, though, it has to be both close to the truth and obviously *not* true. At least on the facts provided here, American law did not authorize imprisonment of the managers of Lloyd's bank or Visa.[9] It could not, nor should it, have been expected to do so.

Business crime in America is all about context. It's how we distinguish the entrepreneur from the predator. Visa was not a crime because consumer credit regulations let banks charge those interest rates. Advertising rules (and subsidized postal service!) allowed Visa to cram its lending products down hungry consumers' throats. And Americans thought people ought to know better than to use money they would never have to buy things they could never afford. Anger at the avarice of salespeople, especially after the fact, does not justify sending them to prison for getting people to buy dumb, risky financial products that the government allowed on the market. If *caveat emptor* (buyer beware) ends up fairly summarizing our attitude toward the business of selling credit cards to consumers, the idea applies only more to experienced bankers buying each other's baroque and speculative securities.

This is not to say that the seller of credit cards or mortgage derivatives, or of any other product or deal in our massive and complex economy, can't commit fraud if he lies to or cheats his buyer. At least with most of America's problems of business crime, however, the crime (meaning what *is* a crime under American law) lies not in the entire market itself, which is usually both legal and encouraged, but in whether a seller in that market played by the rules—rules that often depend, as they must, on what sort of a market it is. Contrary to popular belief, Enron's executives did not go to prison for their inarguable greed and fecklessness in having built a mirage of a company. They went to prison for crossing some lines. For the most part, the bankers of 2006 to 2008 are not in prison because they didn't cross the lines, or at least can't be proven to have done so.

The ancient human idea of crime is about deviance—deviance from social baselines that change and are contingent on contemporary arrangements and values. These days we've given the large business firm and capital markets such primacy in our economic and social order that it's almost impossible to treat those who operate those institutions as ordinary subjects of criminalization—as deviants. We end up in an unsteady state. Law crosses back and forth over a shifting boundary between what is welcome, or even celebrated, and what is forbidden or condemned. This unsatisfying state of legal affairs is not the product of corruption, or lack of nerve, or special justice for the rich, or even, if you see things from another perspective, the demonization of business. It results from an enduring American ambivalence.

Consider Steve Jobs, the legendary founder of Apple. Was Jobs a criminal? Not in the colloquial sense that Americans often speak of such things. He built a product line, and a company, that defined success for the millennial age, in both business and aesthetics. Legally speaking, however, Jobs probably was a criminal—or at least could have been treated as one. He participated in backdating stock options compensation at Apple, including his own, to inflate the options' value and arguably work a fraud on Apple's investors. More flagrantly, he defied antitrust laws by agreeing with Silicon Valley competitors, including Google, not to compete for each other's engineering talent.[10]

The suggestion that Jobs should have been hauled away from Apple and locked in a prison would strike most people as absurd. The world sees Apple, relative to many of the twenty-first century's biggest corporations, as having done a lot more good than harm for the public welfare. If Jobs broke the law, he did so with that driven mind of the innovator that sees rules and structures as there to be broken. He can be forgiven, perhaps, for thinking the law didn't apply to him—that the ends of Apple's innovations justified the means of sometimes stepping over legal lines.

Richard Fuld, the top executive of Lehman Brothers when it went under in the financial crisis, presents a different case. He and his peers at the helms of the big banks seem to have believed that the law—or at least the ordinary economic laws of business failure—didn't apply to them. Unforgivable. And it's inexplicable for many that Fuld did not land in prison, especially given the opulent redecoration of his executive suite at Lehman just as the firm was collapsing into dust. (Apple's offices, on the other hand, are seen as a vision of what the greatness of American engineering makes possible.) Fuld, unlike Jobs, may not have been on the record as having violated the law. But he was unapologetically in charge of what became a national outrage.

Fuld's case is the one that produced my own epiphany about the financial crisis. It came one morning in the spring of 2010 when I opened a pdf file as I surfed the day's business news. That file, a painfully boring looking legal document, was called "Report of Anton R. Valukas, Examiner."[11] It had been filed with the U.S. Bankruptcy Court in Manhattan in a case called *Lehman Brothers Holdings Inc., et al., No. 08-13555 (JMP)*. The document that grabbed my attention was the third "volume" of that more than two-thousand-page pdf, where the report discussed something designated Repo 105, one of those tedious Wall Street deal names. The authors of this report were lawyers at a big New York firm tasked to conduct a financial autopsy of Lehman Brothers by the court overseeing the company's bankruptcy.

Lehman, as we know now, was a much shakier bank than most of the world thought shortly before the firm entered a death spiral that the government's economic chieftains allowed to spin on to bankruptcy, some believe to the lasting detriment of the entire economy. Repo 105 was perhaps the main reason Lehman looked stronger than it was. It was a clever deal structure that Lehman used increasingly and addictively, eventually to the sum of over $100 billion, as the company's mortgage-backed securities books lost value while the air went out of the U.S. housing market.

Repo 105 allowed Lehman to borrow lots more money, yet, in a bit of accounting alchemy, to record that borrowing on its books as operating income from sales. (One executive described these deals in an e-mail as "another drug we r on"; another manager called them "window dressing . . . based on legal technicalities.") The quite intentional result, indeed the only point of using this deal device, was that Lehman's financial reports greatly understated the true leverage ratio of the firm: total borrowing to total assets held, the critical metric for the health of a financial institution.

Nearly ten years earlier, Enron, the company that may forever be the archetype for corporate accounting games, had done the same thing. In the couple of years leading up to Enron's bankruptcy, the company had churned over $5 billion in a kind of deal with its largest creditors, Wall Street banks Chase and Citi, called a "prepaid forward."[12]

These circular deals were complicated on paper but simple in conception. Enron was a major player in the energy trading business. As an energy trader, it held contracts for futures positions it had bought from other traders in commodities like gas and electricity. In the prepaid forwards, Enron sold those futures contracts to the banks and then later bought the contracts back from the banks at a premium—in the same amount that Enron would have paid in interest had these deals instead been loans from the banks. (Chase and Citi weren't exactly energy trading houses.) The prepaid forwards allowed Enron to borrow much more money from its biggest creditors but treat that extra cash as "operating income" on its financial statements. Thus Enron could present itself to investors as less indebted, and less risky, than it infamously turned out to have been when it was suddenly forced into bankruptcy in December 2001.

My epiphany reading the Lehman report that morning in 2010 arrived in two stages. Stage one: They went and did it again. Exactly the same way. But this time they left not just their shareholders but all of us holding the bag. The unprecedented vanishing of America's seventh largest company in 2001, the severe prosecutions with long prison terms, the bitter congressional hearings, the regulatory reforms—none of it did anything to stop this. Enron was only a single canary in the cavernous coal mine of America's financial markets. From the bird's death nobody had learned a thing.

Stage two, following a moment of reflection: Of course they did it again. Because it was perfectly legal. Or at least not criminal. No one who was managing Lehman Brothers is going to land in prison for this financial subterfuge. Just like no one at Enron went to prison for the prepaid forward deals with Citi and Chase. Enron's $5 billion in circular deals with the banks was a big part of the company's bankruptcy. But those deals never made it into the criminal case because they weren't criminal fraud. So too with Lehman Brothers. Even if Fuld, the man at the helm of the signature company of the banking crisis, knew about Repo 105, he won't be prosecuted for it.

With Lehman's Repo 105 and Enron's prepaid forward deals, the financial engineers at each company designed a mechanism for borrowing money without having to call it debt, using accounting and legal rules as a guide. They built something dangerous and ultimately destructive but arguably legal. Those engineers then went to some of the world's most reputable law and accounting firms and asked for a plausible, even if not socially responsible, opinion: It's your business (and indeed moral) choice whether you want to do this but the law and accounting rules, as we read them, don't say you can't.

The careful construction of these deals on the knife-edge of regulations, and the blessing of legal and accounting experts, made it nearly impossible to prosecute Lehman and Enron executives for conceiving and implementing them. Conviction for a serious crime requires, almost always, proof of some form of criminal intent. In the complicated arena of financing the activities of large corporations, in which our economic system has deliberately licensed creativity and risk taking, an executive's claim that he believed in good faith that he was following the rules presents a severe, even disabling, obstacle to prosecution.[13]

Imagine the testimony: "I'm not a lawyer or an accountant. I have a huge amount on my plate. My job is to make the important business calls that in my judgment, whether I turn out to be right or wrong, will maximize profits for our shareholders. I tell my people to hire the best experts to make sure we are going as far as allowed, but not an inch farther, under the rules. I was told that's exactly what we did with these deals." In a situation like Enron's prepaid forwards or Lehman's Repo 105, that sort of assertion is either honest or it can't be proved to be disingenuous in a court of law.

Prosecutors think like any trial lawyer. They calculate whether to bring a case by forecasting how it will play with judge and jury. If there is little chance of proving criminal intent beyond a reasonable doubt, the case doesn't get charged. Indeed, it would be irresponsible and unethical to do so.[14]

This isn't criminal law's fault. The criminal laws that apply in this context could hardly be more capacious or less technical, especially when compared to those of many other advanced democracies. They authorize committing a person to federal custody for up to twenty years per transaction for engaging in any "scheme to defraud."[15] Period. That's what sent Bernard Madoff away for, on paper anyway, 150 years; Enron's Jeffrey Skilling for over twenty years (later reduced to fourteen); and, back in the day, Drexel Burnham Lambert's Michael Milken for two years (down from an original three to ten).

Because the criminal laws in this area are so potentially far-reaching—and, more importantly, because sophisticated commercial activity in American markets involves great novelty and risk—the requirement of criminal intent bears enormous weight, as it should. Only proof of an executive's intent to defraud investors or the public can separate the criminal deal from the merely aggressive, or even stupidly aggressive, one.

As we'll explore, that sort of intent—the kind that can justify locking someone up for a decade or more—requires, at some point in the analysis, the conclusion that the executive knew what he was doing was wrong. This warrants emphasis. It means more than that a deal *was* wrong. It means that it was *known to be wrong* at the time the executive chose to do it.[16] (A different group of accountants opined, after the bankruptcy, that Lehman's Repo 105 actually did *not* work under the financial reporting rules.)

This reflects a simple, foundational principle of the American system of law and government, and those of all modern liberal democracies: citizens must not be imprisoned unless they have chosen to do serious wrong.[17] As the great legal theorist H. L. A. Hart argued in the 1950s, each of us must be able to go about our life knowing and therefore choosing when we are violating society's most solemn edicts.[18] The hapless dope peddler on the street may not belong in prison because drug laws are part of a misguided social policy. But, given largely clear and pervasive American drug laws, even he knows he can be locked up at any moment. This idea, deeply rooted in what is loosely called Western philosophy, is a building block of our political order, one that we neither could nor would want to abandon. Ignorance of the law is almost never a defense, of course. But innocence of deliberate wrongdoing is.

Placing the modern phenomenon of America's capital markets and corporate economy on top of that bedrock principle of liberty severely strains the capacity of criminal law. Legal scholars have long understood, and sometimes passionately argued, this hardly novel point: criminal law's role in the economic sphere, however important, is necessarily a limited one.[19] But neither the public nor experts have fully appreciated this point's many implications for the contemporary problem of business crime.

Who (or What) Should Be Punished?

NOW LET'S take a first look at the second basic question: punishment. In almost every major corporate scandal, there is plenty of blame to go around. The people involved, the corporate institutions in which they worked, and the relative positions of those people in those institutions—as well as their respective roles in what went wrong—seem to offer an array of candidates for punishment.

But when that blame comes to the legal system, and must be channeled through law, obstacles and puzzles appear. In many cases, as the various candidates are considered, each seems an unsatisfying if not unavailable end point for imposing legal blame. As we saw in the case of Candice Anderson, Gene Erikson, and GM, the persons most directly connected to the wrongdoing are not the same as those who, all things considered, bear the most responsibility for it. The criminal law, for arguably good reasons, lacks mechanisms for individually punishing those highest in the chain of responsibility. And punishing the corporation is not a satisfying substitute for individual punishment. As with problems in identifying the crime, only superficially are these problems of punishment due to law.

The history of the corporation in the United States reveals the essential mission of the modern firm: to reduce responsibility. That's not a byproduct or regrettable cost of organizing our economic lives around the corporation. It's the purpose of doing so. The corporation, together with the other major forms of the business firm, was designed to overcome a problem that had slowed industrial society. People lacked efficient and effective means to share capital while controlling and managing personal risks.[20]

The corporation solved this problem. This device created by law offered people a mechanism to limit their personal liability, if things went poorly in a project, to only what they invested in the venture, not everything they had: ten dollars in, never more than ten dollars out. The legal principle of "limited liability" removed fear of many debtors' nightmares from the decision to go into business. The corporate form also allowed people to share limited capital for specific purposes without exposure to each other's other debts, risks, and mistakes—exposure one might bear in a familial, partner, or other noncorporate relationship.[21] By design, the firm made it easier for people to engage in joint economic pursuits without shouldering unlimited responsibility for the consequences of their own and others' actions.

This move—an idea about social organization that came to life when first enshrined in law—helped spark a century and a half of explosive growth. The genius institution of the American corporation proved so successful that it grew to a scale beyond imagination. Capital is the fuel of the modern industrial economy and the corporation is how that fuel is distributed.

The growth in the size of the corporation made the corporate institution even more effective at limiting, or at least diffusing, individual responsibility. So did the speed and ease with which large business firms could change hands, once the economy developed a market for buying and selling whole corporations. This evolved, in less than a century, into the busy modern market for mergers and acquisitions (M&A) with its big, fast-moving deals and frequent turnover in management suites.

Humans have long organized themselves into collective institutions to accomplish complicated tasks, especially commerce. Economists have understood for decades that some form of the modern company is a natural development regardless of legal structures.[22] Great efficiencies result from assembling, monitoring, and managing workers in systems of "team production." To some extent, the phenomenon of the large economic enterprise—and the problems that come from activities organized bureaucratically and in large groups—would be a fact of modern life, even if the legal idea of the corporation had not become the dominant organizing principle for large institutions of production.

But the huge supplies of capital in modern legal systems, especially due to the availability of limited liability, have greatly leveraged the human tendency for teamwork. Philosophies of regulation—particularly in matters of competition law governing, for example, intellectual property and monopolization—have set the boundaries and rules of markets, further propelling the growth of economic enterprises. Under American law, the modern corporation is an invention that has, to say the least, scaled up.

Just after the sudden bankruptcy of Enron, Jeffrey Skilling, the Houston company's former CEO, decided to discard his privilege against self-incrimination and defiantly testify before both Congress and the U.S. Securities and Exchange Commission. Skilling wanted to tell regulators and the public that Enron's failure had been caused not by crimes but by a "run on the bank." (This was a non sequitur; many things can cause investors to break into a run, fraud included.) In a memorable line, while explaining how Enron figured out a way to turn natural gas assets into securities, Skilling testified, "Texas was founded by people running away from the debt collector."[23]

It should be no surprise that, two hundred years or so after the law's abandonment of state punishment for unpaid debts (debtors' prison) and the emergence of the modern business firm, a dominant subject of conversation about the American corporation is the problem of crime. The business firm was invented to reduce individual responsibility. Criminal law is society's most potent tool for imposing responsibility.

Corporations are not people. But they can act and function only through people. Without understanding the behavior of people *in* corporations, there can be no addressing questions of what corporations do and don't do. All human behaviors, at least in modern societies, cannot be fully understood without grasping the institutional context of those behaviors. In a corporation, the relationship between the individual and the institution is especially critical to understanding why people do what they do.

Anyone who has taken a college course in psychology is familiar with one of the important discoveries of twentieth-century social science: people are wired to understand and explain each other's behavior with reference to character and disposition (she ran from the police, so she must not be law-abiding) rather than context and situation (if she ran from the police, maybe the police have a pattern of wrongful arrests in this area). This is a common mistake. Situation generally has far more influence over people's behavior than do their prior tendencies.[24] But the habit of human observers is to interpret what they see the other way around.

This cognitive flaw, called the fundamental attribution error, has been illustrated in dozens of experiments, including a famous series on the Princeton University campus in the early 1970s.[25] In that project, students, including some enrolled in Princeton's seminary, had to walk a route to a meeting across campus, along which they passed by a man lying in a doorway who needed help. The seminary students were no more likely to stop and help him than were the other students. Among the seminary students, the depth of or explanation for a student's professed religious commitments bore little relation to the likelihood that the student would stop. The only thing that really mattered was whether the experimenters told the student before the stroll, per the study design, that he was late for the meeting or instead had plenty of time to get there. Situation influenced behavior more than disposition.

The experiment then went on to illustrate the fundamental attribution error. Subjects placed in the role of observers consistently predicted the wrong outcomes. They kept expecting that the seminary students would be more likely than other students to stop and help the man in the doorway and that, among the seminarians, the ones who expressed deeper and more genuine religious commitments would be more likely to stop. Observers stuck to this forecasting method even when they knew which students sent on the walk had been given greater time constraints. They were determined that altruism would depend on the question of a giving versus a selfish person, not on what might be happening to that person at the particular time and place.

Social psychologists have argued about possible explanations for the strength of the fundamental attribution error. The simplest explanation is salience. We see people, who have names and faces. We don't see situations nearly as well. Sometimes, as when legal and other institutions are involved, situations are practically invisible and we don't see them at all. Social and environmental conditions that influenced the evolution of the human brain may partly explain why visibility still dominates our causal perceptions even when we know about, and are reminded to watch out for, the fundamental attribution error. (In one study, even social psychologists gathered at a national conference exhibited the fundamental attribution error![26])

Misunderstandings about the causes of individual behavior are likely prevalent in how public observers interpret the outcomes of corporate activity. Corporations and financial markets are ever present in our lives. But they're not quite observable. We see their products, their stock prices, and occasionally their buildings and vehicles. But we can't view them as a whole. As Yuval Noah Harari observes in his book *Sapiens*, these incredibly important and powerful modern things are essentially myths. They have no existence in the material world independent of human imagination. They exist only because, in projects of social organization that included the making of laws, people got together and agreed to collectively believe in them.

The people who work in corporations and markets, however, are real beings and are far more visible. They have names and their pictures appear in magazines and on televisions and websites (or pointillized in those *Wall Street Journal* drawings). Or they may be on the other end of the line. Just think of the effort sometimes required to remind oneself, during one of those enervating phone calls, that the service failure is the fault of the cable company, not the benighted call center worker.

This still relatively novel setting for humans is fertile ground for the fundamental attribution error. It's also a place where that error is potentially costly. When it comes to people who work in firms and markets, to miss the situation may be to miss nearly everything. Modern firms and markets are designed to cause the very problems they create. They comprise a machine engineered to capitalize (literally) on human risk taking and material desire.

When we make the fundamental attribution error in this context—when we say, for example, that a bank wouldn't have collapsed if its CEO weren't such a cravenly greedy man—we're blaming people for the flaw of doing what we created the institutions to get to them do in the first place. Naturally, this line of thinking leads to the remedy of criminal punishment, a social practice that exists for the purpose of dealing with individuals who do bad things.

For centuries, Western societies have pursued criminal punishment for two main reasons: to give moral wrongdoers what they deserve and to teach offenders, and others who might offend, not to break the law. These punishment practices are specifically and sharply directed at individuals. They largely ignore context. And the pursuit of these objectives through public legal institutions powerfully reinforces the story that crime comes from people, not situations.

Explanation does not imply excuse. Far from it. Another durable feature of our society is that we hold each other responsible for the wrongs we do to each other—in a moral sense, not only a legal one. I certainly don't agree with determinists who question even the modern idea of free will and, therefore, the wisdom of punishment altogether. If the gunman for the drug gang doesn't get to say, "But where I come from violence is a way of life," then, for heaven's sake, the corporate executive must not get to say, "The pressures of the office made me do it."

The insight from the fundamental attribution error is not that we should stop holding people responsible for crimes because of the institutional contexts in which people commit them. The point is that we shouldn't expect criminal punishment to relieve us of problems precipitated by the forces that large firms and markets exert on those who operate them and, therefore, ultimately, on us. We should continue to punish serious wrongs in order to express and sustain our values—including the boundaries past which we do not wish the capitalist project to travel. But we shouldn't lose focus on the true sources of the problem, or we will never address them.

Many people, quite reasonably, would profess both of two beliefs. They would readily concede that the psychological and situational forces of the corporate world will perpetually tempt decent people to do bad things—for example, to design a faulty starter switch and then cover up the correction for fear of the career consequences of costing the company more or telling the truth. At the same time, they would maintain that the uniquely grave fear of imprisonment can prevail over those tendencies and hold them in check. Criminal law and perhaps only criminal law, they would say, is sufficiently potent to control behavior even in the face of powerful institutional forces.

To maintain the second belief, one must deal with the abundant evidence that corporate workers and managers keep making bad, harmful decisions even though, as we'll see, the law in recent decades has defined more corporate behavior as criminal and imposed longer sentences on those who have been prosecuted for that behavior. But we can leave discussion of this issue to one side because it's beset by empirical uncertainty: since we lack reliable data about the commission (as opposed to the prosecution) of corporate crimes, it's hard to say whether and how deterrence might be working.

There is a deeper problem based in values, not in the instrumental particulars of how law works. If the criminal law is to reach the root causes of corporate crime—the people whose decisions influenced the engineer who chose what kind of starter switch to design—and thus impose legal responsibility where factual (and moral) responsibility is greatest, criminal law must have a way to punish corporate managers. But, in most of the cases we'll discuss, the managers of the corporation did not commit the crime.

That is the nature of the corporation—its tendency to divide and diminish responsibility. But it's also the nature of criminal law, which, even in the age of American mass incarceration, is a product of values based in the idea of liberty. Whatever the outcomes of the flawed criminal justice system, American law does not set out to imprison for substantial terms people who did not think, however briefly, about whether to do something seriously wrongful and nonetheless chose to press ahead. As we will see, such wrongs are difficult to specify—clear lines are hard to draw—when it comes to how corporate managers might be responsible for the criminal acts of others.

Our first question interacts unhelpfully with our second. The social and legal charter that common economic activities enjoy combines with the nature of the corporate institution to complicate, even befuddle, the project of imposing criminal punishment.

It's only natural then that people, and the law, have turned to the possibility of punishing the *corporation*—on top, or even instead, of the corporation's people. Having highlighted the fundamental attribution error, I should add a more generous point about how the modern brain thinks about institutions. The large institutions of modern commerce have been with us for well over a century. They've suffused our lives since the explosion of the consumer economy after World War II. With globalization after the Cold War, their size and influence have grown even faster.

Denizens of the corporate age understand the reality and power of large economic institutions. While corporations themselves may not be visible, their effects on the world certainly are. Vocabulary and discourse have developed to accommodate this understanding.

To illustrate, suppose that a well-known national delivery company, let's call it Speedy, has a business of delivering customers' packages on time. It also has a good reputation and a solid safety record. One day a Speedy driver in Peoria named Frank, while hurrying to a delivery, tragically strikes and kills a child riding her bicycle in the street. What would we say? A Speedy driver killed a child. Or, perhaps, Frank the Speedy driver killed a child.

Now suppose that Speedy is facing tough competition from a new player in the industry, Quicker Delivery. Speedy's management decides that, to keep up with Quicker, Speedy needs to get even faster at delivering packages. The company decides to do this through an incentive program for its drivers. Speedy changes its compensation so that drivers make less money if they don't keep up with a demanding, GPS-monitored schedule controlling each day's deliveries.

After six months of the new Speedy delivery regime, eight Speedy drivers have struck and killed eight pedestrians in six different states. What would we say as we discussed this national scandal? *Speedy* is killing people. This would make perfect sense, even though a corporation cannot drive a truck and can only kill people through the acts of its human agents. In some sense, it might be the only way to accurately describe what's been happening to those pedestrians.

No sooner than people described what was happening, of course, they would be talking about the consequences. One of the first consequences of such a scandal is to blame those thought responsible. Again, people would blame Speedy. The managers and (maybe) the drivers might also deserve blame. But blaming only the managers and drivers would fail to fully respond to what happened. This tragedy unfolded because the corporation, through its managers and employees, and with policies, structures, and practices, created an institution that led to human deaths. Those deaths are—in a real way that people in the corporate age can understand—the corporation's fault.

American law, like the law of some but not nearly all developed countries, has a way to blame Speedy. It's called corporate criminal liability.[27] In the United States, we prosecute corporations even though the police can't put them in handcuffs, a jury can't see them, and a judge can't commit them to a prison cell. The legal rules for holding corporations criminally responsible were developed a long time ago in a quirky way (not coincidentally, at the turn of the twentieth century, during the era of legal reforms that followed the industrial revolution in the United States). But persistence of those rules for more than a century, and increasing reliance on them in recent decades, is a reflection of how Americans have come to understand the relationship between corporate institutions and many public problems.

Maybe the reason many people think of Steve Jobs and Richard Fuld so differently is, in part, that we *do* understand the difference in context—between Apple and Lehman, and the role each of those institutions has played in American life. By the same token, Wall Street bankers' inflated sense of outrage about their demonization following 2008 kind of makes sense. They too get it (perhaps better than anyone). It was the systems not the people; they're being called evil for doing what they thought they were supposed to be doing. Regrettably, many of them have also given themselves a pass on being introspective and self-critical about their role in constructing those systems.

A lot of people don't like American-style corporate criminal liability, as we'll discuss.[28] In policy circles, a coalition between some on the left and some on the right expresses distaste for the idea of prosecuting corporations. Free marketers don't like it because even the threat of prosecutions can be extremely expensive for companies, can impose costs out of proportion to the offense, and can give prosecutors enormous unwelcome influence over corporate managers. Some critics of corporate power don't like it either. They think the human managers of such corporations should be imprisoned more often and that prosecuting corporations can be a distraction from that imperative, perhaps even a deliberate distraction. And they don't like the way prosecutors constantly settle their cases with corporations in order to avoid putting companies out of business. For good measure, some academic theorists don't like corporate criminal liability either because, in their view, it makes no sense to try to punish nonliving things.

These are serious lines of argument that, we'll see, merit careful thought and response. But the arguments also miss how rooted the idea of corporate criminal responsibility is in the way ordinary people perceive the world. That connection between law and reality is likely only to become stronger as the global economy grows.

Despite the heated and too often simplistic rhetoric that fills public discussion of business crime in America, the relationship between these crimes and their contexts is complex—and thus deeply interesting. There's not yet one clear way to think and talk about the role of large corporations and markets in the wrongs that people do, and in what we should do about those wrongs.

Meanwhile, the legal system—largely through the collective actions of the lawyers who work in it—has continued to develop ways to deal with the fact of the large and still growing corporation. For those who would ascribe blame and impose punishment, big private institutions do not present problems only of theory. These institutions also produce severe practical problems. As a consequence in part of being private and big, they are both opaque and complex from the viewpoint of outsiders (and even, alas, their own managers).[29] This makes them hard places to detect crime and enforce the criminal law, even if we assume those laws are clear about what is a crime and what sorts of persons (or things) should receive punishment.

Problems in the enforcement of criminal law are an all-too-familiar subject at present. At some point in the second term of the Obama administration, America reached a flash point with its criminal justice system. The social costs of policing street crime, accumulating relentlessly since the early 1980s, reached a level that triggered widespread public outrage. Americans are understanding better that how the law is enforced is overwhelmingly more important to people's lives than the question of what the law makes a crime.

The insight that enforcement on the ground may be more important than law on the books holds true for the corporate and financial sectors too, in a completely different way. Without wanting to sound glib, we can say that downtown Manhattan is not Ferguson or Baltimore. Cops don't walk the beat up and down the stairs of corporate office buildings. Even if they did, it's not clear how they would see a crime if one were afoot.

To say this is because of privileges of class and race, as real and pervasive as those privileges are in the United States, is too simplistic. That American law bans most recreational drugs may explain in large measure why police departments are empowered to permeate daily life in many urban communities. But there is no equivalent crime that could authorize pervasive, coercive policing of individuals who work in corporate office buildings. There could not be such crimes unless American law banned entire industries, relegating the extraction and distribution of petroleum or the sale of pharmaceutical products to black markets.

The contrast between the street and the boardroom, in this age of the one percent, is stark. Many observers have lamented how the position of corporations and markets in modern American life has produced a special criminal enforcement system. Yet the development of this enforcement system has been predictable. American economic ideas require that industries generating wealth and employing workers be given sufficient space, at least from the most intrusive forms of policing, to be able to do what they do. Giving those industries room to grow as enormously as they have can leave them seeming impenetrable to law enforcement.

The contemporary answer to this problem has been to make firms police themselves. This answer explains the persistence and importance of corporate criminal liability in the United States even more than the public's desire to blame corporations for crimes. Consider the major oil spill of 2010, unleashed by an explosion on BP's Deepwater Horizon rig in the Gulf of Mexico. The government had two tasks in the disaster's wake: to come to grips with the environmental crisis and to impose legal accountability on BP and any responsible managers and employees. The United States government could not do either of those jobs on its own.

The government needed private parties—mostly BP itself, with its gigantic global resources—to get the spill under control and then cleaned up. Nearly as much, the government needed BP's resources to uncover and organize all the evidence of what had happened within BP *itself.* In theory, the government could have accomplished the latter task alone with old-fashioned shoe leather policing. In white collar crime, this usually means subpoenas for documents (literally millions of them) and marching witness after witness in and out of grand jury examinations.

The shoe leather approach would have made no sense. It would have taken years and years, diverted resources from other enforcement projects, and involved innumerable dead ends.

What the government did with BP conforms with what it now does with most large corporations that break the law. The Justice Department held a sword over the company's fictive neck: the threat of full criminal prosecution and parallel civil enforcement lawsuits for every possible violation in the sprawling federal code. Then it said to BP's managers and lawyers, "We will take this sword away, or cut it down in size, if you do a really good job cleaning up the spill and finding and giving us the evidence of what happened here and why. Now show us how motivated you are."

Whether BP did an adequate job of cleaning up the Gulf spill and investigating itself remains, as in almost all these cases, a subject of fair debate. But this government leverage at least has the intended effect. BP filled an office building in New Orleans with expensive lawyers and experts and spent several years, and billions of dollars, working on the remedial job. Once the government was reasonably satisfied, it permitted BP to plead guilty to lesser charges and pay fines and civil settlements that, though enormous, were perhaps lower than BP's worst-case scenario.[30]

Some would describe this repeating scene in corporate crime as a regrettable story about the privatization of public law enforcement in the neoliberal age of government. But that story is incomplete. One cannot account for how government enforces criminal law in the corporate sector without acknowledging the structural constraints the government faces in confronting the complex modern firm. America may or may not have shrunk its government, or important parts of it. Meanwhile, though, the large corporation has indisputably expanded.

ENRON. WORLDCOM. ADELPHIA Communications. Qwest. Dynegy. Tyco International. News Corporation. Hollinger International. Healthsouth. General Motors. Toyota. Volkswagen. British Petroleum. Exxon. Merck, Pfizer, GlaxoSmithKline, Bristol-Myers Squibb. Columbia HCA. McKesson. Hewlett Packard. Apple. AOL. Walmart. Citibank. Goldman Sachs. J.P. Morgan. Morgan Stanley. Bear Stearns. Merrill Lynch. Madoff Securities. BNP Paribas. UBS. Deutschebank. HSBC. Commerzbank. Rabobank. SAC Capital. Galleon Group. Drexel Burnham Lambert. E.F. Hutton. Salomon Brothers. Prudential Securities. Long Term Capital Management. Siemens. Statoil. BAE. Ralph Lauren. Network Associates. Computer Associates. Finley Kumble. Jenkens & Gilchrist. Dewey Leboeuf. Milberg Weiss. Arthur Andersen. KPMG.

That's just a short list of a longer roster of important corporations and investment, law, and accounting firms whose operations have, one way or another, mobilized America's criminal justice machinery over the last thirty years. Probably millions of people have been harmed in some way by actions inside these firms. Some have been killed. We live in an age in which the corporate organization—which is a creature of law that is meant to conform to, and be controlled by, law—regularly malfunctions and causes or allows its managers and employees to break the law.

It's common in discussion of corporate crime to blame the law for what we don't like—from either side of the debate. For several years, an antiregulation think tank called the Washington Legal Foundation has published a document detailing what the group titles the "Federal Erosion of Business Civil Liberties" since 1900.[31] This "Timeline" paints a picture of a century of government campaigns to cut back on the ability of corporations and their managers to do business in the United States. The Justice Department and the enforcement of federal criminal law play the leading role in this group's account, which is characteristic of how those most sympathetic to the political interests of large corporations tend to discuss corporate crime these days.

To those on the other end of the spectrum, and perhaps to most of us, the invocation of the phrase "civil liberties" in a debate about corporate regulation is oxymoronic if not offensive. But, when discussing corporate crime, it's equally unhelpful to say that American law and its enforcers "coddle corporate criminals," and the like. Both rhetorical positions assume what ought to require careful argument: that the criminal law is doing too much (or not enough) in the relationship between Americans and the corporate sector.

If we are going to blame the law, hopefully in the cause of reforming it, we must first understand where the law comes from. The literal account of law's sources, taught in basic law courses, is the three branches of government: Congress writes legislation; the courts make and explain rulings; and the executive branch issues regulations and sets the patterns of enforcement.

Those are the machineries of law, not its actual sources. The government does "our" work, whether or not you or I are actually among the "we" who presently have influence over what government does. The actual source of law in this area is America's social and economic order. That's where we need to look if we want to understand the problem of corporate crime and what to do about it. Happily it turns out in the case of business crime that examining the law, and how it operates in action, shines some of the most revealing lights on that social and economic order.

2

Fraud

I F MALFEASANCE IN the business world has a single concept at its core, it is fraud. Understanding fraud—a simple idea with endlessly complex manifestations—is the key to appreciating the difference between what can lead to prison and what is clever business in competitive American markets. And examining a colorful and diverse array of prosecutions—many of which will be familiar but only dimly understood from the stream of headlines they produced—is the way to grasp what fraud really is.

Wrongs and Frauds

LET'S START with three hypothetical examples. We'll call them Blind Man Bluffed, The Company with the Shaky Assets, and Backdaters in the Valley.

In Blind Man Bluffed, as I wait in line to pay at a store, I'm approached by a man who asks, "Could you make change for a ten dollar bill?" I notice that the man has a service dog at his side and is carrying the type of stick that sightless persons use. I reply, "Sure, here's a five and five ones." I carefully select six one-dollar bills from my wallet, hand them to the man, and take the ten-dollar bill from him. He thanks me, while his dog eyes me suspiciously. I pay the store for my items and walk away from the encounter four dollars richer.

In The Company with the Shaky Assets, I'm the CEO of a big corporation that owns some smaller businesses. These smaller companies do business in volatile industries. I worry about fluctuations in the value of these companies affecting the big corporation's bottom line. My company has been doing well and the price of our stock, of which I own quite a lot, has been rising steadily. I don't want the stock to take a big hit in the event that the company has to report poor earnings due to losses in the smaller companies.

The best strategy for a CEO with this kind of problem is to find someone in the market who will do a "hedging" transaction on the smaller companies. That means, to put it crudely, somebody who will sell the CEO's company a kind of insurance in which the seller of the "hedge" promises to cover any future losses. (Instruments that hedged banks' portfolios of mortgage securities, or didn't, were a big part of what crashed the financial markets in 2008.) My problem is that our small companies are really shaky. No one is going to do that hedging deal with me except at a price so steep that buying the hedge itself will put a dent in my earnings.

I ask my whip-smart CFO, who is my numbers guy, if he can think of any way out of our dilemma. The CFO kicks things around with our company's creative accountants and they come up with a plan. We'll create the separate business (aka the counterparty) that will sell us the hedge. We'll call this new entity Dog. Dog needs to have some assets in it (it needs to be "capitalized"), so that we can say Dog has the ability to make good on the hedge if those small companies fall on hard times and we need to get paid. No problem. We'll fund Dog with our company's stock, which for us is, well, kind of free.

Wait, I say, how can that work? To be a legitimate counterparty in a hedge, doesn't Dog need to be real and actually a different company from us, with hard assets? Otherwise, wouldn't we just be moving something from our left pocket into our right?

My CFO explains that he and the accountants think we can treat Dog as real as long as a small amount of what makes up Dog—like three percent—is actual money that comes from somewhere outside our company. Hmm, I think, whom could we get to put that bit of outside money into Dog? I know the CFO and some other people have a little investment business on the side that we have sometimes done other deals with. I ask the CFO if he would be willing to put his own money into Dog. CFO says he could be persuaded to do it if he were sure he would make money. Don't worry, I tell CFO, the first money the company pays into Dog for the hedging deals will go straight to you to cover your three percent contribution, plus some profit for your trouble.

Within a year, it becomes clear that I've been too clever by half. I thought I'd found a way (Dog) to keep my company's stock from going down. So of course I didn't think I needed to worry about what might happen to Dog if the stock we put in Dog went down. But the market turned against us and our stock fell for other reasons. The inevitable result was that Dog—and its siblings we enthusiastically added to our financial structure by building them with more of our own stock (and that little bit of outside money), Dog 2, Dog 3, and Dog 4—themselves all declined in value. Under the accounting rules, if we didn't think the Dogs were going to be able to make good on all the hedges we bought from them, we would have to start reporting losses in our volatile small companies—and that bad news would only make our stock go down more. A death spiral wasn't out of the question.

At first we staved off disaster by persuading our outside auditor to let us treat all four Dogs as one big Dog, for the purpose of determining whether the Dogs had enough assets to make good on the hedge deals. This helped because not all four of the Dogs had become equally lame. (Some of the graybeards in our auditor's firm thought combining the Dogs like this was flagrantly wrong accounting. But the partner on our account disagreed with them and went along with the idea.) Alas, that move bought us only a few months. Eventually—

and for our investors, though not so much us, quite suddenly and unexpectedly—we had to report big losses on our books from the decline in value of our shaky small companies.

That really spooked the market, which started poking at a lot of other not so great parts of our company that hadn't been scrutinized before. Long story short, a few weeks later the company was bankrupt and I was fired. Many investors were wiped out, including lots of employees whom I had encouraged to invest their retirement savings in our company. That ends the hypothetical of The Company with the Shaky Assets.

Last, we have Backdaters in the Valley. I'm in charge of hiring for a hot tech company that has recently gone public. Our business, which is mostly software, is all about human capital. Geeks are what make money, and the competition for the best ones is fierce. I'm trying to hire a new engineer to lead the development of our next great product, one that has the potential to double our stock price. Like every talented person in an industry that routinely makes multimillionaires overnight, this engineer expects to get paid in part with equity in our company: stock options. We have included a very nice chunk of options in our offer to her. Still, she says our equity package is not quite competitive with another job offer she has in hand.

I could go back to our CEO and board of directors and ask for approval for a larger package of stock options. But I don't want to do that. There will be pushback because of questions about equality of pay packages across positions in the company. If I have to tell her that I tried but couldn't deliver a stronger package, I would risk losing the hire. I decide to take an alternative approach, one that I heard about from an acquaintance at another tech company who has a job similar to mine.

The ordinary practice in public corporations is to grant stock options to new employees at the market price of the company's stock on the day of hiring. (This is called the "strike price.") That way, any increase in the value of those options can, at least in theory, be seen as resulting from the efforts of that new employee. Employee stock options, after all, are supposed to work as an incentive.

On the day we hope to close our hiring deal with the new engineer, our stock is trading at $40. I'm well aware that three months earlier our stock was trading at $30. So I seal the deal with the engineer by telling her that we will date her hiring as of three months ago. This means her stock options are initially priced at $30 per share, not the $40 current market price. In other words, her option to purchase is already worth ("in the money") $10 per share on the day she starts work—on paper at least, more compensation for her without our company having had to pay an additional dime. This idea proves so successful that I use it to hire a handful more superstar Valley engineers and my bosses end up promoting me.

Reactions to these three hypothetical cases will vary somewhat among readers depending on what sort of work you do, your attitudes toward regulation, and your background in matters of law and finance. But a median observer might have the following response.

Blind Man Bluffed is really wrong and probably illegal. Or at least it should be illegal. It's a clear case of taking someone else's money through deception. The gentleman thought he was receiving ten dollars from me when in fact he received six. I knew he wouldn't be able to tell it wasn't ten dollars because I knew he couldn't see. (And I knew his dog couldn't read money.) That was my whole plan. I meant to gain four dollars on the exchange. My deception was particularly craven because I exploited another man's physical disability. Maybe, legally speaking, Blind Man Bluffed is not theft because he happily handed me his cash. But then it has to be fraud. Undoubtedly this sort of thing is what the law of fraud is all about.

The Company with the Shaky Assets is harder. We've made the quantum leap from two people with cash in their wallets to modern corporate finance. The case is loosely based, of course, on a major part of what brought down Enron. (Explaining the mechanics of Enron's version of the Dogs would require half a day, a large whiteboard, and the aid of at least a forensic accountant if not also a CFO who has agreed to plead guilty and testify for the prosecution.) But basic principles about right and wrong, and about what is and is not criminal, shouldn't change as we make the jump from wallets to corporate financial statements.

In The Company with the Shaky Assets, people got hurt because they lost a lot of money when the truth came out about how fragile my company really was. On one account, I hid that truth through the clever and opaque device of the Dogs. And I meant to hide that truth from investors. I wanted to be able to create a steadily rising stock price by reporting reliably smooth earnings every quarter, even while we owned a portfolio of risky and volatile companies. Only the trick of the Dogs allowed me to do that. If Blind Man Bluffed should be treated as a fraud, so should The Company with the Shaky Assets.

On the other hand, though, I wasn't "hiding" the volatility in our shaky companies. I was legitimately "hedging" (insuring) against it. If the accountants let me build the Dogs the way we did, then I was reporting to investors the financial "truth" about my company, which is by necessity a function of how the accounting rules say to report corporate numbers. The reality wasn't that my company had a bunch of hidden shaky assets. The reality was that it had a bunch of prudently hedged assets. I didn't mean to deceive anyone. In fact, what I meant was to avoid future trouble, in the best interests of the company's shareholders. I'm sorry it didn't work out in the long run. But business failure is not fraud.

The key to choosing between these accounts is to focus carefully on the Dogs. If the Dogs were "real," "legitimate," "honest accounting"— whatever term you prefer—and I genuinely believed that in good faith when I authorized them (in other words, I'm not just saying so now that people are accusing me of doing something wrong), then the second view might be fair. And this whole story might not look like a fraud.

But if the Dogs were an absurd stretch and I knew it—if I knew it was silly to think something built from our own stock was real and could last, if I knew that the accountants only went along with our building the Dogs and later combining them because we had the accountants in our pocket, and especially if I knew that promising to get the CFO his "outside" money back right away made the whole thing a sham—

then I'm a fraudster. (In the Enron case, the guaranteed payment to the CFO was also hidden from the accountants.) I meant to deceive investors and, for a time, I succeeded in doing so. The result was a catastrophe, much of which could have been avoided if I'd admitted at the beginning that we had some fragile assets and were going to need to spend some real money to protect against the greater risk those assets posed to our company's future.

Backdaters in the Valley is more puzzling. In one way, I seem to have lied. I made the paperwork say that the engineer started work three months earlier than she really did. That's the sense in which the idea of backdating documents connotes dishonesty. But it's routine in business for parties to a contract to pick a date as the start date for their deal and then formalize the particulars of their agreement later. "Backdating" is a loaded word that can obscure important distinctions among different kinds of cases.

More to the point, even if my backdating of the options documents can be styled as a lie, most lies are not crimes. What I did is certainly not theft because no one had anything taken from him or her. Stock options aren't cash and issuing them doesn't really "cost" a company anything in the way ordinary expenses like salary do. And my job includes, within a range of discretion, deciding what to offer as compensation to new recruits.

If the ordinary practice is to grant stock options at the market price on the date of hiring, it doesn't mean a company couldn't grant options at a below-market price. American law has little to say about how a company is allowed to pay its executives and employees, versus what a company must disclose to investors about pay or what pay mechanisms get favorable treatment under tax law. We could have paid our engineers in dancing elephants if we pleased.

Might Backdaters in the Valley still be a crime, specifically the crime of fraud? After all, as readers may be aware, in the early 2000s some such cases were treated as frauds though prosecutors left many others alone, including the Steve Jobs matter at Apple.

To develop a theory of fraud, one would need to be clear on who the victim might be and how that victim might have been deceived.

The victim is certainly not the person doing the hiring, nor is it the new employee. My bosses are probably not victims either. They high-fived me when I landed the engineer and they didn't lose anything on the deal. At worst, they might have been unaware of the options back-dating and perhaps, when they found out about it, said that I should please loop them in next time.

What about the investors in our company? They certainly didn't know that I was hiring engineers by backdating documents to make sure the new hires got in-the-money options. Did our investors care? If not, they hardly seem to have been deceived because they would not have bothered to think about the question in the first place, much less change anything they were doing based on the answer.

Here is the nub of Backdaters in the Valley. If granting in-the-money options changed anything about the bottom line in our company's accounting and financial reporting, investors might have a very good reason to care. Even if it didn't change the bottom line, investors might be alarmed or dismayed to learn about backdating. They might have liked how we encouraged our employees to devote themselves to the company by paying them only with options priced at market value that would not be worth anything unless the company thrived. (In one of the options backdating cases that was prosecuted, a major investor had asked the company if they ever granted in-the-money options and was told no. The CEO of that company is a fugitive in Namibia.)

Backdaters in the Valley really starts to look like a fraud if I pondered the question whether our investors would care and went ahead with the deal anyway, without telling the CEO or the board of directors. Now I appear to have set out to deceive a group of persons about something affecting their property in a way that caused them harm—or at least exposed them to a risk of harm of which they were unaware and had a right to know about in deciding whether to invest in our company. Incidentally, it would be hard for a prosecutor to get this full picture in view, especially my thinking about the matter, without some evidence that I thought the backdating was wrong when I did it—like me circumventing ordinary procedures for vetting employment agreements or misleading the company's accountants when they asked for backup documents.

These three hypotheticals illustrate that fraud is contextual, perhaps more than any other crime known to American law. The lines can be very fine between ordinary commerce and criminal wrongdoing. And we must continually draw and redraw those lines in light of commercial contexts that change and diversify at accelerating rates. This is the central challenge for criminal law in the world of business: to specify the outer limits of what is permissible within a realm of behavior—entrepreneurial commerce and capitalism—that is not only legal and welcome but is a basic and celebrated building block of our social order.

Taking Each Other's Stuff

IT WILL help to have a summary, in a tiny nutshell, of the legal history of taking each other's stuff.[1] In the beginning in England, the source country for most American ideas about law, simply taking someone else's thing was not usually a crime. The basic worry was more about bloodshed than property. So robbery, which is taking something from someone by using or threatening violence, was the main property crime.

Then society became less intimate and more commercial. Taking each other's things, whether violently or not, became something worth preventing. Theft became a crime called larceny. Then judges had to figure out what counted as larceny. If I lent you my horse so you could carry a message for me to someone a couple of villages over, and you delivered the message but never came back with my horse, did you commit larceny?

Today, the answer is obvious. But when robbery had been the only concept of property crime, this kind of thing apparently posed an intellectual challenge. Judges had to work out how the criminal law should treat a range of ideas about people's relationships to possessions. The result was a proliferation of odd legal rules to deal with different situations: the person with custody of the horse, or the banker who embezzles depository funds, or even the person who is allowed to hold an object she's thinking about buying in a store and then takes it away without paying. Physical possession, in the beginning it seems, really was nine-tenths of the law.

American law has since done away with most of these headaches by adopting simple, modern theft statutes. The problems remain relevant only for the British, who had to reform their property crime laws as recently as 2006 because some of the old legal ideas were creating hurdles for modern prosecutions involving financial misconduct. They're also a bugaboo for new law graduates, who are made by many states' bar examiners to study the old rules because they're confusing and testable in multiple-choice format.

While English law was working out the idea of the crime of theft, the concept of fraud, which had been around in the law since at least the Romans, found its way into civil disputes. (Or, shall we say, quasi-civil disputes. Distinctions between lawsuits and criminal prosecutions were a lot fuzzier then and too complicated to bother with here.) Fraud's leading point of entry was in the law governing debtors and creditors. A "fraudulent conveyance" was, and still is, the very old trick of a debtor unlawfully moving property to another person's control in order to keep it away from a creditor.

Edward Coke is the most famous and influential legal thinker of the Elizabethan age.[2] Apparently one could drop of out of Cambridge in those days—Trinity College for the young Coke—and go on to become one of the top judges in the realm. Coke's lasting influence in law comes from his writings, which include many reports of cases he handled when he served as the attorney general for Elizabeth I (a different sort of job at that place and time, of course). One of those cases concerned a man named Twyne who moved his sheep over to another man's pasture in an effort to place them beyond the reach of Twyne's creditor.[3]

Coke wrote that the judges found Twyne's maneuver to be a fraud in violation of a law recently passed by Parliament. The court took the view that "because fraud and deceit abound in these days more than in former times . . . all statutes made against fraud should be liberally and beneficially expounded to suppress the fraud." Coke explained, "If you ask why are there so many laws, the answer is that fraud ever increases on this earth."

As in many matters, Edward Coke seems to have understood modernity. The man who stashed his sheep in the next field ultimately became the financier with the accounts in the Cayman Islands. And modern courts ended up saying nearly the same things Coke had said in the Elizabethan era:

Lord Hardwicke, a famous English jurist of the eighteenth century: "Fraud is infinite, and were a court . . . once to lay down rules, how far they would go, and no farther, in extending their relief against it, or to define strictly the species or evidence of it, the jurisdiction would be . . . perpetually eluded by new schemes, which the fertility of man's invention would contrive."[4]

A Maryland court just after the Civil War: "The common law not only gives no definition of fraud, but perhaps wisely asserts as a principle that there shall be no definition of it, for, as it is the very nature and essence of fraud to elude all laws in fact, without appearing to break them in form, a technical definition of fraud . . . would be in effect telling to the crafty precisely how to avoid the grasp of the law."[5]

And a twentieth-century federal appeals court: "The law does not define fraud; it needs no definition; it is as old as falsehood and as versable as human ingenuity."[6]

Finding the place where fraud first became a crime in America has, at least for me, been a search for the source of the Nile, one probably not worth the effort. By the time the Civil War had concluded, the concept of fraud as a crime was normal enough that Congress, which in those days mostly left criminal enforcement to the states, didn't hesitate to pass a statute treating as a felony all efforts to pursue fraud through the use of the U.S. mails.[7] With industrialization came more fraud and the mail, no longer dependent on ponies, had proved an easy way to commit it. It still is, judging by the piles of suspect sweepstakes offers that fill some mailboxes, not to mention their vast numbers of e-mail equivalents.

Later, with the spread of telegraph and telephone infrastructure, Congress added a twin statute criminalizing fraud committed via "interstate wires." Much later, with the appearance of the Internet, these federal fraud statutes—which now have maximum penalties of twenty years imprisonment per charge—achieved almost blanket coverage over the American commercial space. Along the way, in the wake of the 1929 stock market crash, Congress adopted criminal fraud statutes for the securities markets that extend into huge portions of the financial industry.[8]

The Modern Idea of Fraud

IN SUM: don't hurt me became don't take my stuff, which in turn became don't cheat me out of my stuff. "Don't cheat me" isn't a law and doesn't even sound like one. But criminal fraud laws don't say much more. The federal statutes used to prosecute most of the big corporate fraud cases prohibit engaging in a "scheme or artifice to defraud" or engaging in a practice that "would operate as a fraud or deceit on any person." As far as Congress is concerned, the federal law is "don't commit fraud" while using the postal service or wires, or in securities markets, or in connection with federally insured banks.

The courts have put a bit of flesh on the bones of these laws, mostly by drawing from the law of fraud as it has developed in England and America in the centuries since Edward Coke. Lies must be "material," meaning that they must be about things that would influence the decision of a buyer or seller. For a felony criminal conviction, the fraudster must act with the "specific intent to defraud," meaning at least that frauds can't be committed accidentally—they require that one think about deceiving someone and want to accomplish that. And there has to be something that is the object of the fraud—what the perpetrator is trying to get or take away, usually property but sometimes less tangible things like valuable information or legal rights.

Despite thousands of pages of written judicial opinions, that's all we really have from the courts in terms of hard-and-fast rules about criminal fraud. Even the kind of fraud that can land someone in prison can't really be broken apart or boiled down any further. It's one of those legal ideas like obscenity (Justice Potter Stewart's now clichéd "I know it when I see it") or probable cause. Perhaps the most we can say is that fraud is deception, with the getting of something from another as the object of the deception. After that, one can only understand the legal concept of fraud through example—which is both the job of the rest of this chapter and what makes fraud so interesting.

Given its history, it should be no surprise that fraud is both a malleable and irreducible legal concept. As commerce and industry grew and became more complex, social and economic interactions became more impersonal and required more regulation. Theft law had to evolve to deal with a variety of methods of taking other people's things. As outright theft became more predictably subject to regulation and punishment, taking property by cheating and deception became a more common problem. Fraud gradually became a crime and, eventually, a serious one.

But fraud remained a general offense because methods of cheating and deception kept evolving as modes of business and commerce changed. It became clear to legal thinkers that this would always be true. Fraud is thus the residual property crime: Don't take other people's stuff by means of cheating and deception that are (or perhaps even *should be*) criminal.

In developing this idea of fraud, the law set a hard task for itself.[9] To police deception in the always evolving world of modern business requires laws capable of hitting a moving target. Deception, after all, is causing someone—through words or action—to hold a belief that is not accurate. This describes many common activities in the rough-and-tumble of commercial affairs, including advertising and negotiation. "Our network has the clearest cell reception available." "This is my final offer, I won't go a dollar higher." "The property has spectacular ocean views." "Look at the happy sexy people in this beer ad, you can be like them." "Our company is on a fantastic growth trajectory and the sky is the limit."

In making fraud not simply unlawful but also criminal, punishable by long terms of imprisonment, the law made a hard task even harder. Making behavior eligible for prison time imposes special legal demands, primarily constitutional ones, including that the prosecutor must have proof beyond a reasonable doubt. The law must also fairly warn people of where the line is between going to prison and remaining free. That's especially important when criminal law is policing conduct in areas like business and politics that are far from categorically illegal.

Being clear with law is pragmatic too. Excessive doubt about what is a crime might cause lots of people to forgo productive activities. As critics of the ends-over-means utilitarianism of Jeremy Bentham and his followers have sometimes pointed out (unfairly to the careful arguments of serious utilitarians), the best way to deter murder might be to lock up every tenth person, guilty or not. This way everyone would remain safely at home for fear of random arrest. But at what cost to social productivity, much less liberty?

When it comes to fraud, we've ended up with a deep tension between law that is vague enough to be flexible and specific enough to be predictable. Apply that tension to modern corporate commerce and the law has a vexing task before it. Fortunately our legal system decides cases one at a time, according to their facts. That is the only way to feasibly handle this challenge. To understand fraud one needs to look at the *frauds*, not the rules about fraud.

Over the last thirty years, Americans have watched with fascination, disgust, amusement, and anger as a parade of accused fraudsters have been led out of the financial world and into the legal system. Michael Milken. Ivan Boesky. Kenneth Lay. Jeffrey Skilling. Bernard Ebbers. John Rigas. Dennis Kozlowski. Richard Scrushy. Samuel Waksal. Martha Stewart. Frank Quattrone. Raj Rajaratnam. Rajat Gupta. To name a few of the more notorious cases of the late twentieth and early twenty-first centuries. At the same time, Americans have questioned why others have not been marched in that parade.

It's an obvious mistake to lump all these figures into a single category of the corporate malefactor. The concept of fraud is, in most of these cases, the analytical tool that helps us understand how to view each case on its own terms and with reference to right and wrong.

To keep the following tour organized, we'll divide the world of corporate fraud into five categories: Ponzi schemes, looting the corporation, accounting fraud, buyer-seller fraud, and insider trading. So as not to hide the ball, the conclusion I would draw from this brief tour is this: Fraud cases can be hard, and sometimes unsatisfying, because they're the theater in which we stage our unresolved conflicts about entrepreneurship and capitalism. Ingenuity and greed, when combined, are powerful and productive forces that, for most of us, are not themselves wrong. But they can lead those under their powers down a path to iniquity. The concept of fraud, which has the job of setting boundaries, is, perhaps paradoxically, both simple and unstable.

Ponzi Schemes

ONE KIND of fraud is so famous it goes by a proper noun, taking its name from Charles Ponzi, the legendary perpetrator arrested in Boston in 1920. Ponzi schemes are an interesting subject for psychology. Why do people continue to fall under the sway of these things even though a Ponzi is the one kind of fraud most people easily understand and the methods of which never change? Some good books have been written on Ponzi schemes, including the biographies of schemers like Ponzi himself or Ivar Kreuger, the "Swedish Match King."[10] To stop Ponzi schemes, or at least intervene in them earlier, we would need to figure out a way to dampen the "irrational exuberance" of the unsophisticated investor—the "I might win the lottery" mentality applied to playing the securities markets.

Ponzi schemes are not such an interesting subject for understanding how law should deal with modern corporate crime. This is fraud one step removed from theft. I get you to give me your money by promising to invest it profitably in something that doesn't exist. You may end up with a profit but, if you do, it won't be because my promise was honest. It will be because I have made the same false promise to a next round of victims whose money I have used to pay you. That's how I keep my lie a secret and continue to lure in new marks. As we all know, eventually I'll be discovered and the later victims will be left holding the (empty) bag.

The story of Bernard Madoff, and especially his relationships to his victims, is tragic and fascinating.[11] It remains incredible that in the sophisticated world of early 2000s New York investment advisers, it was possible to invent a nonexistent fund and get people to pour billions of dollars into it. It is equally unbelievable that this could have been done under the noses of regulators of the financial markets, who had sniffed around Madoff's operation (even taking his testimony under oath!) and smelled nothing wrong.

Trust is a complex phenomenon, subject in part to market forces (Madoff thrived during a bubble) but also to enduring features of human behavior and the mind. Madoff's case, though, tells us little about fraud as a legal idea—about the crime itself. There was nothing to dispute in the Madoff prosecution once his jig was up. That's why he pled guilty and threw himself on the mercy of the court. (A court that, as discussed in a later chapter, was predictably unmerciful.)

For understanding modern corporate fraud, the important thing about the idea of a Ponzi scheme is to see what it's not. Often people see things that look dubious in the business world and say, "That's basically a big Ponzi scheme." Like mortgage-backed securities before 2008: The banks kept the game going with lax consumer lending that inflated American housing prices. Loose lending was fueled by selling loads of risky securities backed by those same home loans. Eventually and unavoidably, as many have said, the music would stop.

But even the massively overleveraged borrower is not engaged in a Ponzi scheme. Borrowing for expansion, even very risky borrowing, fuels new business growth in the capital system. If the borrower is not lying to get loans, and the lender does not care to worry too much about how much risk the borrower is taking on (pricing the loans accordingly, of course), there's been no fraud. Madoff's fraud was not that he persuaded lots of overly excited people to give him their money while expanding his fund at a dizzying pace. It was that he misled his investors about what he was doing with their money.

Borrowing like mad to expand—and cantilevering a business by using each piece of expansion as collateral to borrow still more—is basically the same as what the term "pyramid" usually describes: one of those marketing programs in which each new sales recruit is rewarded when she brings in two new recruits. Most pyramid schemes are not Ponzi schemes. If people are not purposely misled, a pyramid is not typically a fraud. It's at worst a business plan destined to fail, and therefore a bad investment.

Looting the Company

ANYONE WHO followed corporate crime in the early 2000s will remember the $6,000 shower curtain. Dennis Kozlowski, the former CEO of an electronics and security systems conglomerate named Tyco International, ended up sentenced by a New York state judge to serve eight to twenty-five years in prison. Kozlowski was convicted of defrauding Tyco out of millions of dollars in lavish perks or, if you prefer, nontraditional compensation.[12]

The case against Kozlowski, which produced two drawn-out trials, one involving a misbehaving juror, sprawled across a wide array of things the company did for his benefit. These included the inevitable private airplane rides for him and his family, the purchase and over-the-top decorating of a corporate pied à terre in Manhattan (with things like that shower curtain), and half the bill for a two-million-dollar, upmarket toga party in Sardinia to celebrate his wife's birthday. It's so often the vivid details that cement attitudes toward these cases. At the birthday party, it was the female-figure cake with the exploding chest and the Adonis ice sculpture with the vodka "spout."

It's an amazing but true fact about the American corporate system, and its regulatory structure, that almost nothing prohibited Tyco—which the irrepressible Kozlowski had built from almost nothing—from "paying" him with all of these things. As long as disclosure and approval processes are followed, and everyone pays the taxes they owe, nauseatingly high levels of executive compensation—even essentially immoral ones—are not illegal. (At most, really egregious cases might prompt shareholders to file a lawsuit against the company's directors.) If there's a legitimate idea behind this system it's the theory that, as long as investors can see whether a company is wasting money on its executives, investors will be able to choose to take their money elsewhere.

The prosecutors in Kozlowski's case charged that Tyco hadn't properly approved all of Kozlowski's perks. So this was a case of "looting": the company didn't award him the baubles; he used his powerful position to extract them from the company. Kozlowski insists to this day that the jury got it wrong. He says that Tyco's accountants and board of directors were well aware of what was going on, that he had no reason to think every item was not properly approved, and that he engaged in no lying or concealment that might have suggested he knew he was up to no good.

The trickiness in cases of executive looting comes from two realities about the large American corporation. First, executive compensation at the biggest companies is routinely profligate and, for the most part, not substantively regulated. As long as pay is properly approved and disclosed, the sky's the limit. So it's almost never possible to say that a CEO like Kozlowski defrauded his company because he seems to have been piggish, or even unforgivably tacky.

Second, American companies, especially fast-growing ones, tend to be led by charismatic, aggressive CEOs with big personalities. And boards, who are effectively chosen by management even though elected by shareholders, tend to be less independent and industrious than they should be. In looting cases, it can be difficult to work out whether the gaudy decorating job was within some general area of board approval and, more to the point, whether the executive really acted with criminal intent in taking something from the company to which he knew he wasn't entitled.

An attitude of *la compagnie, c'est moi* is one our business culture encourages—by venerating the great leader who single-handedly creates a massive success story. This is perhaps why Steve Jobs never thought he was doing, or could do, anything wrong.[13]

Take Conrad Black. He was a sort of poor man's Rupert Murdoch—though Black had a private plane and a house in Palm Beach, so it's more like a less-rich man's Murdoch.[14] He owned a media business based in Canada that included lots of North American newspapers. He had the smarts to know in the early 2000s that he ought to get out of that game. Under Black's direction, his company began selling its paper businesses one by one. Some of these deals were small and involved weekly community newspapers in places like Mammoth Lakes, California.

Black and his associates structured some of these newspaper sales to include millions of dollars in payments to them in exchange for agreements personally not to compete in the future with the new owners of the papers. It was absurd to think that Black would have any interest in competing with a weekly paper in rural California. In some instances, the buyers hadn't even asked for these agreements, which were bizarrely inserted into the sale documents at the request of the seller without changing the bottom-line price. The payments were just a way for Black and his people to channel more of the sales price into their personal pockets.

Federal prosecutors in Chicago charged Black with defrauding his company by diverting part of the proceeds of these newspaper sales to himself. He mounted an expensive and vocal defense that succeeded in knocking out many of the charges, some at trial and more on appeal. Black, long a successful author, has written a bulging memoir of the case in which he settles scores and warmly recounts his relationships with the common folk in a federal prison in Florida. Still, Black was convicted for looting the company through one of those noncompete payments in one of the newspaper sales.

The case looked flagrant at first because the noncompete payments were ridiculous. But prosecutors ended up with a tough road against Black. It can be hard to prove that an executive who presides over a company in near dictatorial fashion, even a public company (Black's was public but he personally owned the largest portion of it), means to deceive anyone because he doesn't run something by a complacent board of directors.

After all, if a board decides in its business judgment to pay an executive a percentage of the proceeds from every asset the company sells off, that board is, ordinarily, free to do that. Black and his codefendants said that was what had happened: these payments were really "management fees." They came up with the noncompete story, they said, because they hoped that classifying the payments that way would lower their tax burden in Canada. Even if the Canadian tax dodge were illegal, it was not the type of fraud under United States law that the Chicago prosecutors had charged.

Embezzlement has been a crime for centuries, and a fairly simple one. If the bank teller or store clerk takes a few bills home at the end of the day, that's just stealing from the bank. But if a bank manager's job includes taking customers to lunch and she has control of an account for that purpose, it becomes harder to prove that she's stealing when she takes home some cash—or a few extra steaks from the lunch place.

For the powerful modern CEO of the big corporation, in an era of large and complex compensation, the legal concept of theft works poorly. The law needs to use the concept of fraud. For fraud, there needs to be some deception. Modern CEO pay itself may look to many people like bald looting, especially when compared to worker pay. Whether or not a modern CEO's pay package ought to be said to be a pillaging of her corporation, her conduct cannot fairly be treated as criminal unless it's been hidden from, and has not been approved by, the directors who govern the corporation and the shareholders who own it. To be paid way too much—however one wants to measure that—may be selfish, greedy, tone-deaf, wasteful, and bad for business. But it's not a crime.

Fraud by the Numbers

"SHOW ME the books" has been a standard demand in negotiations to buy a business or lend it money for probably as long as there have been businesses and writing implements. And it's always been possible to lie with numbers. If a farmer puts "20" next to "pigs" on an inventory he gives you before you buy his farm and it turns out he had only 10 pigs, you've been defrauded.

A lesson from the first century of American industrialization, brought home by the stock market crash of 1929, was that a reasonably safe and attractive capitalist economy requires that investors have faith in the numbers. The great reform of American securities regulation in the 1930s, one of the cornerstones of the New Deal, was based on two simple ideas. Investors will be better protected and more willing to advance their funds into markets if corporate numbers—the profits, losses, assets, and debts that are the vital signs of any business—are both transparent and reliable. Transparency was promoted by adopting uniform systems for corporate accounting and reporting of financial results. Reliability was promoted by adopting tough new sanctions for fraud in financial reporting.

The New Deal reforms in American capital markets are largely a success story. Recessions aside, American investment markets have had some amazing boom times since World War II and they attract capital from far more people and places than they used to. But fraud is a chameleon. The more complex the surroundings, the harder it becomes to identify the animal. The interaction of modern accounting systems and modern corporate finance have produced a kind of lying through numbers that keeps getting more sophisticated. This kind of fraud never seems to go away.

Bernard Ebbers is the fallen man who built a small regional phone company in Mississippi into Worldcom and then saw it disappear in 2002, in what was then the largest bankruptcy in U.S. history.[15] He is still in prison. Ebbers committed a massive and flagrant accounting fraud that was not all that far removed from doubling the number of pigs on a farmer's inventory. This makes his case a good place to start.

Worldcom ran into trouble when the dotcom bubble of 1998 to 2001 popped. Demand for the company's broadband lines suddenly dropped hard. Ebbers would not tolerate a big dip in reported earnings. It would puncture the Worldcom story he had brilliantly written. It also would put him in personal financial distress because he had used almost all of his holdings in Worldcom stock as leverage to expand his own investment portfolio, which included slow-to-sell assets such as art and property.

Ebbers and his advisers avoided having to give their shareholders bad news for a little while with a mix of questionable but ticky-tacky accounting strategies: moving a bit of this over there, changing estimates of value on this or that, and pushing a few things forward to future quarters. This approach bought the company a little time, but to maintain the story they needed something bigger.

Scott Sullivan, who was the CFO of Worldcom, proposed a secret billion-dollar switch. The company would stop treating as an operating cost the money it spent leasing space on transmission lines of other telecom companies and instead record that money as a capital expenditure. Ebbers agreed. On a company's financial statements, this makes a massive difference. Operating costs are, well, costs—like the electric bill or the coffee employees go through in the break room. Capital expenses, like the construction of a new factory, are recorded more like investments and can be depreciated over time, meaning they're not subtracted from earnings all at once.

Worldcom was hemorrhaging money, and this switch of a billion dollars from one part of the books to another hid that basic fact. The case involved only a slightly teched-up version of the old play of the business that has two sets of books—the false one to show to outsiders and the hidden one that keeps track of where the money actually goes. Once prosecutors secured Sullivan's testimony, and could prove what Ebbers knew, it was no surprise that Ebbers landed in prison. The court that rejected Ebbers's appeal even ruled that it wouldn't have mattered if Ebbers could have argued that the accounting rules might have allowed Worldcom to treat its leasing payments as capital expenditures. The ultimate issue, the judges said, was whether Ebbers was fooling Worldcom's shareholders and knew it. A massive switch in accounting like this, without anyone knowing about it, is a heads-we-win, tails-you-lose approach to financial reporting that is fraud.

Unfortunately for prosecutors and the courts, the relative simplicity of Ebbers's scheme is not common in the large modern corporation.

If the executives who committed accounting fraud at Worldcom were playing three-card monte, the financiers at Enron were running a full-fledged casino.[16] Among the prosecution team on the Enron case it became a standard line early in the investigation that every accounting fraud case that had come before had been algebra to Enron's calculus. (In other words, be patient with us while we investigate, please.)

Fully explaining the Enron fraud requires a book. In my opinion, the *Fortune* reporters who covered the company's collapse wrote the best one.[17] For our purpose of understanding fraud, the important thing is to see why some of what Enron's managers did was criminal and some of it was not. Contrary to popular belief, and "house of cards" analogies prevalent at the time, the whole company was not crooked.

The Enron executives who were prosecuted did not go to prison for running a fake company. The prosecutions were based on specific accounting maneuvers that crossed the line from risky or aggressive management of the company's finances into fraud. And the main thing that pushed those strategies across the line was the knowledge and intent of the managers who pursued them. Two examples should help explain the nature of the case.

First there is the complex effort to hide losses in Enron's bad investments that was represented, roughly, in the story of The Company with the Shaky Assets from the beginning of this chapter. From one perspective, the entire structure looks bogus. How could a company use its own stock—the value of which rests largely on the market's belief about the company's present and future strength—as the *collateral* for hedging its own volatile assets? Because expert accountants at Arthur Andersen, which was then one of the world's most respected auditing firms, said their reading of the accounting rules permitted it, as long as the collateral also included a little money from somewhere outside of Enron.

Those accountants were compromised by their fees. They were probably wrong about the rules—though the deliberate novelty of the scheme ensured that the outcome under the rules would be ambiguous. Wrong or not, however, the thing was hugely complex and the accountants said what they said to Enron's executives, who were not accountants and could plausibly say they were relying on the advice and reputations of the best experts money could buy. The scheme crossed the line into fraud mainly because, as you may recall from the example, the company promised Enron's CFO Andrew Fastow, who agreed to contribute the necessary slice of "outside" money to the deal, that he would be paid back immediately. He took no real risk. That fact, which was hidden from even Enron's submissive accountants, blew up the whole structure, making it invalid under even the most aggressive reading of the accounting rules.

This might sound like a technical basis for separating a crime from ordinary corporate finance. But fraud is about deception. And deception—at least deception that is wrong and deserves moral blame—is a purposeful act. The deceiver is a person who deliberately tries to put one over on someone else. If a corporate executive managing the complexities of a big company's books thinks she's following the letter of the accounting rules—even if she's doing so to paint the rosiest picture she can—then she may not be intending to lie to anyone. Or, at the least, it may be extremely difficult for a prosecutor to prove beyond doubt that she had that intention.

Accountants don't have a stack of get-out-of-jail-free cards that they can sell. Bernard Ebbers was clearly engaged in a massive deception at Worldcom, and he knew it, even if he could produce some expert who would say Ebbers had an argument for what he was doing with those leasing costs. The more complicated the accounting gets, however, the harder it becomes to say (and prove) that the executive did not genuinely believe that the approval of the accountants meant he or she wasn't doing anything deceitful.

That's why our second Enron example, discussed in chapter one, didn't result in any criminal charges even though it was of even greater consequence. The biggest part of Enron's business, and the one that drove its explosive growth and celebrity status among companies in the 1990s, was its energy-trading operations. As a trading company, Enron's credit rating was critical because a trading company is always borrowing, so to speak, from those with whom it trades. A trading company with a solid credit rating attracts more business and can demand better terms on its deals. One with a falling credit rating loses counterparties very fast and can collapse as a result. Some may recall the sudden death of the hedge fund Long Term Capital Management in the late 1990s, a business from which Enron was at pains, sometimes misleadingly, to distinguish itself in the minds of investors.

A corporation's creditworthiness, like anybody's, is based in large part on how much debt it already has. No lender wants to wait at the end of a long line of creditors when there may be nothing left by the time he gets to the payment window. The more money a company borrows, the more risky it becomes, the more its credit rating goes down, and the more costly it gets for the company to borrow more. In theory, that is. If the credit rating agencies (Standard & Poor's and Moody's are the big ones) don't look hard enough, they may give a company a credit rating it doesn't deserve. And lenders and others doing business with a company may rely too comfortably on what the rating agencies have said.

As we saw, Enron, its accountants, and two of the big banks in New York (Citi and Chase) figured out a way for the Houston company to borrow more money from the banks—billions of dollars more—without reporting it as debt. In those deals, the prepaid forwards that involved special companies set up in the Channel Islands between England and France (an offshore tax and regulatory haven), they used accounting alchemy to turn borrowed money into operating income.[18]

Enron sold a huge amount of energy futures positions to Citi and Chase in exchange for cash that Enron did not want to have to borrow. Recall that these deals were structured so that Enron would later buy all those futures positions back from Citi and Chase. And the difference between the price at which the banks bought Enron's "forward positions" and the price at which they sold them back would be exactly what it would have cost Enron to borrow the same amount from the banks. If it looks like a loan, walks like a loan, and quacks like a loan, one would think, it's a loan. Structured with enough steps in between, however, the accounting rules (arguably) didn't treat it as a loan. And Arthur Andersen was not willing to say this could be misleading even though the rules technically might allow it.

Proving criminally fraudulent intent on these transactions—even though they helped to disguise how fragile Enron was—would have been nearly impossible. Multiple accountants' approvals appeared all over the deals and the rating agencies themselves had been consulted in advance. Before Enron paid the banks for these transactions, it of course wanted to know if the rating agencies would nonetheless treat the deals as, in substance, borrowing and thus lower Enron's credit rating.

The rating agencies—not surprisingly given what we learned about their later role in the mortgage securities market—said they would not treat the deals as debt. Had Kenneth Lay, Jeffrey Skilling, and Enron's financial engineers been charged with deliberately deceiving the market by using the billions of prepaid forward deals with Citi and Chase, the testimony of those credit raters would have hobbled the prosecution.

This explains in part why Richard Fuld and the other leaders of Lehman Brothers were not indicted for fraud in connection with the collapse of that firm. As we saw in the previous chapter, one of the principal ways that Lehman kept itself afloat in spite of its increasingly grave exposure to mortgage-backed securities was that financing and accounting device called Repo 105. It was basically the same thing as Enron's prepaid forwards: a way to borrow money but treat it as operating income instead of debt.[19] Repo 105 had the accountants' paws all over it and thus was a poor basis for a criminal case against Fuld and other top managers who were not accountants and could plausibly say they delegated the question of whether these deals were permissible.

At this point, you would be right to want to blow up the entire American corporate accounting system. So it's important to remember that the project of mandating and systematizing corporate financial reporting that commenced with the New Deal reforms has been a success. Americans enjoy the world's most transparent and routinized markets. But it remains true that the regulatory system does not seem to be able to control corporate finance. Indeed, the accounting rules only appear to make that beast bigger and more powerful, as the creature continually adapts itself to become more resistant to the effects of the rules.

Laws against criminal fraud give the legal system a backstop: punish the wrongdoers even if they have an argument that they followed the Byzantine accounting rules. Courts, as in the Worldcom case, have wisely said that option is available.[20] Technical compliance with GAAP (Generally Accepted Accounting Principles) is not an absolute defense to fraud in corporate financial reporting.

Even interpreted this way, however, fraud prohibitions don't solve the problem in cases like Enron's prepaid forwards or Lehman's Repo 105. Principles of American law most of the time prohibit imprisoning someone who did not mean to commit a crime. With criminal fraud in corporate financial reporting, that means having the specific intent to defraud the market, something that is very hard to prove. When an executive gets an opinion from an independent accounting firm on a really complicated issue, his intent is often not just hard to prove. It may have been absent altogether.

The corporate accounting regime, together with the failure to regulate accountants' independence effectively, remains the problem. And that problem of complexity and outmaneuvering is a direct result of what that regime is trying to accomplish: control of an industry (corporate finance) that is competitive, lucrative, and, at least in some form, essential to the existence of markets for raising the capital needed to start and operate businesses.

No Bankers in Prison

NOW WE can take on what's been the $64,000 question in corporate crime for some years: why are no bankers in jail for what caused the 2008 financial crisis? In its most common form, this is a question about fraud. Specifically a question about buyer-seller fraud, which is fraud in the form of the simple example of Blind Man Bluffed from the beginning of this chapter: a seller intentionally deceives a buyer into purchasing something that's not what the buyer thought it was.

The big question from the 2008 crisis—summarized by the exclamations of "fraud!" from Steve Carell's character in the film version of

The Big Short—goes like this.[21] The banks caused a financial, and then general economic, crisis by leveraging a bubble in housing prices into a big bubble in securities—one of historic magnitude. The bursting of the latter bubble immediately placed big financial institutions, whose routine lending is essential to the survival of the economy, in peril of rapid failure. The banks created the securities bubble, at great profit to themselves, by making and selling massive quantities of investment products that were backed, directly and indirectly, by cash flows from home loans.

The banks and other mortgage dealers inflated that bubble further by loosening lending standards in order to create more home loans that could produce more cash flows for the assembly and sale of more securities—which brought in more proceeds that could be lent out to more mortgage borrowers. And so on. The banks kept on doing this while knowing that a sharp national decline in housing prices would crash that securities market and imperil financial institutions. Somehow the law must make someone who was responsible for that a criminal.[22]

While a film can paint with a broad brush and freely tap into abundant, justified anger about these events, a legal theory of fraud needs to proceed in steps. The first is to identify who has been defrauded. There are several candidates here. None, it turns out, works out cleanly.

Start at the "bottom," with the home buyers. People who are lent funds they may be unable to pay back are generally not the victims of fraud unless they have been lied to about how much they will owe (for example, if a bank hid the truth about interest rates that would later balloon). If an interest rate is illegally high, borrowers may be victims of usury. But that wasn't the case here, just as it wasn't in credit card and other consumer debt markets, even if everyone later saw clearly that rates, among other features of loans, should have been more strictly regulated.

People who bought mortgage-backed securities from banks seem like the more obvious candidates as victims of fraud. But to make a bad wager, even a downright stupid one, is not to be defrauded. The average casino gambler may become convinced that she can beat the house, in part because of the lure of the casino's advertising and its other ploys to get her in the door and keep her there. She's under an illusion, deceived in fact. But she has not been defrauded. There must have been some intentional and wrongful deception worked upon the fraud victim—either a lie or the concealment of important information that the seller was obligated to disclose. This is where the case of the mortgage-backed securities, and the many baroque products derivative thereof, runs into problems.

As we all know, deception and expectations about disclosure vary a great deal by market. The candor a buyer expects from a seller is not the same on the used car lot or in the bazaar as in the surgeon's or lawyer's office. Negotiation and trading are competitive activities in which each side seeks to gain advantage over the other. Especially with financial products, a trade doesn't happen, by definition, unless the seller and the buyer have different beliefs about the future value of the product.

The buyers of the mortgage-backed securities were, for the most part, other traders at other banks and related financial institutions.[23] Those traders were mostly familiar with the nature of those products, the risks involved, and conditions in the housing market. In many instances, they may themselves have sold the same products. Unless the seller of the security lied about the nature or quality of the mortgages underlying the product, even the late-in-the-game player who was still buying when the rest of the world was selling is dumb but not defrauded.

Surely these well-informed buyers understood that other financial institutions might be taking different positions in the market—shorting the home loan business even as they continued to sell long positions to other banks—even if those financial institutions were doing so quietly. But it wouldn't matter even if the buyers didn't know that. The ordinary buyer of a product in an arm's-length transaction doesn't have a right to be told where else the seller's money is going.

The exception proves the rule. The most notable case that went to a trial (and not even a criminal trial) was the SEC's charges against a Goldman Sachs banker for selling a mortgage-backed securities product called Abacus.²⁴ In that deal—presumably in contrast to most others, since few others with similar facts have been found in spite of the strong incentives for disappointed traders to sue—Goldman misled a German bank that bought the Abacus product about how the underlying mortgages were selected. Goldman told the buyer that the mortgage loans packaged in the particular securities had been reviewed and approved by a "selection agent," an independent company with some credibility in the mortgage securities market.

This was true. But Goldman did not say that the mortgages had also been selected with the "help" of Paulson & Co., the now famous hedge fund that made billions by going short on mortgage-backed securities, including in this very Abacus deal. In effect, a gambler was being asked to place a wager on the Packers not only without being told who was betting on the Vikings (why should the gambler have a right to know that?) but *also* without being told that a big Vikings bettor was helping the Packers' coach decide who would start on Sunday. Michael Lewis's *The Big Short* recounts the amazing story of Paulson and others who made a killing on the collapse of the home loan securities market.

The SEC won a jury verdict against the Goldman banker who constructed the Abacus transaction, a trader who called himself "Fabulous" Fabrice Tourre. But it was a civil case only. Even under that low burden of proof—more likely than not, as opposed to beyond a reasonable doubt—the jurors said they had qualms about finding against the banker. They sympathized with the defense portrayal of a midlevel guy who was just doing his job like anybody else in the market.

Another civil case brought against a Citibank trader for concealing information about a similar securities product resulted in a loss for the SEC at a jury trial. Likewise, the Justice Department lost a criminal trial against some Bear Stearns bankers who, late in the game, sold mortgage-backed securities while chortling to each other in e-mails about the trashiness of their products and the teetering market for such securities.

The Justice Department passed on the Goldman Sachs case, which probably wasn't strong enough for a criminal prosecution. The evidence was less than decisive that the selection agent would have withheld its seal of approval from the Abacus deal if it had known about Paulson's involvement in selecting the pool of loans. More importantly, this one case was unusual for the seller's concealment of a fairly egregious sort of fact.

The problem in the market for mortgage-backed securities wasn't lies. It was that the buyers didn't have enough incentive to ask the sellers the hard questions that either would have resulted in real, provable fraud or would have stopped these deals long before they got out of control. And the biggest problem of all was that the people left holding the bag—those affected by the collapse and bailouts of many of America's largest financial institutions—weren't even parties to these deals. If someone is hurt because she deposits or invests her money in a bank that makes stupid investments, she's not the victim of fraud unless the bank has deceived her about how it invests its money. Likewise, if she invests her money in a pension or mutual fund that invests in banks that make bad decisions, she's not the victim of fraud unless the pension or mutual fund has deceived her about what it used her money to invest in.

The 2008 collapse of debt securities markets was many things, including proof of a massive regulatory failure and a fiesta of foolish risk management. But it was not, at least writ large, fraud. There may have been some frauds committed along the way—a lie here about mortgage underwriting standards, a tricky cover-up there about how loans were selected for a particular security.[25] Perhaps if the government had looked harder for more of those cases there might have been a few more prosecutions. The pursuit of those cases has not come to a conclusion, at least as to mop-up work on a few deals and traders who may still be caught in clear lies that would support indictments.[26]

The public record on lies and concealment about underwriting practices in particular—the banks' efforts (or lack thereof) to verify the creditworthiness of borrowers whose loans were securitized—is frustratingly inconclusive. Documents from the Justice Department's civil settlements with large banks such as Bank of America, as well as a federal judge's massive written opinion in a government lawsuit against the Nomura group of financial companies, are filled with descriptions of shoddy underwriting practices and misrepresentations about those practices. But these documents from civil suits, and others like them, have not demonstrated where the evidence of knowledge, intent, and hands-on involvement—in the processes of both reviewing the mortgages and selling the securities—would have been sufficient to prosecute named individuals for criminal fraud.[27]

The most serious obstacle to fraud prosecutions was the nature of the market for mortgage derivative securities itself, which was a meeting place for some of the world's most sophisticated and risk-hungry buyers and sellers of some of the industry's most bespoke products— products that were, it bears emphasis, perfectly legal for banks to own and trade.

Contrast the sale of mortgage-backed securities prior to 2008 with a more recent banking fiasco: the manipulation of benchmark interest rates, including the influential London Interbank Offering Rate (LIBOR).[28] LIBOR is actually quite simple. It's an index consisting of an average of the interest rates, measured to the hundredths of a percent, that about fifteen big banks pay to borrow funds from each other on any given day. The only way to get the information for this index is for the banks to report to the banking authority in London what they're paying in interest as they borrow money from each other.

Unfortunately, there is (or at least was) no straightforward math for measuring this. The banks had to use some judgment and do some estimating. This presented an irresistible opportunity for traders at many of the banks whose jobs and incentives were to buy and sell interest-rate swaps in amounts and configurations that would earn those traders the heftiest possible bonuses. These were deals to hedge against volatility in lending rates. The traders priced their agreements using LIBOR as the benchmark. The price in an interest rate swap would be set as, for example, LIBOR (that is, whatever LIBOR would turn out to be on the date the deal concluded) plus "six basis points [hundredths of a percent]."

If a trader could influence the number his bank reported, he could change the LIBOR rate a tick or two just as he was due to get paid on a deal he had made, for example, six months earlier. That would be kind of like your bank being able to change the Fed's prime lending rate precisely when your payment is about to come due on your "prime plus a quarter point" home equity loan. The traders developed relationships with the people at their banks who had the job of reporting the number to the London banking authority, and even with traders at other banks, that allowed them to influence the content of the banks' submissions.

Horribly, the traders did this a whole lot, the banks had no effective mechanism for preventing it, and the problem became epidemic. The rate rigging was so widespread that, unlike in the case of the mortgage-backed securities market, the government has found itself awash in flagrant messages among the bankers that have invited criminal charges.

Such as: "I'm not setting libor 7 [one hundredths] away from the truth . . . I'll get [United Bank of Scotland] banned if I do that," to which the response was, "OK . . . not asking for it to be 7 [one hundredths] from reality . . . any help appreciated." Or: "Mate ur getting bloody good at this libor game . . . think of me when yur on yur yacht in monaco wont yu." And: "Morning skipper . . . will be setting an obscenely high [LIBOR rate] again today," to which the response was, "Oh dear my poor customers . . . hehehe!!" And my favorite, one fellow who ended up indicted, responding to a request from a trader: "Sure no prob . . . I'll probably get a few phone calls but no worries mate . . . there's bigger crooks in the market than us guys!"

With that kind of evidence, one might think, most people's grandmothers could get a jury to convict. The interesting thing for thinking about the problem of fraud in corporate crime, however, is that even the flagrant case of LIBOR manipulation is not crystal clear. These traders, like the ones in the mortgage-backed securities market, were dealing among themselves in a sophisticated and specialized market in which most if not all of the banks appear to have been monkeying with how they reported their interest rates. After a trial in London in early 2016, a jury acquitted five of these traders of all fraud charges in the face of a record of such snickering messages.

That everyone is a criminal should be no defense. Indeed, it could suggest a conspiracy among the banks to rig the market for interest rates in violation of antitrust law. But it does raise questions about whether traders who dealt with other traders who were manipulating LIBOR were really in the dark about rate manipulation in a way that would make these trades fraudulent. "Hey, you sold me these interest rate products while you were tinkering with the interest rate behind the scenes" could end up looking like crocodile tears. Some of the indicted traders have tested their cases with juries even though their written statements seem to have left them caught red-handed.

As we've discussed, fraud is a question of deception. And deception is always a question of context. Just think about how often in one's daily commercial experiences, much less in life generally, one isn't fooled for a moment by someone else's careful silence, selective report, or even bald-faced lie. Occasionally that might be because someone has tried to commit a fraud and failed. But most of the time it's because someone, whether she was ethically upstanding or not, has played a game of business or social affairs the way that game gets played.

This is why many problems at the higher reaches of finance that seem to be ones of buyer-seller fraud are not—despite some extremely harmful downstream effects in markets—frauds at all, or at least are not criminal cases because they're not, beyond a reasonable doubt, intentionally fraudulent.

Insider Trading

IF WE did one of those picture association tests using a photo of a man standing in a business suit with handcuffs on, a lot of people would probably say "insider trading"—the offense of trading in securities on the basis of material, nonpublic information in violation of a duty not to use such information for personal gain. Insider trading has become an archetype for crime in corporate America. If we then asked viewers of the picture to describe a typical case of this crime, a lot of examples might start with two guys on a golf course.

As it happens, one of America's most famous golfers recently found himself, as they say in the law enforcement business, "under the micro-scope" with regard to insider trading. It seems that Phil Mickelson likes to hang around a bit with a man named Billy Walters, a Las Vegan who is a remarkably successful gambler, including in the risky area of sports betting. Walters likes golf, which paradoxically is a sport that operates on the honor rule and is also a betting man's game.

Reportedly, Walters and Mickelson both traded profitably—surely no coincidence—in options linked to Clorox stock just before the price rose on news that the famous corporate "raider" Carl Icahn was plan-ning a takeover bid for the company. The government investigated, presumably on the theory that Walters, who seems to have some con-nection to Icahn, got a tip from Icahn and then perhaps shared it with Mickelson over a friendly, and no doubt heavily wagered, game of golf.

The case seems have gone nowhere. And not only because investi-gators couldn't prove that Walters received an insider tip about Icahn's play for Clorox. As we'll see, even if Walters had received such a tip, and even if Walters had said, "Hey, Phil, nice drive and, by the way, buy Clorox and bet on the Jets," Mickelson probably would not have been guilty of insider trading. Even insider trading, that most classic of busi-ness crimes, is far from simple.

The crime of insider trading brackets the roughly thirty-year era of corporate crime that concerns this book. The industry of business crime prosecution got rolling with the insider trading prosecutions of the 1980s, brought by Rudy Giuliani's U.S. Attorney's Office in New York against Michael Milken, Ivan Boesky, Dennis Levine, and others during the heyday of the leveraged buyout, junk bonds, and Drexel Burnham Lambert.[29]

After a long period of steady but fairly normal enforcement, insider trading prosecutions have exploded in the last several years in the world of Wall Street hedge funds, brokerages, and even law firms. Preet Bharara, who has Giuliani's old job, has raised the alarm about "rampant" insider trading in the financial industry and has used wire-taps and other aggressive strategies to bring nearly a hundred cases in the government's biggest white collar crime initiative since the 2008 financial crisis.[30]

Here is a fact that will surprise most people who aren't lawyers: federal statutes—the laws made by Congress—include no express prohibition on insider trading. This activity that seems so prototypically crooked was made criminal relatively recently, and in a roundabout way. Insider trading seems like it ought to be the easiest case among business crimes—an unambiguous prohibition everyone can agree on. But it turns out to be yet another instance of law struggling to figure out where and how lines should be drawn among competitive and evolving practices in financial commerce.

The crime of insider trading grew slowly between the 1960s and 1980s, rooting itself in the general rule against fraud in securities trading, the famous "Rule 10b-5." This rule says it is illegal to "employ any device, scheme, or artifice to defraud" in a securities transaction. Another provision of securities law says that anyone who does so "willfully" may be imprisoned. The idea that made 10b-5 the home for insider trading in American law—one initially conceived by creative lawyers at the SEC—is that the inside trader defrauds the person with whom she trades a security because she conceals something (that she has inside information) that the other person has a right to know, and would want to know, before deciding whether to trade with her. Insider trading, on this theory, is a particular kind of buyer-seller fraud.

This makes insider trading law very different from what a lot of people think it is. Many trades made with inside information are legal. Recall, from examples like banks trading mortgage-backed securities with each other, that frauds involving concealment or nondisclosure require a story about how the seller who is keeping her mouth shut has an obligation to open it and disclose the information at issue, and thus deceives the buyer when she remains mute.

In modern markets, not every seller of securities has an obligation to tell every potential buyer everything he or she knows. This must be true. Otherwise, there would be no reason or reward for anybody to do research and the whole investment analysis and advising business would collapse. The business of trading itself might no longer have appeal and the death of investment analysis, foibles of analysts aside, would leave us with a far less transparent corporate sector.

In any event, being industrious to get a leg up in markets isn't bad behavior. If I go wandering around Best Buy stores for weeks and figure out that people don't like the latest smart phone, I should be able to bet against the phone manufacturer's stock. I should be allowed to make that bet even if no one else in the market has bothered to do the same work and the investor herd is mindlessly advancing in the other direction.

Insider trading is not, therefore, trading on information that no one else in the market has. Buyers and sellers in securities markets do not have a general duty to lay all cards on the table. Insider trading is buying or selling while having information one has an obligation to disclose to one's counterpart in the market (whether or not one is dealing with that person directly).

So who has that obligation to disclose (or to refrain from trading)? And when do they have it? The law first said: only corporate insiders who are trading in their company's stock with the company's own shareholders. There was nothing especially novel or controversial about saying that a corporate executive has special duties of candor toward the shareholders who own the company that employs her.[31]

That covers everyone's idea of the classic inside trade: Jeffrey Skilling dumps his Enron stock when he knows that the company's finances are going south and the share price will soon tumble. If one borrows in a rough way from ideas in the law like being an accomplice to a crime or conspiring to violate the law, this theory of fraud sweeps in a lot more people, like lawyers who work for the company or friends of the executive whom he tips so they can trade their own stock before the bad news comes out.

Yet this theory of insider trading as fraud leaves out a lot of people. To take two famous cases, what about a *Wall Street Journal* reporter who tips his accomplices to important, price-moving information about companies when the paper hasn't yet published that news?[32] Or a law firm partner who trades in the shares of a company that is not his firm's client but that he learns is about to be bought by another business that *is* a client of his firm?[33] Neither of these people has that special relationship of corporate employee to shareholder, nor is either of them involved in a trading scheme with someone who stands in that relationship.

The courts invented a broader theory of fraud to deal with these cases. The *Journal* reporter and the law firm partner have not defrauded their counterparties in the stock market. They have deceived, and thus defrauded, their *employers*—the newspaper or the law firm—by stealing the employer's information for their own use, in violation of their duties as employees and without disclosing that fact to their employers. This is, if you like, embezzlement of information as fraud. A stretch, to be sure, as Justice Clarence Thomas pointed out in a dissenting opinion in the key Supreme Court case, *United States v. O'Hagan*.[34] But the idea, called the misappropriation theory of insider trading, has thrived.

To recap this somewhat counterintuitive story, the law against insider trading is not "don't trade with nonpublic information." It is "First, don't trade in your own company's stock with nonpublic information and, second, don't trade any stock with nonpublic information that you got at work." Also, no end runs around these two rules: "Don't trade with any nonpublic information you got from someone who gave it to you so you could trade when it would have been illegal for the other person to do so."[35]

In a funny and not at all accidental way, this meandering and awkward theory of insider trading as fraud has arrived about where we might have set the line if given a clean slate. In other words, what kinds of trading with informational advantage *should* be crimes? Most people would think: definitely the CEO who trades ahead of bad earnings news; definitely the law firm partner who trades ahead of the merger; and maybe even the *Wall Street Journal* reporter who trades ahead of a market-moving story.

But not because people would look at the facts of those cases and immediately declare, "That's fraud—I know it when I see it." More likely because people think those are all cases of cheating. Industriously getting the upper hand through dogged research is the American way. Having an advantage because you happen to know a guy, or work somewhere, is not.

The law of insider trading has tried to balance these two ideas: fair play in markets and good old competition and questing for profit. On a curious recursive logic, insider trading prohibitions are believed necessary to persuade investors that markets are fair, so that investors will continue to play in the markets, so that markets will not consist solely of cheaters, so that investors will continue to play in the markets. The economist George Akerlof was awarded a Nobel Prize for theorizing this general problem of a "lemons market."[36] At the same time, the rule cannot prohibit all trading with informational advantage because such a rule would eliminate incentives for trading based on research.

The result is a pattern of prosecutions that could strike the reasoned observer as unprincipled if not inexplicable. Rajat Gupta ends up in prison while Steven Cohen does not.[37] Gupta was the former CEO of the prestigious McKinsey consulting firm who landed a seat on the Goldman Sachs board of directors. For reasons that remain hard to grasp, Gupta leaked information about Goldman board discussions to his associate Raj Rajaratnam, who traded on those secrets for the profit of his own hedge fund. Gupta was a classic inside trader: the corporate board member who finds out good news before it hits the market and buys up the stock or, as in Gupta's case, tips off a friend who buys.

Gupta's was an easy case for insider trading, on both general intuitions about cheating and on the legal theory of insider trading as fraud. As a board member, Gupta had, the judge who sentenced him said, "stabbed Goldman in the back." Gupta had to be sent to prison in spite of his otherwise exemplary career as a business manager and an effective and sincere global philanthropist. And in spite of the fact that, incredibly, he made no money from his tips to Rajaratnam.

Steven Cohen—ruthlessly, by all accounts—ran a multibillion-dollar hedge fund, SAC Capital, that made money by making profitable bets on where the market was going. More than a few of those bets, it turned out, were based on leaks from people in various industries with whom SAC's employees had cultivated relationships. Several of Cohen's traders were convicted of insider trading for recommending and executing transactions that made Cohen hundreds of millions of dollars. Prosecutors never got to Cohen because they couldn't prove that Cohen knew that his traders' recommendations to dump or grab particular securities at certain moments were based on illegal tips from corporate insiders.

Cohen was running an investment fund in an industry that exists for the purpose of capitalizing on lots of little advantages in knowledge that come from lots of places, most of them the legitimate, smart investment analysis with which the law of insider trading has no quarrel. Prosecutors, who never caught Cohen on tape or in an incriminating e-mail, couldn't rely on the argument that Cohen surely knew his traders' recommendations came from people who tipped them off in violation of the law. Too much of what hedge funds do has to be treated as allowable research—in which the shady "research" can be buried—lest the rule about insider trading become that no one is allowed to seek profit from the fruits of her labor.

The wrong of insider trading may seem like a clear fixed point in the rules for capital markets. But it too turns out to be an unstable and evolving idea. Even now, the law is continuing to search for just where the line should fall between informational advantage that is the reward for industrious effort and illegitimate profits that flow from privilege in status or relationships.

The newest results of this effort have been disappointing. In December 2014, the most important court for the law of insider trading, the U.S. Court of Appeals for the Second Circuit (the appellate court a few blocks from Wall Street), reversed the convictions of two hedge fund traders who profited handsomely in 2008 from advance tips on quarterly earnings news that was forthcoming from the tech companies Dell and NVIDIA. The facts were a paradigm of insider trading: wealthy traders who enjoyed profits only because of their connections to corporate employees who improperly leaked confidential information.

According to the appeals court, the legal problem in the prosecution of these men, Todd Newman and Anthony Chiasson, was that the information about Dell and NVIDIA came to them downstream through a chain of tips. In these situations, the ultimate recipient of the tip who trades on it has to know that the person who originally leaked the information upstream did so improperly. The idea, under the misappropriation theory, is that insider trading is fraud only if the person taking the information from his employer and disclosing it to others does so improperly—to trade for business or favors, not, for example, to blow the whistle about wrongdoing. The legal test for impropriety is whether the person disclosing the information did so for "personal benefit."

In the case of the fund managers Newman and Chiasson, the court said those who trade on downstream tips have to *know* that the leaker of the information originally disclosed it for personal benefit and the prosecutors failed to prove that in this case. Other recently convicted inside traders, including one of Steven Cohen's employees, have attacked their convictions as likewise failing this test. In effect, the rule for tipping in the clubby world of high-end Wall Street funds has become don't ask, don't tell. If someone provides information he "heard from a guy I know," without any details about who that person is or why he leaked it, then downstream "tippees" are free to trade away.

Many have suggested that it is finally time for Congress to step in and make a specific law against insider trading. However difficult the details of that project prove to be, the decision in the Newman and Chiasson case has compelled me to agree.

Who Belongs in Prison?

IN MY course on business crime, I usually finish our extensive unit on criminal fraud by asking the students what they have concluded about how the legal system selects cases for criminal prosecution. If the law of fraud is so general—"don't commit fraud," and you might go to prison if you do it really intentionally—and fraud itself is so darn elusive—shape shifting with context and identifiable only against its particular background market—then how can any lawyer, much less client, predict who and what will be prosecuted?

One recent fall, when I posed this question at the end of a long discussion of the Goldman Sachs Abacus deal and the LIBOR manipulation cases, a student raised his hand and, no doubt picturing Snidely Whiplash of Bullwinkle fame, said, "I think we look for some evidence of mustache twirling." Yes, that's it.

Fraud cases need a perpetrator, a victim, a story about deception, and some harm or at least potential harm. But, in the end, the cases that prosecutors think deserve prosecution, that juries think deserve guilty verdicts, and that judges think deserve serious punishments, are the ones in which the evidence—what we often call the "smoking gun"—shows that the defendant knew what she was doing was wrong.

There are two reasons that moral intuition leads people assigned the job of prosecutor, juror, or judge to focus on the mustache twirling, even though the law of fraud has nothing to say about mustaches. These reasons are two sides of the same coin. First, people who think about the wrongfulness of what they're doing before pressing ahead, then go ahead anyway, are morally bad actors—people who have chosen to do wrong to others. Second, the serious worry, enshrined in America's Constitution and its rule-of-law foundations, that a person should not lose her liberty except when she has chosen to cross a line is assuaged if we think somebody knew what she was doing was wrong.

Actually, the focus on mustache twirling might also have something to do with the essence of the law of fraud. If this chapter has established anything about fraud in business crime, it's that an effort to deceive someone in a market becomes fraud only if the norms of the particular market make that behavior wrong. It all depends on context: the used car lot versus the lawyer's office. One way—maybe not the only or ideal way, but perhaps the best available one—to figure out whether a sophisticated, sharp practice in a specialized market is wrongful is to see if the people engaged in that practice themselves understood it to be wrong.

There's plenty to complain about in this approach to identifying each new fraud, not least its heavy contingency on the available evidence in any particular case. But it may be the best we can do. And it's an accurate depiction of how the American legal system grapples with the hard job it has been given of separating merely "aggressive" new business practices from criminal fraud.

We've given American law and its ministers the important but vexing task of specifying criminal wrongdoing within a vast and complex world of competitive economic activity that is not only legal but is welcome, celebrated, rewarded, and to some extent a matter of liberty and right. Fraud is the principal conceptual tool for that task. There are others as well, to which we now turn.

3

Loopholing

AMERICANS HAVE HAD a growing feeling over the last twenty years or so that, in the fight to control big industry, law is getting its rear kicked. Many regulation projects that are immensely important to safety, health, and the creation and fair distribution of wealth—maintenance of a solid banking system, control of consumer debt markets, production and sale of safe food and medicines, collection of tax revenues, extraction of natural resources for energy production, and others—have turned into endless games of cat and mouse.

It's not clear who is the cat and who is the mouse. Whack-a-mole is perhaps the better metaphor. The ingenuity, wealth, and personnel at the disposal of large corporate enterprises allows them continually to devise new ways of doing business and generating profits that seem to undermine each legal effort to control the risks and harms that are byproducts of their activities.

Crises and disasters produce regulation. Regulation produces new ways of doing business. New ways of doing business produce new problems. And we seem to end up more or less back where we started. A

New Yorker cartoon that struck a chord in the early 2000s had two shirt-and-tie guys leaning over a desk looking at some papers, while one of them said, "These new regulations are going to completely change the way we get around them."

Chasing the Geniuses of Wall Street

THIS CYCLE of regulation chasing innovation has been most evident along the corridor between Washington and Wall Street, populated by the men and women who operate the big banks, the hedge funds, the SEC, the Fed, the Treasury Department, the congressional committees, the White House, and the important courts for business litigation. These determined and ambitious people are engaged, sometimes competitively and sometimes cooperatively, in an important and often seemingly impossible enterprise: to maintain a vibrant financial sector that both fuels growth with capital and is stable and safe enough to protect the average investor and the economy as a whole.

Consider the arc of financial regulation from the Enron fiasco to the Obama administration. Enron shocked the world when it collapsed in late 2001 because, at least for a generation or two, no one had thought that the seventh largest (and by some accounts the most admired) corporation in America could evaporate almost overnight.[1] People believed that the stock prices of the Fortune 500 were realistic, or at least not fiction, because they were based on numbers that reflected a company's actual earnings and debt—and the market's beliefs, however exuberant at times, about what those numbers might mean for future growth.

Enron, and the accounting scandals that accompanied its collapse, gave the lie to this belief. Some corporate finance and accounting managers had been devising schemes to exploit complexity and ambiguity in accounting rules. These elaborate schemes were, at bottom, simply lies designed to boost their companies' stock prices. The lies got past professionals like investment analysts, raters of credit, lawyers, and auditors who are supposed to be watchdogs. The rapidly increasing fees earned by these "gatekeepers" (and paid by their clients) made their conflicts of interest so acute that some were willing to risk severe reputational damage for the rewards of keeping clients. It turned out that the regulatory system itself, especially the accounting rules and the enforcement regime for holding companies to those rules, had supplied a roadmap to companies like Enron for how to make themselves look stronger than they were.

In addition, the stock option—a popular and seemingly great idea to align managers' interests with those of the shareholders—ended up fueling what it was supposed to prevent. The motive for CFOs and CEOs of public companies to exploit the accounting system was to inflate their stock prices or, more commonly, to prevent their stock prices from falling when things went sour. Huge stashes of stock options caused managers of companies like Enron to care so intensely about stock price that they were willing to commit fraud. Enron even installed screens in the elevators of its Houston office tower that displayed the company's market price in real time. In some cases, like those of Kenneth Lay at Enron and Bernard Ebbers at Worldcom, managers could not afford any decline in their companies' stock because they had gone deeply into personal debt using their options compensation as collateral.[2]

The immediate response was a flurry of legislation and regulation, primarily the Sarbanes-Oxley Act of 2002 and the huge number of new regulatory rules that it empowered the SEC to enact and enforce. These laws were, of course, products of the sausage factory that is Congress. No one approaching financial regulation as a science would have designed a corrective to the Enron-era accounting scandals in this way. But the laws included major reforms intended to prevent another Enron: new controls on the off-books special purpose entities (SPEs) that Enron exploited to hide debt; a ban on corporations making loans to their executives; a requirement that corporate officers personally certify the accuracy of financial statements at pain of criminal sanction; a new intrusive regulator (the Public Company Accounting Oversight Board [PCAOB, pronounced "peek-a-boo" in Washington acronym-ese]) for the accounting industry with powers to punish wayward auditors; and lots of new rules about disclosure of executive pay.[3]

The crisis of 2008 seems to have washed from public memory that, for a while, reasonable people worried that Sarbanes-Oxley had imposed a much too expensive and legally scary regime of accounting and financial reporting rules.[4] A big topic in the period around 2004 to 2006 was whether United States law was driving capital to London and other offshore markets, at great cost to the American economy. Just a couple of years before the banking industry and then the economy utterly collapsed, many considered it a real question whether Congress had *overregulated* in response to Enron.

As it turned out, the energy giant's collapse was only a preview. What happened with the big banks in the period between 2006 and 2009 was, in many ways, Enron on a grand scale. Leaving aside chapter two's narrower legal question—whether the banks committed the kind of criminal fraud that Enron's managers did—the methods of and motives for the financial engineering that was so disastrous at the banks were strikingly similar to Enron's.[5]

Enron figured out a way—much of it maddeningly legal—to leverage its financial statements with its own stock price, believing that this essentially crazy idea would work out because the company's skyrocketing stock would never come down. With credit default swaps (CDSs) and credit default obligations (CDOs), the banks found a way to create massive markets in side bets on American housing. This had the effect of quintupling down on the American economy's running bet on real estate prices. The financial engineers at the banks were able to convince themselves and their bosses that this would work because the booming real estate market would not go down. (Or at least that their banks would not be the biggest losers when it did.) Real risks—ones that looked incredibly obvious in hindsight—got redefined as highly improbable "black swans" and corporate financial models accordingly generated rosy earnings and balance sheet numbers. Both inside and outside the banks, industry specialists took false comfort from sophisticated quantitative tools, like "value-at-risk" (VAR) measures. The fancy models only obfuscated the extent of the banks' reliance on flawed assumptions about the markets in which they were doing business.

Enron and other companies of the earlier era had managed to compromise and co-opt nearly everyone in a position to play the skeptic. Exploding fees clouded the judgment of lawyers and accountants. Hunger to stay in Enron's good graces and win work on the company's deals compromised the judgment of "buy side" investment analysts at the Wall Street banks. The financial press jumped on a story about a cool, innovative company that was using strategies from the dotcom boom in the energy sector. The credit rating agencies liked the steady flow of work that rating Enron's financing deals provided. Regulators in Washington did not have the resources or ingenuity to get onto what Enron was doing and they faced relentless pressure, building since the early 1980s, to defend any action seen as impeding profits.

So too with the Wall Street banks and the housing bubble. In fact, the circle of compromise and responsibility spread much wider than it had during Enron's era. Americans are painfully aware of how booming markets in residential real estate, and secondary investment markets created off of those primary markets, co-opted nearly every relevant institution in the public and private sectors, as well as huge numbers of retail homeowners and investors. Easy money was gushing from the system and few people had any motivation to play the skeptic.

Then, in 2008, from the March collapse of Bear Stearns to the September bankruptcy of Lehman Brothers, the bubble deflated, shocking the markets (as with Enron) and dealing a crippling blow to the global economy. So we regulated again, this time with the complicated and bitterly contested Dodd-Frank Act. The debate around Dodd-Frank included considerable agonizing over whether Congress had made a serious mistake—one that should be reversed—in 1999 when, with President Clinton's support, it passed the Gramm-Leach-Bliley Act. That law removed barriers to commercial banks getting into the securities trading business, rules put in place by the Glass-Steagall Act of 1933. The pendulum of financial regulation, inscribed with successive senators' names, keeps on swinging.

Dodd-Frank is hardly a great work of imagination in governance, designed to remake a fundamentally flawed system.[6] Like Sarbanes-Oxley before it, the bill was more like a tactics manual written by generals determined to win a war recently lost. Dodd-Frank, among other things, limits and makes more transparent many of the innovative products and practices in the banking sector that produced the mortgage-backed securities business. Once again, law attempted to train new spotlights on parts of the financial industry that had been lurking in shadows.

Predictably, the conversation about risks and regulation in the financial industry has moved on—to practices different from the ones that Dodd-Frank had in its sights. The banking industry has the money to attract some of the world's smartest people. Those ambitious minds will hunt for new dark corners in which previously undiscovered profits can be extracted from trading markets. The process of lawmaking and regulation creates some of those corners, leading the industry to find new practices in a pattern academics call "regulatory arbitrage."

Worries about banking practices that arose almost as soon as Dodd-Frank was signed into law include the exploitation of new software and hardware technologies to squeeze profits out of low-margin, high-volume trades executed with milliseconds of timing advantage over other traders.[7] This category of trading strategies, which already has led to proposed new regulations, includes many variations, among them what have been called high-frequency and flash trading. What the tech whizzes of Wall Street have been doing has produced a lot of head scratching as to whether their practices can be described as insider trading or market manipulation under long-standing securities laws. Even the SEC has appeared puzzled about the extent to which high-speed trading activities require new regulatory frameworks.

That game of derivatives traders at big banks manipulating LIBOR and other global interest rates also postdates the financial crisis. Thanks to some enforcement actions here and in the United Kingdom, we have learned about continuing activity that raises questions not only of fraud in individual trades but also collusion among the banks in possible violation of antitrust laws, as well as accounting fraud in how banks reported their trading earnings to their shareholders.

The volume of global transactions potentially affected by these manipulations is staggering.[8]

Similarly, traders at global banks colluded to manipulate benchmarks that control the prices of deals in the currency markets, a sector that trades $7 trillion worth of financial instruments *per day.* Journalists have asked whether J.P. Morgan and Goldman Sachs—banks, not mining or food companies—have been "pulling another Enron" or engaging in "Enron 2.0" by using clever strategies to move prices in global markets for commodities such as aluminum, cotton, wheat, coffee, and oil.[9]

These are just a few issues in banking that have drawn attention in the years following Dodd-Frank. By the time you read this, undoubtedly some new strategy will have been deployed. Indeed, as soon as we know about the latest innovation in trading markets that might raise worries, it's no longer the latest. These strategies—produced by operations that are the financial equivalent of the Skunk Works, Lockheed Corporation's famous aircraft design hatchery—yield their highest profits only so long as they remain closely kept secrets.

The Flaws of Law

SOME WOULD say this story is not about law, it's about politics. Law fails to keep up with the problems corporations produce because corporations, especially financial firms, are powerful in Washington. If Washington could overcome obstruction and move faster, and if corporate interests did not have so much influence over the content of legislation and the decisions of regulatory officials, the cat-and-mouse game would look different.

But the problem is not just a form of corruption. It goes much deeper than how we finance campaigns for office or appoint the personnel who run government agencies. The problem is structural.

Even without the messiness of democracy, law would be a flawed technology. Laws can never quite reach their intended targets, for two reasons. First, human ingenuity and foresight are always limited, especially when predicting the paths that our creative species will take. Laws must anticipate futures that the people who make laws cannot clearly see. Legal rules will inevitably end up confronting innovations for which they were not designed.[10]

Second, law is made from language, which itself is an imperfect technology. Generalizations in words can't exactly express the ideas that give rise to them. "Don't pollute" is not a law. It's an idea for a law. A law would be something like, "Anyone who discharges any of the following ten harmful substances into a public waterway in more than the specified amounts shall be fined." In reality, once lawmakers thought hard about how to design a law to deal with water pollution, it ended up with far more words. Take a look at the hundreds of pages of the Clean Water Act and its implementing regulations—if you can bear it.

Two ideas central to Americans' relationship to government amplify these limitations of law. The first is an idea about individual liberty: each of us is entitled to know in advance what the law is and what the consequences might be for us if we choose to violate it. In other words, in a liberal democracy we can't deal with the problem of limited foresight by waiting to see what we end up not liking and punishing it later. That would be making law *ex post facto*, in the words of the U.S. Constitution.

The second important idea is about capital enterprise and the economy: law should be limited to what is necessary to further the general public welfare so that law does not wastefully limit industry and growth. It's not an acceptable solution to the imperfections in language to intentionally write laws to cover much more than they need to—like making one big law that says "don't pollute" and leaving it up to the EPA and the courts to enforce that law enough but not too much. Although one might not know it from looking at our biggest-in-human-history legal system, a principle of American regulation—of any system that starts with commitments to liberty and representative government—is "First, do no harm."

These basic limitations of law are evident in the field of business regulation more than anywhere else. Grasping those limitations and the dynamics they create is essential to understanding many white collar crimes. Law's structural limitations leave gaps, and the gaps produce the problem of loopholes. Some loopholes in law are the products of brute politics. If big agriculture lobbies Congress for an exception in the corporate tax code that applies only to certain soy products, we might call that the "soy loophole." But that kind of loophole, like it or not, is an intentionally designed gap in the law.

The more interesting and challenging loopholes—the ones that explain so many forms of business crime—are found by the people the laws govern rather than designed by the officials who create the laws. They result from the limitations of lawmaker foresight and of written language. And they pervade business law in America.

What Does It Mean to Obstruct Justice?

CONSIDER THE case of Frank Quattrone, an investment banker who became a symbol of insider Wall Street greed during an earlier bubble, the dotcom boom of the late 1990s.[11] Quattrone, who worked for what was then Credit Suisse First Boston (CSFB), was one of the biggest bankers in the market for initial public offerings (IPOs) of Silicon Valley tech stocks. When the Internet first started changing the world, the stock market was awash in these IPOs, many of which were extremely lucrative for early investors.

Often a new tech company stock would hit the market at an initial offering price and, within the first day of trading, the price would be bid up in multiples. A famous example was Globe.com, a now defunct website for personal web pages, which hit the market at $9 per share and reached $97 the same day. In this kind of market, financial institutions that received initial allotments of these IPO shares were practically guaranteed easy money. Quattrone, as the lead banker on a lot of these deals, often got to decide who received those initial blocks of shares.

When this boom crashed, the government pored over the wreckage. One issue regulators scrutinized was whether Quattrone and others at CSFB had engaged in "spinning," a form of potential corruption in which investment bankers doled out initial allotments of IPO shares as a reward to players in the market who reliably brought other business to their banks. Quattrone was never charged with wrongdoing in connection with the spinning investigation. But for a while it looked like it could be a serious legal problem for both him and CSFB.

Shortly before the end of December 2001, in the midst of the spinning investigation, a supervisory banker at CSFB sent a group e-mail within the firm in which he wrote, "Subject: Time to clean up those files. . . . With the recent tumble in stock prices, and many deals now trading below issue price, the securities litigation bar is expected to [sic] an all out assault on broken tech IPOs. In the spirit of the end of the year (and the slow down in corporate finance work), we want to remind[] you of the CSFB document retention policy." The banker had first sent a more colorful draft of the e-mail to Quattrone for approval, writing, "Today, it's administrative housekeeping. In January, it could be improper destruction of evidence." Quattrone's response was to tell him that he "shouldn't make jokes like that on email!!"

When the supervisor's final e-mail went out to the CSFB staff, Quattrone endorsed the advice, replying to all, "having been a key witness in a securities litigation case in south texas i strongly advise you to follow these procedures." While both Quattrone and the author of the group e-mail were aware of regulatory attention to the IPO allocation process, Quattrone was in a crucially different position. Just one day earlier, CSFB's top outside lawyer had informed Quattrone, and directed him to keep confidential, that a federal grand jury investigation (that is, a criminal inquiry) of the spinning issue had commenced. The lawyer told him that, given Quattrone's position in the case, he would likely need to get his own lawyer.

Did Frank Quattrone obstruct justice by encouraging destruction of evidence in a federal criminal investigation? Or did he simply encourage savvy document handling practices in an industry rife with legal risk and a cutthroat cadre of plaintiffs' lawyers? The prosecution of Quattrone didn't settle this question because it was fought to a draw. A first trial produced a hung jury. A second trial yielded a conviction for obstruction of justice but then a reversal on appeal because the judge, the appellate court said, had not given the jury a demanding enough legal standard for determining whether Quattrone acted with criminal purpose. The government then settled with Quattrone, letting him have a deferred agreement in which he agreed to stay out of trouble in exchange for a later dismissal of the charges.

The famous obstruction-of-justice prosecution of the Arthur Andersen accounting firm did not answer this question either.[12] The conduct in *Andersen* was eerily similar to that at CSFB, though it resulted in destruction of much more evidence. Aware that the SEC was investigating its largest client, Enron Corporation, for accounting improprieties, but that the SEC had not yet formalized its investigation and issued subpoenas, several partners at Andersen repeatedly encouraged employees who worked on the Enron account to follow a "document retention policy" that previously had been ignored. One partner explained at a training session that the advantage of doing so was that the destroyed material—notes, drafts, e-mails, everything except the final file—would be "gone and irretrievable" in later legal proceedings and "all we did was follow our policy." When the SEC finally served Andersen with a subpoena for its Enron records, an e-mail went out to the employees telling them to "stop the shredding" because "we have been officially served for our documents."

A nearly hung jury, which included an odd foreman who was keen to write a book and talk to the press, concluded that Andersen obstructed justice by destroying records relating to Enron's accounting. But the Supreme Court reversed the conviction two years later because a trial judge, again, gave the jury legal instructions that failed, the Court said, to require a sufficiently venal mental state for document shredding to rise to the level of criminal obstruction of justice. Because Andersen was effectively out of business, the case was never retried.

A reasonable view of the Quattrone and Andersen cases is to say of course this is obstruction of justice. There's no difference between a banker or accountant shredding a document when securities regulators are sniffing around and a drug dealer throwing his ledgers in the fireplace when he hears the cops banging on the door, or even the fleeing murderer wiping fingerprints off the weapon before he throws it off a bridge. You can't destroy evidence when the authorities are on the way.

But the analogy doesn't quite hold. The murderer and the drug dealer do not go about their business in what we would call a regulated industry. In fact, they're quite intentionally regulated out of business entirely. The only laws that apply to them are ones that criminalize their conduct—banning it entirely. Legal risk for them poses a simple calculation: Don't get caught or prison is nearly certain.

Investment bankers and auditors of Fortune 500 corporations work in industries with a different relationship to legal regulation. They're governed by criminal laws that threaten imprisonment for serious wrongdoing like fraud and obstruction of justice. But those criminal prohibitions are the least commonly applied of the many laws they confront. On a daily basis, managers and employees in these industries pursue their professions in the shadow of sprawling regulatory schemes that emanate from a variety of sources in state and federal law, as well as systems of professional licensing and self-regulation. They also get sued all the time by other businesses and individuals. Bankers and accountants spend a fortune every year on legal advice, employing large in-house legal staffs and expensive lawyers at national law firms.

How does the basic intuition that you can't destroy evidence when the cops are on the way work for industries in which, most of the time, some kind of cop is always watching? A banker or auditor cannot be expected to save every document because there is always a risk that it might be relevant to a government or private legal action. If that were true, the legal rule would be that workers in these industries must live like pathological hoarders, crushing themselves under the weight of their own paper trails.

More to the point, these businesses ought to be allowed to do things to minimize their legal risks. If they're not allowed to get rid of their drafts in part because drafts left lying around later help their adversaries in litigation, then on the same principle they would not be able to think about what kind of language to leave out of an e-mail because it might later be used against them in a lawsuit. The investigative report on the starter mechanism disaster involving GM, released in 2014, recounted that lawyers, sensibly I suppose, had instructed employees not to describe the company's autos in memos with terms such as "rolling sarcophagus."[13]

Yet this is not what Quattrone and the partners at Andersen were up to. They weren't going about a routine practice of cleaning up so that fewer evidentiary morsels would be there for a hypothetical plaintiff's lawyer some day. They were destroying, or encouraging destruction of, records in specific parts of their firms relating to specific lines of business that were already under legal scrutiny. They thought they could do the thing they probably knew, or at least suspected, was wrong—destroy the evidence when the investigation is heating up—by claiming they were only doing the thing they thought must be permissible—just "following our document policy."

In other words, they thought they had found a loophole in the rule that you can't destroy evidence when the police are on the way. If that loophole in obstruction-of-justice law existed, it was there because of a problem that plagues the law of white collar crime: criminal law has to draw lines around areas of social and economic activity that, unlike dealing drugs and homicide, are largely legitimate.

Neither the Quattrone nor the Andersen prosecutions answered the central and very hard question: when does a corporation's ordinary destruction of documents become criminal obstruction of justice? The answer cannot be that it becomes a crime only when, and as soon as, the person doing the destroying has received a formal subpoena or has knowledge of such a subpoena—which seems to be what Quattrone and the partners at Andersen thought they had cleverly figured out. Such a rule would create a perverse incentive to rush destruction of evidence whenever regulatory or legal action started gearing up. This would actually be bad for firms. The government would have to go underground with its investigations, treating bankers and auditors like drug traffickers and sneaking up on them with search warrants at dawn.

The Supreme Court thought it found at least a partial answer in the Andersen case. The Court said that the trial judge set the bar too low when she told the jury that if it concluded that Andersen's partners and employees destroyed the Enron records to keep them away from the SEC, then the firm could be convicted of obstructing justice. This fact was obvious from the e-mail communications. At least one Andersen partner admitted it at the trial. And the trial court and the prosecutors reasonably believed this rule to be the correct reading of then federal law.

That rule, the Supreme Court said, would still criminalize routine destruction in everyday business motivated even in part by a desire to have fewer documents around in the event of legal proceedings. The Court ruled that the judge should have required the jury to decide whether the Andersen partners acted with "consciousness of wrongdoing" when they told employees to destroy documents—that they gave their instructions to keep documents from the SEC while knowing that the withholding was "wrong." The Court did *not* say that they specifically had to know doing so was a crime.

The Court's answer was frustratingly circular. It sounds as if the rule is whatever someone thinks it is: destroying documents to keep them from regulators is criminal if you believe it is wrong. But maybe that is the best the Court could do. There is no basis *other* than the mental state of the person doing the destroying to set a workable limit on permissible destruction of corporate records. And since all responsible companies—including CSFB and Andersen at the time of these cases—have policies that require retention of all relevant records when a specific legal action is threatened or has been filed, employees who destroy in that sort of context ought to know that they're doing something exceptional and wrongful, not routine and permissible.

A Loopholing State of Mind

IF ACCOUNTING or investment banking were black market industries, it would be pretty easy to say that destroying business records is always obstruction of justice—because those records would consist of nothing but evidence of crime.

Of course that's not the case. If we want to be able to do things like invest in public companies that have books audited by outside firms, or trade in shares of exciting new technology ventures, we must live with several realities. Most of what auditors and bankers do is legitimate and welcome. Some of it is wrong and harmful. The law will have to draw, police, and adjust the lines between the two.

State of mind—the thinking of people who plan their activities in the shadow of regulation—is at the center of efforts to manage those lines. Examining mental states provides the law with a means of identifying those who harmfully exploit loopholes—those who are the "conscious wrongdoers." Unfortunately, entrepreneurial individuals can find further loopholes in legal rules about state of mind.

Start with a case from outside the world of business crime, the infamous "torture memos" of the Bush Justice Department.[14] Simultaneously—and certainly by design—the White House and the CIA each asked the Justice Department for a legal opinion: the former on the meaning of the federal statute criminalizing official torture abroad; the latter on whether certain interrogation methods, including waterboarding, constituted torture under that criminal statute.

The lawyers wrote two memos. One memo, to the White House, said that an interrogation method counts as torture under the federal statute only if the interrogator means to inflict pain commensurate with that involved in organ failure or near death, or mental suffering equivalent to temporary loss of sanity. The other memo, to the CIA, said waterboarding, at least up to a point, does not inflict that kind of pain or mental suffering. This conclusion was based on facts about waterboarding (mostly accounts of its effects in American military training) that the CIA itself provided to the lawyers who wrote the memo.

These two memos created a virtual immunity from criminal prosecution. To take a less charged example, suppose a law says, on its clear terms, don't operate your leaf blower with the purpose of offending your neighbor. Jessica can only violate this law if she has in mind the idea of offending her neighbor. Jessica doesn't like her neighbor. She goes to her lawyer and explains when, where, and for how long she plans to operate her leaf blower, and at what decibel level. The lawyer looks at the leaf blower law and tells Jessica that, in the lawyer's opinion, what Jessica plans to do does not legally count as offending her neighbor under this law.

If Jessica then goes ahead with her plan, she cannot possibly have in mind that what she is doing is offending her neighbor under the law—because the lawyer just told her that, legally, it's not. That is, unless the whole thing is a sham. Picture Jessica meeting with Saul, the corrupt lawyer from *Breaking Bad*, and assume we somehow have a recording of their ordinarily privileged conversation. The proof shows that Jessica knows that the lawyer did not believe for a moment that the law could plausibly be read as meaning that her leaf blowing would not offend her neighbor, and she knows that the lawyer gave her an opinion to the contrary to immunize her from prosecution.

What the authors of the torture memos did may have been immoral, dumb, and also bad legal work. But it was only criminal—grounds for prison, not just loss of law license—if, as they sat and wrote those memos, they thought their analysis was not even within the range of straight-faced legal argument. And how could a prosecutor possibly prove that, short of simultaneous e-mails in which the lawyers snickered to each other about the implausibility of what they were doing?

What happened with the torture memos happens in business lawyering all the time. In what was probably the most significant criminal tax case ever prosecuted, the government convicted lawyers and accountants, including several from the multinational KPMG firm, for giving some big and abusive tax shelters sold to wealthy individuals the same kind of legal absolution that the Justice Department lawyers gave to waterboarding.[15] The difference in the KPMG case was that the government had good evidence that the lawyers and accountants knew, even as they gave their opinions that the shelters were legal, that they had pushed well beyond even the ample boundaries of fair argument under the Byzantine U.S. tax code.

Ignorance of Law

IN RESPONSE to examples like the torture memos and the KPMG prosecution, you might ask what happened to the venerable principle that ignorance of the law is no defense. If someone knows what she is up to but thinks that it's not a crime, when it is indeed criminal, she doesn't get to escape prosecution later by claiming she made a mistake. "I didn't know it was a crime to sell that bag of heroin to my friend at work" is not a winning defense, even if the defendant persuades a jury that this wrong belief about the law was genuine.

Ignorance of the law isn't a defense to white collar crimes either. But there's a major caveat. Because the law of white collar crimes has to draw fine lines between permissible conduct and criminal behavior in economic and social contexts that are often legitimate, mental state becomes a crucial distinguishing factor in the law.

How might we distinguish, for example, between the factory owner who should be fined for releasing more nitrogen into the river than his EPA permit allows and the one who should go to prison for doing so? We could send them both to prison, of course. But it might be wiser to fine the factory owner who mistakenly went a bit over his permit one month, while imprisoning the one who knew and intended to exceed his permit, hoping or scheming not to get caught—as we wouldn't want, in the Andersen and Quattrone problem, to treat everyone as a criminal who, for whatever reason, happens to destroy a document at work.

This reliance on mental state to identify the genuine white collar criminal sometimes produces laws that cannot be violated without some knowledge of the law—exceptions to the ignorance-of-the-law rule. Tax is the prime example. Harold Cheek of Dallas was a pilot for American Airlines and a man of peculiar views.[16] He listened to a number of people who were peddling "tax protester" advice—the sort who assert that the federal income tax is unconstitutional and therefore not law. Cheek decided, he said, that his W-2 wages from American Airlines were not taxable income. Accordingly, he took a very large number of exemptions to prevent withholding by his employer. He then failed to pay the taxes he owed on his salary.

Cheek was prosecuted and convicted for tax evasion and got his case all the way to the Supreme Court. The Court ruled that, because tax law is infamously specialized and complex (though not the concept of W-2 taxable wages!), a jury in a criminal tax case must be told that the government has to prove not only that the defendant failed to report taxable income but also that the defendant *knew as a matter of law* that the item in question was income under federal law. Meanwhile, Cheek was retried with the new instruction and convicted again. The second jury apparently did not believe his claims about his alleged reading of tax law.

A downside of using mental states to draw lines is that those lines can be exploited. The particular states of mind involved in white collar offenses can actually be manipulated, including through the procurement of legal advice. The lawyer's advice to Jessica about the reading of the leaf blower law meant she did not have the state of mind to violate that law. The document shredder who's been told by a lawyer that he can continue routine destruction does not intend to obstruct justice. The factory owner whose lawyer has read the permit as allowing release of a chemical does not intend to exceed the permit even if that reading turns out to be wrong. The taxpayer whose lawyer has said the check does not count as income does not knowingly evade taxes when she doesn't report it. And the pharmaceutical seller who markets the drug for the unapproved use does not do so intentionally if he has been incorrectly told that FDA approval included that use.

This structure in the law of white collar crime places great pressure on the regulation of the legal profession, as well as other professions such as accounting. In the KPMG tax shelters prosecution, attorneys and accountants crossed the line because they were willing to provide opinions to clients that were beyond the range of plausible argument in their fields. Professionals are supposed to be deterred from this behavior—for which clients can be willing to pay a lot of money—by the prospect of criminal prosecution and by the potential of loss of license to practice. The latter deterrent requires that professional regulatory organizations, like the state bar associations that license lawyers, be willing to sanction professionals not only for the most egregious violations, like theft of client funds, but also for providing shoddy legal advice.

Unfortunately these organizations have been far too hesitant to bring such actions. To be fair, it can be difficult to prove that someone knew his judgment was wrong on a matter within a range of opinion. Even a bar disciplinary action against the lawyers who wrote the Justice Department torture memos would have been difficult to win. Their arguments about how to interpret the federal torture statute were weak and one-sided—especially in light of the prestige of their employer and the moral seriousness of the subject. But they were not clearly outside the range of lawyer's argument. Had they been writing a brief to a court on behalf of a client charged with violating the statute—which was decidedly *not* their role—their work would have been acceptable.

Crimes of Loopholing

AMBIVALENCE ABOUT innovation and aggressive wealth creation intersects with the exceptional American commitment to law and legalism as a basis for social organization. A dilemma resides at this intersection. On one hand, we abhor crafty loopholers who thumb their noses at the state's efforts to prohibit their conduct. On the other hand, we encourage, or at least allow, businesspeople to seek out legal advice, pay handsomely for it, and design innovative transactions and business processes that comply with (or choose your word: evade, avoid, undermine) regulatory regimes.

Even the core crime of fraud fits this pattern. We saw how fraud polices the line between sales practices that are acceptable means of doing business in modern markets and those that are wrong, harmful, and deserving of punishment. Fraud law exists—and it persists in very general and open-ended form—in order to deal with the problem of the innovative wrongdoer. It is, therefore, perhaps the most powerful antiloopholing weapon of all.

Loopholing problems are not unique to white collar crime. Narcotics regulation, for example, must contend with the problem of "designer" drugs that are not explicitly banned. Most business crimes, however, are in their structure crimes of loopholing.

Law professors and think tank people, on both the left and the right, have been complaining for years about the federal criminal code.[17] If one includes, as one must, not only the statutes Congress makes but also the mountains of regulations the executive branch issues, federal law infamously contains more criminal offenses than any person has been able to count—over four thousand by one estimate. A criminal justice reform bill introduced in Congress in 2015 included a provision that would require all federal crimes to be counted and listed in one place—a law to count the laws! Many more of these crimes relate, in one way or another, to business activity than street crime. It's been said that one can hardly sneeze in this country without violating some sort of federal law.

The "overcriminalization" situation is lamentable. The political process for making federal crimes has been ad hoc, reactive, ill considered, and dysfunctional. But it's not quite as alarming as a description of law on the books might sound. Most Americans are not federal prisoners, even with the embarrassing and wasteful overgrowth of that population. This is because federal prosecutors rely, in both street crime and white collar enforcement, on a relatively small number of bulwark criminal offenses.[18] Most federal prisoners are serving time for violating a few shopworn drug, immigration, and firearm statutes that have fueled the federal criminal justice machine since the American "wars" on crime and drugs were launched in earnest in the late 1970s.[19]

Few if any offenders are in prison for crossing the line of laws that are most often described as exemplary of Washington's excesses in criminalization, like prematurely tearing the tag off a mattress or misusing the image of Woodsy the Owl. The majority of serious federal white collar cases—and therefore the vast majority of corporate crime prosecutions in the United States—involve one or more of these crimes: securities, bank, government contracting, or other fraud; bribery, especially nowadays foreign bribery; money laundering; tax evasion; criminal violation of environmental or food and drug laws; and obstruction of justice.[20] Most of these prevalent white collar crimes share a common structure, as antiloopholing devices: laws targeted at people who are trying, in various ways, to get around the law.

Bribery or Politics?

CORRUPTION PRESENTS a problem of loopholing on two levels. The businessperson who pays a bribe to get a deal done is seeking to improve on the terms of the deal, especially price, that otherwise would have applied in that market. She's loopholing the market for her product or services. In addition, because bribery law sometimes must draw lines between corruption and the ordinary business of government, the entrepreneur seeking advantage will tend to structure her dealings with government officials to try to get what she wants while staying on the right side of the law. She's loopholing corruption law.

The biggest loophole of all—one that many believe has swallowed in one gulp the American political system and the regulatory problem of corruption—is the United States campaign finance system. Consider the hypothetical case of Charles, head of a big New York bank, who is worried in the wake of a market crash that Washington might impose expensive new regulations. Charles starts giving the maximum he can to the campaign fund of Laura, a senator who chairs a key banking committee. Charles also organizes fundraisers for Laura that pull in a lot of campaign cash. Every chance Charles gets—and he gets more than most people—he bends Laura's ear about how new regulations will be wasteful, damage the industry, cost jobs of average workers, and so on.

Laura has reliably looked out for the interests of the banks, which is why Charles has continued to contribute money to Laura's campaigns.

But the political pressure for reform is intense this time. A package of new laws has come to the decision point before Laura's committee during an election year in which Laura is on the ballot. Charles calls Laura and says he's likely to throw another $100,000 to a PAC that is running negative ads against Laura's challenger if Laura can assure Charles that she will block the bill in the committee.

Has Charles committed a crime? The answer under present law is: not until Charles said what he did in that last phone call. Indeed, even the last phone call might not have pushed this across the line into bribery if Charles had simply told Laura about the PAC contribution and then proceeded to "change the subject" and lay into her about blocking the banking bill.

It's hard to see why the law should draw the line as it does. Everything Charles is doing, in whatever form, looks like buying votes in Congress. Charles's purpose is abundantly clear. It's easy to follow the money. And no one doubts that the money influences what Laura does on Capitol Hill. If you think the line can look fuzzy when it comes to Congress, try educating yourself about what goes on in Albany, New York—a state in which the great majority of the campaign funding comes from industry groups with business before the legislature.[21]

As long as we have money in politics, and lots of it, law needs an instrument for drawing the line between bribery and politics as usual. The present tool is the idea of a *quid pro quo*, meaning this-for-that. A quid pro quo is a kind of contractual exchange in which one person offers or gives something in return for a specific official action. Charles's campaign contributions alone are not quid pro quos, the law says, but coupled with the substance of his phone call with Laura they are.

The Supreme Court explained this rule in a case that involved Mike Espy, who was Bill Clinton's secretary of agriculture.[22] An old college buddy of Espy's was the chief lobbyist for Sun-Diamond, a Big Ag company in California concerned about some decisions Espy's department was about to make. The friend arranged with some men at a DC lobbying firm to funnel money from Sun-Diamond into an account for retiring the campaign debts of Espy's brother, who had run unsuccessfully for Congress. The friend also gave some nice gifts he thought Espy would like, including fancy luggage and tickets to the U.S. Open tennis tournament. The government charged the giving of the gifts to the secretary not as bribes—proof of a clear quid pro quo was, not surprisingly, lacking—but as illegal "gratuities" under another statute that punishes less severely the giving of something to an official as a "reward" for past action.

The Court reversed the conviction, ruling that it was not enough, as the government had argued, to prove that Sun-Diamond gave Espy the gifts because of his position as ag secretary. The government had to prove that the gratuities were given because of a specific official act Espy had taken. It was much harder, of course, to prove that *that* is what was in the mind of the college buddy lobbyist when he threw the tickets to Espy.

The loopholing problem here is plain. Until corruption is redefined to include the whole idea of private money in politics—something that, after a series of Supreme Court rulings, would now require amending the Constitution—criminal law needs to be able to give people in business and government a clear line so they know the difference between politics and crime. Today, that line is "no quid pro quo agreements." Of course, drawing that line also makes it clear how to get what you want without breaking the law. Just make sure to have an ongoing relationship in which both parties understand what is expected and there is never any need to discuss the particulars of the deal—quids, quos, or otherwise.

The problem becomes even harder if the law wants to regulate corruption in the private sector. If the line between campaign funding and bribery seems tricky, consider the line between a "bribe" and money offered to close a business deal. Even in a case as egregious as the baubles thrown at members of the International Olympic Committee to get them to pick Salt Lake City to host the 2002 Winter Games, a long and costly prosecution foundered at trial.[23]

The bribery law in the Salt Lake City case, which might well have bothered the jury that acquitted the defendants, prohibits any effort to confer a benefit on an agent (employee) without the consent of the agent's principal (boss), "contrary to the interests of the principal" and "with the purpose of influencing the conduct of the agent." In non-legalese, that means that it's a felony, at least on paper, for someone who sells a product for corporation A to offer a buyer for corporation B tickets to tonight's game for the purpose of getting the buyer to stop haggling and close the deal (and without clearing the ticket offer with the buyer's boss first).

That's a law that would seem to need refinement. Maybe that explains why commercial bribery prosecutions are so uncommon. The Justice Department's 2015 indictment of world soccer chieftains in the FIFA case made oblique reference to New York's commercial bribery statute, a law similar to Utah's. (In spite of its far reach, FIFA, as a private organization, is not within the purview of public sector bribery laws.) But the backbone of the government's legal theory in that case is fraud, not bribery: that the officials diverted into their personal bank accounts payments from event sponsors that, in theory at least, belonged to FIFA the organization and its member groups.

Since the late Bush and early Obama years, the Justice Department has launched a determined campaign to police business bribery globally, especially bribes paid by large multinational corporations in developing economies in which the practice is business as usual. The government's weapon in this campaign is the Foreign Corrupt Practices Act (FCPA). Congress passed this law as part of the post-Watergate reforms of the mid-1970s. The law was originally meant to address concerns about secret corporate money in politics. After its passage the statute was left mostly dormant for twenty years. In the 1990s, for a variety of reasons including the signing of an agreement among many countries to adopt and enforce anticorruption laws, the FCPA became active. It now accounts for a substantial part of corporate crime enforcement and defense in the United States.

The FCPA addresses bribery of foreign officials. But, as with the bribery statutes that apply to U.S. elected officials, it pivots on the requirement of a quid pro quo. The problem in foreign bribery prosecutions is not the lines between things like a fancy business dinner and a bribe—though there are such cases and those lines do worry compliance supervisors at big companies. The real problem is systemic. The FCPA, and similar statutes enacted by developed countries such as the United Kingdom, attempt to impose a Western, progressive, good government definition of corruption on societies that have long tolerated bribery.

The objective of the United States and other signatories to the bribery agreement is to change international business culture, even to transform the problem of corruption in developing economies. Some would say this is fantasy, others that it could end up doing more harm than good, perhaps by discouraging companies from investing in the developing world.

But there is a worthy argument in its favor. On the streets of cities such as Delhi and Shanghai, one might find a lot of support for the idea among people whose environments and economic prospects are made worse by the actions of corrupt governments. Whatever the merits of this anticorruption campaign, a lot of people will be caught in tight places as the plates of global commerce shift and legal norms about business corruption are contested. One such tight place is the Chinese criminal justice system, where the head of pharmaceutical giant GlaxoSmithKline's China operations found himself held in custody and ultimately convicted in a scandal involving the company's Chinese sales force paying bribes to doctors to prescribe GSK's medicines.

So far, fear of FCPA prosecutions, and therefore quick settlement with the government, has been the norm. If some business defendants begin to challenge these prosecutions by fighting over the statute's legal definitions, the courts will have to sort out contestable questions about corruption versus old-fashioned business, and about bribes versus bills that must be paid to turn the lights on or pour the concrete, in diverse economies that don't see these matters through American or British lenses.

The most noteworthy FCPA prosecution is the global bribery scandal involving the German corporation Siemens, which does a lot of business in large government contracts.[24] Bribery became a business plan at Siemens. Managers at the massive company openly maintained accounts to fund a program of bribing foreign officials that, as best could be determined, involved over $1 billion in payments in more than sixty countries. The bribery was so pervasive that, until prosecutors and the press got onto it, no one at Siemens seemed to think that there was anything particularly wrong with it. Maybe that was because payments to government functionaries had so long been treated as ordinary in Argentina, Venezuela, Bangladesh, and the other countries where Siemens routinely paid bribes. In fact, until the late 1990s, Germany's own laws treated bribes as a deductible business expense on corporate tax returns.

Wal-Mart Stores, Inc. has been embroiled in a scandal involving people in its fast-growing Mexico operation engaging in an apparently systematic program of bribing local officials to obtain permits for store construction.[25] Probably everybody bribes local officials to get construction permits in Mexico, but Walmart is supposed to be a pillar of American corporate values that doesn't engage in such things. What got Walmart in trouble in this case more than the bribes, which were dwarfed by those in a case like the Siemens prosecution, was the company's failure to report itself to the Justice Department when it first discovered the problem. Failure to report a violation is not a crime itself, under the FCPA or in general. But the Justice Department relies so heavily on corporate self-reporting that a case like Walmart's has to be hit with a heavy sanction to send the right message to other companies that find evidence of crime by their employees.

Apparently Walmart's business model of obsessive cost cutting extended to legal fees. Attorneys from a prestigious law firm advised Walmart to investigate thoroughly information about potential corruption in its Mexico operations. Reportedly, executives at the company's Arkansas headquarters instead tried to make the problem go away. It came back to bite Walmart, in the form of a disgruntled employee who walked into the *New York Times* with a gift-wrapped story about scandal at a company that many people love to hate.

An interesting feature of the statute that controls these foreign bribery prosecutions is that it requires—perhaps in an effort to narrow the law—that the person offering a quid pro quo do so "corruptly," that is, with a corrupt state of mind. Notice the circularity. Corruption, at least under this statute, is defined as a quid pro quo offered with corrupt purpose. Because so few individuals or companies have taken FCPA cases to trial and up to the appellate courts, we have little from the courts about what this means. Corrupt payments are payments made with corruption in mind. One court has defined "corruptly" under the FCPA as "a bad purpose to violate the law."[26] Bad purpose. Conscious of wrongdoing. It's the loopholer that these laws, and the judges who interpret them, seem to be after.

These sorts of oddities in white collar criminal laws are not all attributable to poor drafting skills among the scriveners of Capitol Hill. They reflect ambivalence and uncertainty about, for example, what should count as criminal corruption versus acceptable practice in international commerce. The persistence of a term like "corruptly" in the FCPA is recognition of the need to draw that line. It's also a punting of the ball downfield with a deliberately vague term, in the hopes that future cases and the work of the courts will produce a clearer answer.

Evading Taxes or Avoiding Them?

NOWHERE DOES the word "loophole" come up more than in tax law. Again, some loopholes are things the government does not tax because somebody or some industry got the rule they wanted. But the unintended loopholes that taxpayers and companies, especially those who can afford smart lawyers, seek out are the ones that make criminalizing sophisticated tax evasion so difficult.

As with banking regulation, it's a near scientific property of law that tax laws will produce new ways of structuring activity designed to reduce taxes. The tax code is the most arcane, overweight, and deadening body of law known to the American legal system. Tax law, especially as it applies to complex corporate finance and investment, is a foreign language, inscrutable to laypeople and only dimly comprehensible to lawyers who are not specialists in it.

Tax law is this way because of politics, of course. But the political story is not as simple as a divided Congress that keeps adding to the heap, bit by bit, and can't summon the will to wipe the slate clean and write something that makes sense. (Though there's plenty of that inertia.) Tax law is a complex web of picayune rules because the project of taxation is entirely pragmatic. It has no first principles.

With fraud, bribery, or environmental crimes, for example, one can identify some idea of right and wrong that animates the legal project: don't cheat people out of their money, don't corrupt government officials from their loyalty to the public, don't ruin each other's water and air. With tax evasion, what is the basic wrong? It might be "don't fail to pay what you owe" or "don't fail to pay your fair share." But that just completes a circle of logic, pointing back to existing tax laws themselves, which would be the only place to discover what counts as one's fair share. This is why we all think we have the right to expend as much effort as we choose to find out how to pay as little tax as possible. Anyone who volunteered to pay the government more than he owed would be, to put it charitably, silly.

Given the nature of tax law, it would be a bad idea to criminalize every instance of someone not paying what she or he owed. It's too easy to make a mistake. And the laws themselves are the only place to look to figure out what one owes. Our moral compass can tell us that it is wrong to shirk the obligation to pay taxes. Certainly any corporation that embraced such a position would, without controversy, deserve to be treated as a criminal. But even the most accurate moral compass cannot calculate adjusted gross income.

Tax evasion therefore requires a criminal state of mind. The only logically available one, as the Supreme Court figured out in the absurd case of the airline pilot Harold Cheek, is the intent to violate actual tax law. One cannot intend to break a law one does not know about. So knowledge of the relevant tax laws is required for criminal tax evasion. This crime is an exception to the principle that ignorance of the law is not an excuse.

This is where lawyers come in. If tax law is too complicated for laypeople to understand—at least when it comes to complicated finance rather than W-2 wages—then if a lawyer tells a client that tax law allows something, the client apparently cannot commit tax evasion if the client does what he's been told is allowed. As in the examples of the torture memos and Jessica's leaf blower, the client will lack the criminal intent to break tax law.

Thus we have the tax shelter industry, the highest art form in loopholing. Its practitioners, who include both lawyers and accountants, design elaborate financing structures that are woven through and around the gaps and ambiguities in tax law—like spiders that build their webs in the nooks and crannies of the garage. They then provide their clients with opinions that say these structures do not violate tax law. A client who has been told by a lawyer that her activity complies with tax law cannot have the intent to violate the law when she pursues that activity. This sounds like a business in selling legal immunity—not so far removed from the corrupt priests of old who sold indulgences to those desperate to avoid perdition.

The situation is fortunately not quite this grim. Lawyers and accountants who provide bogus tax opinions can lose their licenses to practice and even be prosecuted criminally. That risk, in theory, should cause professionals to stand up to the pressures of clients and the seduction of fees. The client who is desperate to pursue the really shady offshore tax shelter will be unable to find a lawyer or accountant willing to absolve him. Even the clients who obtain legal opinions remain at risk of prosecution because the law, not surprisingly, says that a taxpayer's reliance on a legal opinion does not count if the taxpayer didn't give the lawyer all the relevant facts or knew the lawyer's opinion was bogus.

These prosecutions—which turn on a thorny combination of states of mind and highly technical tax rules—are hard to put together, much less win under the criminal standard of proof beyond a reasonable doubt. Still, the government has prosecuted and won some cases on the argument that complicated tax shelters marketed by prestigious firms were means of criminal tax evasion. Some people who used to hold partnerships at fancy national law and accounting firms have served federal prison time for designing and selling these things. That is no trifle.

But taking on the tax shelter industry with criminal cases cost a great deal, including years of litigation in the prosecutions of people from KPMG, Jenkens & Gilchrist, and other firms.[27] That group of cases involved tax shelters that included something called FLIP or OPIS, a "defective-redemption" shelter. It was structured so that a tax-payer's redemption of stock from a Cayman Islands company would, its designers intended, not qualify as a stock redemption under U.S. tax law. This shelter created a "synthetic loss" under tax law, allowing the client to claim a deduction that greatly reduced taxes owed.

To convict the defendants in the KPMG case, the prosecutors had to establish not just that FLIP/OPIS—which will require at least a couple of aspirin for anyone determined to sit down and figure it out—did not in fact work as its designers intended under tax law. They also had to prove that the designers of FLIP/OPIS *knew* their construal of the tax laws was bogus. This is a bit like trying to convict a neurosurgeon for committing perjury in testimony explaining the details of an operation to remove a brain tumor. It can be done. But the close cases are going to be lost.

As the tax example shows, the incorrigible problem of loopholing in business crime does not exist solely because of damnable lawyers and hopeless lawmakers, though they certainly make matters worse. The problem is structural. It arises the moment law sets for itself the task of punishing some people for crimes within practices of business and commerce that are, in the main, not only perfectly allowable but often expressly encouraged by government, law, and prevailing social norms.

White Collar Money Laundering and Extortion

IN THE business world, criminal law performs plenty of its core function: punishing bad people for bad acts. But, as it roams through the realms of business, government, and politics, criminal law inevitably is engaged in a project of regulation. Of course, in one sense all criminal law is regulation. The point of homicide law is to reduce deaths. Ordinary regulatory projects, however, don't set out to eliminate all of something, as the law might for heroin or meth production. They're more often projects that distinguish among things: safe medicines from unsafe ones, benign effluents from ones that poison drinking water, fair litigation tactics from ones that obstruct judicial process, lawful tax avoidance from evasion, and so on.

Including criminal punishment in these regulatory projects requires making the same kinds of distinctions. Indeed, finer distinctions, because criminal law should select for the severe penalty of imprisonment only a subset of what civil regulation has deemed problematic. This leaves white collar criminal law engaged in the same ongoing war with loopholers that plagues most regulatory projects. We've seen here how that problem explains what goes on when the legal system deals with the problems of obstruction of justice, bribery, and tax evasion—and even in as core an offense as fraud.

The problem of loopholing explains many other offenses commonly charged against people engaged in business activity. Money laundering laws make it a crime to conduct a wide variety of financial transactions—from bank deposits to real estate purchases—with the proceeds of crime. These laws started, mostly in the 1980s, as a seemingly clever tool for attacking narcotics trafficking networks along their exposed financial flank. Prosecutors then began to use these laws to make life difficult for those pursuing complex fraud schemes, tax evasion, financing of terrorist groups, circumvention of laws on export and import of weapons and other controlled materials, and even alien smuggling.

These policing efforts triggered repeated innovations in methods of global finance designed to evade money laundering controls. The drug dealers figured out how to use retail money transmitters instead of regulated banks. The terrorists substituted microlending practices for mainstream banking. The tax cheaters ran to the Cayman Islands and the Swiss banks. And the government kept on chasing them to new places, with some successes. It looks as if the next redoubt will be dark corners of the web, where bitcoins are traded anonymously and untraceably.

When it comes to legitimate commerce, even a seemingly basic crime like extortion can present loopholing problems. Of course, when Tony

Soprano's loan shark threatens to break the legs of a debtor who is in arrears, we have a simple violent crime (even if he tries a little thuggish loopholing by phrasing it as "be a shame if anything happened to those legs"). But where is the line between hard-nosed threats in business negotiations and criminal extortion? Judges have struggled with this one. It's probably not extortion to tell someone you will sue her unless she writes you a fat check. That's usually called settlement. But it might be extortion if you know the suit you're threatening to bring has no merit. It certainly would be extortion if your threat was to induce prosecutors and police to arrest the person for a crime.

In spite of the colloquial sense in which we talk about the bills of plumbers and cable providers, it's not extortion to demand a great deal of money to give somebody a unique item that is of little value to you but enormous value to her. That's just driving a hard bargain. It might seem unfair but it's not illegal.

Consider the case of a man who bought a private plane financed by a bank loan that was secured by the plane.[28] He missed his payments and the bank repossessed the plane. The bank, not being in the aircraft business, failed to collect the craft's logbooks when it took the plane. Later the bank figured out that not having the logbooks would make it a lot harder to move the plane on the secondary market. When the bank went back to the debtor, he demanded a substantial payment for the logbooks.

Instead of the payment, he got a criminal prosecution that ended up before a federal court of appeals. The court said this was extortion because a debtor has no legal right to refuse to cooperate in a creditor's recovery of collateral. As is common when defendants lose close cases, he had some bad facts, like having told a witness that what he was doing felt kind of like kidnapping for ransom. "Coercion" and "extortion" are loaded terms that do not themselves answer the deep puzzle about what kinds of pressure on others, in what circumstances, are criminal rather than tough luck.

The law professor's favorite example of this puzzle is the "blackmail paradox." Why was David Letterman's producer free to tell the world that Letterman was sleeping with his staffer, and Letterman would have been free to offer his producer money to keep his mouth shut, but the producer committed a crime when he asked Letterman to pay him to keep quiet? Academic journals are full of efforts to find a more satisfying answer to that question than "because it's what the law of blackmail has long said." The producer's conduct probably would have been legal even if, setting himself to the task of loopholing, he had gone to Letterman and said, "I know about the affair, what are you going to do about it?" and then accepted an offer of hush money from Letterman.

Loopholes in Perpetuity

NO ONE wants to go to prison. Aside from the pain of it, prison is bad for business. The enforcement of criminal law, which aims to put people in prison, is thus full of problems of evasion. The whole thing is an endless contest. Those most determined to win the game are probably the hardened professionals who run the outlaw networks of international narcotics dealing, human trafficking, organized crime families, and terrorist groups. In one sense, these people are loopholers too—when they kill a witness, bribe a cop to get a heads-up about a raid, or use a system for communicating over the Internet that can't be traced.

In business crime, however, the loopholing problem is much harder for law to handle. People bent on pursuing unwanted activities that are embedded within legitimate business enterprises start by thinking about how to do something so it's not a crime in the first place. That approach really isn't an option for drug dealers, Mafia bosses, terrorists, and alien smugglers. And the government cannot respond by banning entire realms of legitimate social and economic activity because some portions of them have turned out to be problems.

So, in business crime we're guaranteed the constantly repeating drama of fights over whether something that has produced, or some are saying should produce, an arrest is really a crime at all. And as long as the definitional and line-drawing questions remain unsettled, enterprising business people will devote resources to finding novel and profitable ways to skirt those lines.

A society could choose to deal with this problem by compromising on the rule of law. It could say that from now on we're going to have a few basic criminal categories: fraud, bribery, extortion, obstruction of justice, pollution, selling dangerous products. Our prosecutors, judges, and jurors will decide, case by case and after the fact, whether each person who ends up in cuffs belongs in one of those categories. We give you, ladies and gentlemen, Lloyd Blankfein of Goldman Sachs. Fraudster? Here is Tony Hayward from BP. Criminal polluter?

Such a system, of course, would not only be unconstitutional as a matter of settled American law, but would signal a sea change in the values of our liberal democracy. Not to mention that it might have large and unpredictable effects on the economy.

When it comes to controlling what we don't like and don't want from our modern corporate system, let's be sober about what we can expect from the criminal law and its endeavor to define deviance. The categories "bad" and "illegal" make a Venn diagram, especially in the business world. In a relatively narrow band where these two categories overlap, there are the things that the law calls crimes. Then there will be lots of things that law regulates but, prudently, does not criminalize. And there of course will be lots of things that are distasteful and even unethical but not necessarily illegal. The entrepreneurial mind will forever seek undiscovered refuges along the seams in this terrain.

4

Corporations as Criminals

NOTHING CAPTURES THE American dilemma of criminalizing business conduct more than how criminal law, and its current methods of practice, treat corporations themselves. To see how, we'll begin with the recent malfeasance and legal troubles of two of the world's most massive companies, British Petroleum and General Motors.

BP

ON APRIL 20, 2010, BP's Deepwater Horizon rig exploded in the Gulf of Mexico, killing eleven people and releasing nearly five million barrels of crude oil from the ocean floor into a strained and economically important ecosystem.[1] The losses from the Deepwater Horizon explosion, probably impossible to calculate with precision, run into the billions.

If terrorists had done this, the story about how the accident was caused and who should be held responsible would have been straightforward: simply a matter of forensics, however technical. But because a corporation did it—no rational individual, of course, actually *wanted* such a thing to happen—explanation, including where accountability resides, is far more complex. As with many calamities, the best account of causation in the BP affair combines immediate events with more gradual developments. The rig blew up because the men in charge failed to call ashore for help when all signs pointed to an impending and disastrous failure. The events of that terrible day unfolded, and were not brought under control, because BP (and its subcontractor on the rig, Transocean) did not do enough as an organization, in the Gulf or elsewhere, to prioritize accident prevention while pursuing an aggressive corporate strategy to find deeper offshore deposits.

This story yields no easy account of responsibility for the tragic deaths and extensive environmental damage that BP and its employees caused. One might start by blaming the people who "did it": the workers on the rig that day. But they didn't want to destroy their own rig. They had every reason to avoid such a horror. Some of them died in the explosion. For the most part, they were doing their difficult and dangerous jobs as their employers had trained and instructed them.

The names Robert Kaluza and Donald Vidrine are not likely familiar. They were not at the center of the public's understanding of the BP case, even though they are the two BP employees federal prosecutors said were responsible for failing to alert others of the escalating problem at the well. Kaluza and Vidrine were charged with the *homicide* offense of manslaughter. A third BP employee, David Rainey, was indicted for obstruction of justice for concealing information after the accident about how much oil was flowing out of the well site on the floor of the Gulf. Few people seemed to closely follow the prosecutions of these men, which became tied up in pretrial wrangling and did not seem crucial to anyone's reckoning of responsibility for the Gulf spill.[2]

In the spring of 2015, a federal appellate court ordered the homicide charges against Kaluza and Vidrine dismissed. The court's questionable reasoning was that when Congress wrote the maritime manslaughter law to cover any "person employed on any vessel," it meant people who operate the boat, not others working on board. (No one disputed that an oil rig is a "vessel" under this law.) Apparently, at least in federal court, your captain but not your cruise director may be prosecuted for negligently causing your death at sea.

The rig workers were, in any event, cogs in BP's machine. One thus might be inclined to lay responsibility on the corporations that owned the rig, drilled the well, profited from the enterprise, hired and trained the workers, and made the critical decisions about equipment and safety. First, though, one needs to be clear about who or what is being blamed. Is it the managers and executives at BP who were in the chain of responsibility, extending from the well all the way to the top? Or is it the corporation "itself" or, if one prefers, the company "as a whole"?

The trouble with blaming the managers and executives is that, as in many cases of corporate crime, it's difficult to pinpoint who within the massive, bureaucratic global organization that is BP both knew enough and was in charge enough to be the right target for blame. This isn't just a lawyer's problem, a mere difficulty of proof. It's a problem of responsibility and culpability. The higher you go in BP, the more responsible the managers seem to be—but the less they knew and were involved day-to-day in the Deepwater Horizon rig.

As one ascends the corporate ladder, the case for responsibility becomes more and more "you didn't do your job well" and less and less "you did the following thing that caused that terrible explosion and spill." People, especially highly paid people, certainly deserve blame for not doing their jobs well. But that kind of blame does not fit well with the condemnation associated with the stiffest legal sanctions, especially criminal punishment that includes imprisonment.

It's natural in a case like BP's, then, to reach for a story of blame and responsibility that targets the corporation itself. At the end of 2012, after years of investigation and negotiations, the Justice Department and BP reached a criminal settlement in which BP—the corporation—agreed to plead guilty to serious felonies. These included criminal violations of the Clean Water Act, as well as rare corporate charges of homicide, under the same federal statute that the court said did not fit the rig engineers but which expressly applies to any "owner" of a vessel.[3]

A legal representative of the company—a BP North America VP who had nothing to do with the accident—walked into court and said "guilty" to a federal judge on behalf of a nonhuman legal entity that has no capacity to speak, feel guilty, suffer pain, or be confined in a prison. BP was criminally fined over four billion dollars—an exceptionally large fine that is still only a fraction of the tens of billions the company ultimately will have paid in cleanup and liability costs. The public was told, in banner headlines, that BP was a criminal corporation—homicidal, to be specific.

Many changes were made at BP, especially in the company's safety operations. BP's access to new offshore drilling contracts was impeded and the company and its shareholders sacrificed much profit. The stock price took a big hit and a giant energy company shrank to a less giant one. But BP went on with its business and the stock gradually recovered. In my town, where gas stations that sell the company's products are ubiquitous, I didn't see anyone avoiding the pumps and neither, truth be told, did I. A consumer might want to boycott BP because of the Gulf spill. But it's not as if the effectiveness of BP's gasoline became suspect because the company was adjudicated a felon.

GM

THE MORE recent fiasco involving the deaths of drivers of General Motors cars, while still unfolding, presents a similar dilemma of causation and responsibility within a massive corporate organization.[4] If the crashes that resulted were not so horribly tragic—none more so than that of Candice Anderson and Gene Erikson—the conduct within GM would be almost comical, in a Keystone Cops way.

Years of engineering designs and redesigns, accident reports and reconstructions, litigation teams, meetings, documentation efforts, and corporate reporting procedures reduce to a stunningly simple problem. As noted earlier, the spring inside a starter—the place where the key goes in the car—wasn't strong enough. A simple coiled bit of metal was the reason that when drivers knocked a leg into a key chain that had heavy doodads on it, the thing could rotate out of the run position, causing the engine to turn off and preventing the airbag from deploying. With hundreds of past crashes still under investigation, it appears that over one hundred people died when a starter was rotated unintentionally or an airbag otherwise failed to deploy.

It is inexcusable that GM would design and use such a lousy starter switch when making a better one would have been easy. It's much worse, though, that GM's managers failed to figure out this simple problem and fix it in the face of nearly *nine years* of lawsuits and mounting evidence.

As we saw, there is a traditional villain in the GM story. The engineer responsible for the switch corrected the design—no doubt after realizing the problem, though he claims, incredibly, to have forgotten the whole thing—but he did not document the change as required by GM procedures. The engineer's act of concealment ended up throwing GM lawyers and investigators off the trail of the bad starter switch and prolonged the problem.

But many other people at GM were responsible for the junky switch and the failure to discover the simple explanation for the deadly accidents. They included numerous lawyers at the company who tracked the relevant lawsuits, as well as senior managers who presided over an organization in which such a major problem could develop without anyone raising the alarm with top executives. Even the general counsel, responsible for all of GM's legal matters, was not told. And Mary Barra, who was appointed the new CEO of the company in January 2014, and looked a bit like Sisyphus when she stood up and talked about her plan to make a "new GM," had been unaware of the problem in her previous position as head of product development.

Assume for the sake of argument—there's a good one to be made—that what was done at GM that killed those drivers deserves, generally speaking, to be treated as a crime. Who is the criminal? One could try to find a legal theory on which to prosecute the engineer who concealed the change in switch design. But that hardly seems an appropriate end to the matter, just as prosecuting the rig supervisors alone at BP would not have been an adequate response to the Gulf spill.

One can go up the management chain at GM, as one could at BP. But the problem at GM, even more than at BP, is one of "you should have been a better corporate manager; your communication channels were lousy." When it comes to the approach to safety that resulted in deaths, the culpability of GM's senior managers, even more than for BP's top executives, is for sins of omission rather than commission.

GM seems an even more fitting case than BP for saying that it was really the corporation that killed people, that is responsible, that deserves to be blamed and punished. As discussed, federal prosecutors have charged GM with crimes: lying to the government and defrauding customers, but not homicide. (Recall that ordinary forms of manslaughter are not federal crimes.) GM has agreed to pay a $900 million penalty and profoundly overhaul its safety procedures while subject to government monitoring. If the company does not fulfill its promises under this criminal settlement, it might be prosecuted and follow BP's path, with someone from its legal department walking into a courtroom and saying "guilty" for the company.

No matter what, GM will go on making cars. America needs the jobs GM provides to the industrial, swing-state-filled Midwest probably more than the petroleum BP pulls from the floor of the Gulf. At least since World War II, Americans have well known that GM jobs are not replaceable except at great pain. As the saying goes, what's good for GM is good for America.

The Dilemma of Corporate Criminal Liability

THE IDEA of the corporation as criminal is a puzzle. Many people, especially in academic circles, argue that criminalizing corporations makes no sense.[5] Companies can't be imprisoned, the argument goes. And they don't do bad things themselves: They have neither the minds nor the bodies needed to commit crimes like manslaughter, assault, theft, and fraud as the law defines those acts. Only the people who work for corporations commit crimes, so the law ought to punish only them. The law cannot hope to deter corporate crime except by making those people fear punishment. Besides, look at the waste of what happened to the Arthur Andersen accounting firm in the Enron case, when it was prosecuted and went out of business. Criminalizing a corporation can wipe out wealth and eliminate the jobs and retirement savings of people who did nothing wrong.

This argument runs into a simple ground truth. The American people, and the world, blamed BP for the Gulf disaster and GM for the killer ignition switch. They were right to do so. Only impoverished accounts of these fiascos would describe them as caused by a few careless workers who had a bad day. There's no explaining Deepwater Horizon or the Chevy and Saturn crashes without attributing them to the corporate institutions that, *through* their employees, made those disasters happen. BP's careless approach to safety and aggressive drilling led directly to the explosion in the Gulf. GM's sclerotic bureaucracy and inability to compete in the small car market except on lower prices produced unsafe cars that killed drivers. The company's cover-your-rear culture—investigators learned about the "GM nod" (everyone at the meeting concurring that "we should do something about that") and the "GM salute" (everyone pointing to the person next to them as the one responsible)—suppressed the starter switch problem for years, as the deaths multiplied.

This is the dilemma of criminal liability for corporations. Some corporations ought to be criminalized, even if they cannot be imprisoned. And prosecuting corporations can wipe away the wealth that the government licensed them to create for their shareholders and employees and the American economy in the first place.

Organizations cause bad things to happen. We know this from our experiences with our institutions of education, employment, charity, and government. Even the best institutions are deeply imperfect, or dysfunctional, as we often lament. When we organize ourselves into groups for even the noblest purposes, we can't help but produce some ill effects. Behind their glittery logos and public images, big corporations are as dysfunctional as any other social institution.

Institutions may be made by people, but they're not human. There always will be something irrational, or at least unsatisfying, about trying to punish a paper entity—a bit like kicking the chair over which one has stumbled in the night. And it will always be a legal truth that the principal punishment available for corporations is monetary penalties, a legal sanction that could as easily be imposed in a society that lacked any criminal law or criminal justice system.

Over the last three decades American legal practice has reached an unsteady compromise on the problem of fitting ancient Western practices of criminal punishment with the modern corporation.[6] Institutions can and do cause crime. That is surely right as an empirical matter, whether or not one can develop a satisfying account of the moral responsibility of something that does not live and breathe. However, firms cannot be imprisoned. And severe sanctioning of firms—in financial penalties and reputational harm—can deter wrongdoing but also can over-deter, in the sense of needlessly wiping out economic value.

So the law makes corporations eligible for conviction—by saying that a company is criminally liable anytime an employee or other agent of the firm commits a crime as part of doing her job and at least partially to benefit the company. Then the government almost always bargains away that liability in exchange for tailored changes in the corporate institution. Those changes are designed to get the right amount of cooperation from the firm to ensure punishment of the human wrongdoers involved, deterrence, and prevention of future wrongdoing. Almost always, the corporation is also required to admit publicly to what it did—to face up to its failures as a first step to correcting them.

Lawyers call these arrangements "deferred prosecution" or "non-prosecution" agreements. The terms misleadingly imply immunity. The agreements are onerous, detailed, usually made public, often filed with courts, and can include large financial penalties equivalent to, or even beyond, the fine a judge would impose in a full prosecution.

Some legal professionals see this practice as a win-win, or at least as preferable to the alternatives of either institutional immunity or excessively costly punishment. The public gets a remedy that addresses the problem that institutions can and do cause crime without the cost and waste associated with flogging something that feels no pain.

Nonetheless, few people within or outside the legal system are happy with this practice. Many in the business world think the Justice Department abuses its power to threaten corporations with criminal prosecution. Prosecutors, they say, get lazy and careless because their corporate cases are never tested at trial. Companies, especially those with public shareholders, face such enormous pressure to put criminal problems behind them and to take no risk of conviction that they roll over and settle from the moment a criminal investigation gets started. Also, these critics say, prosecutors don't have the knowledge or training to undertake the technical and ambitious tasks, at the center of most of these settlement deals, of supervising the overhaul of corporate management.

More commonly, there remains a deep public sentiment that corporations are "getting away" with crime—that they're not held responsible for it in satisfactory ways. This feeling has surfaced in debate about whether the government should require firms to confess—that is, to explicitly admit criminal wrongdoing, and even to plead guilty in front of judges though that act cannot lead to the usual next step of incarceration.

BP pled guilty (to some charges). Other large corporations have been formally convicted in pollution and bribery cases. But in most prosecutions, the corporate confession has not included saying "guilty" in front of a judge. One might think that a plea is only a legal formality. But many people argue that a corporation bears greater stigma, and demonstrates fuller and more public acceptance of its wrongdoing, if its confession includes a plea of guilty (through a senior representative) on the record in open court.

The impetus to blame corporations formally is not only to slake primal anger. Just as we understand from our own experiences that institutions produce harm, we understand that our own associations with organizations are part of how we define our identities, construct our self-images, and build our resumes. No one who is not a professional criminal wants to work for a criminal organization. Social condemnation can produce shame, introspection, and change for people in their organizational roles as it does in their individual and private ones.

Consider, for example, the intense feelings on both sides of the devastating scandal over sex crimes by a football coach at Penn State University.[7] Thousands of stakeholders in the university continue to insist that a rush to judgment by the NCAA and an investigator hired by the board of trustees unjustly destroyed the school's reputational capital. Those people feel as strongly as do the victims and their supporters, who blamed the institution and its football culture for enabling a serial rapist.

The threat of corporate criminal liability and its ultimate imposition can deter wrongdoing within business organizations and can lead to reform of organizations, industries, and markets. If this were not true, the savviest managers of America's biggest and most successful corporations would not spend so much time worrying about how to avoid what they call, often extravagantly, the "death sentence" of a corporate criminal prosecution. And those managers would not routinely agree to undertake the intrusive and costly reforms of their businesses that they accept in settlements with the Justice Department.

The reputational effect of a criminal conviction of a corporation—especially through a jury verdict but arguably also through a guilty plea—gives corporate criminal liability its special potency. That effect counters an argument economists have made that monetary penalties, which come with civil sanctions too, are the most the law can impose on corporations anyway.

But the potency and scope of reputational effects is also a problem. A reputational sanction, as academics call it, is not like a sentence of imprisonment or a fine. A judge can't order a ten percent reduction in a business's reputational capital. A corporation can't agree in a settlement to give up twenty percent of its good name with its customers and business partners. Once unleashed, the reputational sanction that falls on the corporation branded criminal cannot be controlled. And that sanction can be set loose by an investigation, an indictment, or even an article in the *Wall Street Journal,* long before there is any legal determination of guilt.

Arthur Andersen

AMONG LAWYERS, the story of Arthur Andersen has become *the* story of criminalizing a corporation, with the result that the tale is repeated in apocryphal form.[8] Look at what happened to Arthur Andersen, this story goes. The government indicted them in the Enron case and they went out of business. Thousands of people who had nothing to do with any wrongdoing lost their jobs. Years later, the Supreme Court reversed the accounting firm's criminal conviction but it was too late to save the jobs. Therefore, the government should rarely if ever charge a company with a crime. After all, prosecutors at the Justice Department are not supposed to be running the U.S. economy.

As someone who studies corporate crime for a living and was also one of the prosecutors on the Andersen matter (two other lawyers and I tried the case), I agree that the Andersen case is important to understanding the limitations of corporate criminal liability. But not for the usually cited reasons.

Arthur Andersen was not a corporation at all but rather a partnership, a venerable brand among what was then the "Big Five" accounting firms paid to audit the lion's share of America's corporate books. Andersen's partners—its senior employees—owned the firm. It had no public shareholders. It was a service firm with little in the way of nonhuman assets. Andersen thus was vulnerable to the risk of client and partner flight. This has been true of America's large and increasingly unstable law and accounting firms for a long time. Andersen and its peers in the big five were exceptionally at risk among professional partnerships because the core service they sold—certification of the reliability of corporations' books to investors—depended heavily on their reputations for honesty and reliability.

In the fall of 2001, Enron Corporation shockingly collapsed in the midst of an historic scandal over its accounting practices. Andersen was Enron's auditor and Enron was Andersen's biggest and most lucrative global client. Andersen was in serious trouble. Because of two prior accounting scandals involving major clients, Andersen was already subject to a "consent decree," a probationary status with the chief regulator of the public auditing profession, the Securities and Exchange Commission. Just weeks after Enron's implosion and an ensuing SEC investigation, the obstruction-of-justice problem came to light—the "follow the document policy" shredding and deleting by Andersen personnel who audited Enron.

Now Andersen was in really big trouble. Aside from the prospect of crippling civil liability over its role in auditing Enron, criminal charges for Andersen looked possible. Corporate clients, required by law to keep their quarterly audits going, began to abandon Andersen. The firm's partners, many of whom had portable clients, became restless. Andersen's lawyers approached the Justice Department and said the firm needed to know, as soon as possible, whether there would be any criminal charges in the Enron affair. Prosecutors obliged by setting aside the larger Enron project for two months and conducting an all-hands investigation of the document destruction at Andersen.

The result was the discovery that Andersen partners and employees, at both the firm's Chicago headquarters and in Houston, had deliberately urged rapid destruction of Enron records as the SEC investigation started. They seemingly thought they could use that loophole of invoking the previously ignored document policy until they were formally served with the SEC subpoena that prompted that "stop the shredding" e-mail. But federal law sensibly prohibits the destruction of evidence by persons who can see that a legal proceeding is on the way.

The prosecutors, whose obligations encompass the general public interest, told Andersen that forgoing a criminal case against the firm would be impossible to justify. The conduct was another display of the firm's chronic attitude toward its chief regulator. The Enron matter was of surpassing importance. Senior managers at Andersen counseled the document destruction. And strong deterrence of this type of obstructive conduct is vital to evidence production in corporate regulatory matters, a process that depends on companies to preserve their documents and disclose them to the government when directed.

Nonetheless, the Justice Department offered to negotiate a plea agreement. When Andersen rejected that, the government suggested a deferred prosecution agreement that would require no plea of guilty. Andersen again declined, insisting that even a factual admission of criminal wrongdoing in a settlement agreement with no guilty plea would destroy the firm's reputation and put it out of business. When asked what specifically they sought, the firm's representatives said they needed the government to publicly clear the firm of wrongdoing—something prosecutors generally don't do and certainly couldn't do in this case.

The government indicted. More Andersen clients and partners headed for the door. Prosecutors again suggested a deferred prosecution agreement and Andersen again refused. The firm asked for and got a rapid trial, and a federal jury in Houston heard the evidence and convicted Andersen of obstruction of justice. That sealed the firm's fate, if there had been any hope of survival left—which seems doubtful given the bleeding that already had occurred from the mortal wound of having been Enron's accountants.

Two years later, the Supreme Court reversed the conviction and ordered a new trial because of faulty jury instructions.[9] Contrary to the apocryphal story, the Court did *not* absolve Andersen. It rendered a novel decision, one that prior federal courts and even Andersen's trial lawyers had not foreseen, about an awkward obstruction-of-justice statute that Congress, in any event, had made moot by reforming the laws between the Andersen trial and the Court hearing the firm's appeal.

The Court ruled that Andersen's employees could not have obstructed justice merely by destroying documents to keep them out of the SEC's Enron investigation. For the evidence destruction to be criminal, the late Chief Justice Rehnquist wrote in one of his last opinions, the workers must also have had in mind a "consciousness of wrongdoing." Because Andersen was out of business and a new trial would have been pointless, it can't be known whether a jury told of this requirement would have convicted the firm.

The story of Arthur Andersen does not carry the moral that prosecutors shouldn't indict a firm. Its moral is that the reputational sanction that makes criminalizing a corporation different from suing it is powerful and cannot be controlled. Potent reputational effects are what get a company's attention when the prospect of criminal liability looms. But if an orderly settlement that controls those effects can't be reached, then the reputational sanction must be applied in spite of its far-reaching consequences. Otherwise there would be no credible risk of criminal liability for corporations in the first place.

Once those sanctions are unleashed, their effects depend on factors beyond the control of the legal system, most importantly the nature of the firm and its business. BP survived being called a criminal. GM will too. So did the massive Siemens Corporation, in spite of pleading guilty in a huge global bribery scheme. The auditing partnership Arthur Andersen, already gravely wounded from its relationship to the notorious fraud at Enron, did not.

(Not) Prosecuting the Banks

THE POTENT but tricky relationship between prosecuting companies and punishment through reputational damage illuminates controversy over how the Obama administration handled the Wall Street banks after the 2008 financial crisis.[10] Assume for argument's sake that a question discussed in chapter two was settled in favor of prosecutors: the investment banks' sale of mortgage-backed securities in certain circumstances was criminal fraud. If so, the banks deserved abundant blame for the conduct of their traders. It's hard to think of an example of wrongdoing within corporate organizations that could more appropriately be laid at the feet of the institutions, and their management and compensation practices, than the time bomb that was the 2005 to 2008 mortgage-backed securities market.[11]

This is not news. Americans were justifiably furious at J.P. Morgan, Citibank, Goldman Sachs, Merrill Lynch, Lehman Brothers, Morgan Stanley, Bear Stearns, and their corporate accomplices and partners for wrecking the economy. They wanted the legal system to call the banks criminals. Perhaps the most infamous statement during this time was the admission by a senior Justice Department prosecutor that worries about the survival of these bloated and dangerous institutions kept him awake at night.[12]

There is embarrassing circularity in the story of the government and the investment banks. Many people remain unsatisfied because the word "criminal" has not been attached to the banks. But the government has secured a series of settlements of civil lawsuits over MBS deals in the lead-up to the financial crisis. The settlements are unprecedented in size for the Justice Department: $13 billion from J.P. Morgan, $7 billion from Citibank, and $16 billion from Bank of America. The agreements are on top of a $20 billion settlement with the same banks, and others, over the servicing of individual mortgages.[13]

These historic settlements pale by comparison to the total costs of the financial crisis. But what really throws the civil fines into question are the all too familiar words "TARP" (Troubled Assets Relief Program) and "bailout." Just a few years earlier, the government disbursed a total of over $100 billion to those same three banks as part of a desperate, and most think necessary, effort to avert a total collapse of the American economy. The telling fact is not that the government's panicked bailout payments dwarf the settlement proceeds from its later lawsuits. (The banks repaid the bailout money in full, plus a few billion in profit to the government.) It's that the government was in a position to righteously insist in 2012 that the banks pay steep penalties for their conduct in the MBS market only because the government had moved heaven and earth in 2008 to save the same banks from liquidation as a result of their self-inflicted exposure to that *same market*.

There would have been something illogical, at the least, about the government pursuing criminal prosecutions of big Wall Street banks in 2010 or 2011 when the same government, in an effort to save the world economy, had spent over a trillion dollars in 2008 and 2009 to keep those banks from failing. If the essence of criminalizing corporations is to punish their reputations, the point of criminal prosecutions of the banks could only have been to really hurt them. Not just fine them, reorganize them, and reregulate them. Not even break them apart in some orderly fashion—an option that may have been a serious mistake not to pursue. But just hurt them, with unpredictable consequences for everyone else.

There was another problem with prosecuting the banks, a common complication in the prosecution of corporations. Human felons lose legal rights, like the right to vote or own a gun or remain in the United States without citizenship. So-called felon disempowerment—though justifiably subject to criticism and reconsideration—has been fundamental to the American legal system. Federal law, which regulates the bulk of the day-to-day business of corporations in most major industries, includes dozens of statutes and rules that say felons may, and often must, be barred from doing important things for public safety and well-being like marketing pharmaceuticals, auditing corporate books, running nuclear power plants, making weapons for the Pentagon, and operating federally charted banks. These laws apply to corporations in the same way they do to people.

Taken individually, laws ejecting criminally convicted companies from certain kinds of business seem like common sense. No one wants a criminal making her heart medication or getting her tax dollars for selling airplanes to the navy. Taken as a whole, however, these laws complicate the prosecution of business crime. The all-or-nothing potential of corporate criminal liability, and its reputational consequences, is magnified by the potential for debarment, which can work like capital punishment for a company.

If Pfizer breaks the law in marketing an antidepressant drug, should the consequence be that its antiseizure medications are no longer available to patients? If Siemens criminally bribes the government of a South American nation, should the result be that VA hospitals are no longer able to update their CT scanning equipment? If Citibank's derivatives traders market a fraudulent securities product, should the bank no longer be allowed to extend credit to small business owners? The structure of these regulatory regimes combines with our deep dependence on large corporations to make criminal prosecution, in some circumstances, simply not feasible or sensible.

Convicting Corporations

POTENTIAL TARGETS of corporate prosecution must be evaluated on two dimensions that may have little to do with the nature of the crime: firms' reputational capital and their regulatory environments. In other words, are the investment banks more like Arthur Andersen or more like BP? In the years after the financial crisis, and for many years before, the conventional wisdom about the banks, on Wall Street and in the legal profession, was that they were more like Arthur Andersen. Financial firms sell their reputations to their clients and they're among the most heavily regulated businesses in America. A criminal prosecution, it was thought, could easily mean the death of a big bank.

In recent years, this view has taken a surprising turn—in part because the American people, who naturally do not base their views on what the legal profession tells them, kept insisting that a criminal justice system in which big banks were too big to fail and too big to prosecute was not acceptable. The Justice Department became sensitive to criticism that it was presiding over a system based on a double standard.

The turning point was the case of HSBC, the British megabank discovered to have permitted global customers to launder hundreds of millions of dollars in drug proceeds through its depository system.[14] After a thorough investigation and extensive negotiations, the Justice Department reached one of those nonprosecution agreements with HSBC. In December of 2012, HSBC paid a then record penalty (nearly $2 billion) and agreed to reform itself under the government's close supervision, with extensive and costly improvements to its money laundering compliance operations. Prosecutors thus avoided imposing a criminal conviction, with all the consequences that might have dealt to diverse stakeholders in the bank who had nothing to do with the money laundering.

For many concerned with corporate crime, the HSBC deal was the last straw.[15] Put simply, the Justice Department was accused of coddling money launderers in the banking industry while continuing without interruption its decades-long practice of slamming common retail drug dealers with stiff prison sentences in part by charging them with money laundering. (For a more colorful version of this critique, see Matt Taibbi's book *The Divide*.)

The criticism seems to have stung. In its next two big bank cases, the Justice Department extracted corporate guilty pleas after tough and complicated negotiations that included banking regulators around the world and, apparently, the president of France. The government prosecuted Credit Suisse for being an accomplice to massive tax evasion by wealthy Americans and BNP Paribas for allowing businesses to use its bank to evade U.S. sanctions on Iran and the Sudan. In 2014, both banks pled guilty to federal felonies in settlement agreements with the Justice Department that included, like the HSBC deal, big financial penalties and extensive reforms designed to improve compliance.[16]

The surprise was that the guilty pleas in the Credit Suisse and BNP deals did not devastate the banks. This was partly because the Justice Department took care to include relevant regulators in the negotiations, ensuring an orderly process that would not cause either bank to lose licenses necessary to keep its doors open. Debarment rules in regulatory regimes are a serious complication for the prosecution of corporations. But in some cases they can be handled delicately through negotiation. (That raises the question, of course, whether the intended teeth of a criminal conviction have been pulled.)

Even with regulatory complications worked out in advance, the formal admission of these banks in a court of law that they were federal felons might have been expected to drain their reputational capital. That didn't happen. Credit Suisse is still open for business. It's still very big. And its stock price is about where it was before the bank's guilty plea. So too for BNP, the stock of which has fallen a bit but is still well above where it was after the global banking meltdown.

The lesson seemed to be to stop fearing what had been known as the Arthur Andersen effect. Even the accounting firm KPMG, while not required to plead guilty, survived a criminal settlement agreement in which it publicly admitted to having helped clients cheat the federal government on their taxes.

Maybe twenty or thirty years ago a big financial services firm would have been more like Arthur Andersen, a business with a fragile reputation that could not survive its customers learning that their money had been trusted to the safekeeping of a felon. That's apparently no longer true. The big banks' reputations have fallen so much, and their serious legal problems have become so commonplace, that a criminal conviction may be no big deal. And the global economy is so dependent on a small number of financial services firms that it's not feasible for all the money in one of these institutions to get up and walk away. Where would that money go? Nobody thinks that BNP and Credit Suisse are full of venal cheaters while the other big banks employ only paragons of rectitude.

Not too long after the Credit Suisse and BNP Paribas guilty pleas, and the market's orderly response to those convictions, the Justice Department announced a remarkable set of five deals in which Citigroup, J.P. Morgan, Barclays, Royal Bank of Scotland, and UBS all agreed to plead guilty to serious charges of conducting an antitrust conspiracy among traders in global currency markets. What had once been thought to be Armageddon is now common. Which raises the question whether the reputational penalty of corporate criminal liability can turn out to be uncontrollable in *both* directions: too powerful when it came to a firm like Arthur Andersen, then not powerful enough now that banks are regularly convicted of felonies.

Making criminals of corporations—at least the big ones that employ us, give us returns on our investments, and make the economy hum along—requires us to confront the duality in our relationship with them. Their power and our dependency on them make them especially justified targets of retribution when they abuse that power and break the law. But punishing them is only meaningful—truly retributive and likely to deter—if it leads to painful consequences like loss of reputational capital and business. Those are the very consequences that, because corporations are *not* people, flow back on us—as employees, shareholders, customers, and stakeholders in the economy.

Some celebrated what the Justice Department did with Credit Suisse and BNP with a declaration of "finally." These deals could as easily be mocked as empty ritual: the formal corporate plea of guilty is offered to the public as if it were genuine punitive justice only after an agreement has been carefully negotiated to ensure that the consequences of that plea will not differ much from the outcome of one of the Department's widely lamented nonprosecution agreements. The truth is that resolutions like those with Credit Suisse and BNP—or even more severe ones like that with BP over the Gulf spill—don't solve the dilemma of how to deal with the crimes of big corporations. These cases only further expose that dilemma.

Prosecuting People

THERE IS another approach. One can argue, as many have, that prosecution of corporations is a largely symbolic practice, ineffectual and beside the point. When it comes to meaningful blame and effective deterrence, the real issue is whether the people who make the critical decisions that produce harms and disasters like those at BP, GM, and the big banks are held accountable. It's important to remember, and too often forgotten in popular treatments of this subject, that being unable to imprison a corporation does not entail that individual wrongdoers walk away. Or at least it shouldn't.

Many critics of the Obama Justice Department have said that the real scandal in a settlement like the HSBC money laundering affair is that no *person* at HSBC went to jail. An outspoken federal judge in New York published an opinion piece lending sharp legal analysis to this complaint.[17] Since federal law makes a corporation liable for a crime only if an identifiable employee of the corporation commits a crime as part of doing his job for the company, he noted, it's legally impossible for a corporation to be a criminal without a specific person being at least eligible for prosecution. Therefore, in a case like HSBC, the Justice Department did not just fail to prosecute people, it *chose* not to.

Prosecutors, who for good reasons cannot provide public autopsies of cases that never go to court, defended themselves with standard lines about how "we follow the evidence where it takes us" and "when we have the proof, we bring the case." What this means is that the prosecutors in a case like HSBC decided there was enough evidence to lever a settlement from the bank but not enough to win a trial against an individual. Or, less convincingly, that they thought the sum total of the bank's money laundering violations was extremely serious but that any one violation by a bank employee was too technical or of too small consequence to warrant imprisonment of that person. Still, as the editorializing judge pointed out, some would consider it as disturbing for the Justice Department to muscle settlements out of companies in weak cases as for the Department to abandon prosecution of individuals out of laziness or impatience once it has extracted a splashy financial penalty from the corporation.

The Justice Department has again showed its sensitivity to this type of criticism. Just as the HSBC deal was followed by the Credit Suisse and BNP guilty pleas, the failure to prosecute HSBC employees has been followed by individual prosecutions of bankers at Credit Suisse, with perhaps more to come in the BNP case.[18] Years after the government secured the massive settlement from the Siemens Corporation, the government finally prosecuted a group of former Siemens officials for their roles in the company's bribery scheme.[19] The Justice Department has said publicly, in a September 2015 memo issued by Deputy Attorney General Sally Yates, that it intends to put more pressure on its prosecutors to include individual prosecutions in corporate cases.

Prosecuting individuals is important—to the legitimacy of corporate crime enforcement as well as deterrence. Imagine you have a job at a major, heavily regulated corporation, a pharmaceutical company let's say, that involves serious legal risk. In considering legal risk, you would have to think about the possibility not only of lawsuits but also a criminal prosecution, which is not so rare in your industry. Let's say that you run the massive sales division of the company. You're well aware that almost all the big pharma companies have had troubles with the federal law that bars drug companies from marketing "off-label" uses of their drugs to doctors. (The law, as most patients know, leaves doctors free to prescribe for unapproved uses.) This prohibition applies whether those uses are relatively benign ones like taking an antidepressant to help with weight loss or harmful ones like taking OxyContin for insomnia. The law includes criminal penalties.

You would personally have to worry about a few kinds of criminal cases. A salesperson might violate this law and wind up being prosecuted. For you, that would involve at least a failure on the job. That salesperson's crime could, in turn, be attributed to the company. If a prosecutor decided that this was more than an isolated incident, the company could end up in criminal trouble—its worst legal nightmare short of its drugs harming people—because of a failure in the division you run. If lots of salespeople violate the off-label marketing law, and there's evidence that you knew about and perhaps encouraged them to push the medicine that way, the government could choose to prosecute you.

Obviously you will worry about the last case—the prosecution of you—first and most. Prosecutions of lower-level employees and of companies will certainly encourage corporate managers to be diligent. No one wants to lose her job, especially due to a scandal or even an accident for which she bears responsibility. And no one wants to be associated with an institution that has been labeled criminal.

But these employment and reputational consequences pale in comparison to the prospect of federal imprisonment, which means the loss of one's freedom and so much more. Prosecution of a corporate manager for criminal behavior on her watch undoubtedly offers the most powerful deterrent to corporate crime.

The Problem of the Guilty Mind

GREATER DETERMINATION to prosecute managers does not eliminate the problem with which we began this chapter. The higher you go up the corporate ladder in a case like BP or GM, the more "responsible" managers are in the sense of the buck stopping on their desks. Yet the less responsible they are in the sense of the criminal knowledge and intent that Western legal systems require as a precondition for substantial imprisonment.

Imagine that you're that pharma company sales division manager and the government says it's going to seek to have you imprisoned because a handful of salespeople, among an army of thousands under your command, pushed a medicine to doctors for a use not formally approved by the FDA. If you were prosecuted on that basis, you and your family would feel like victims of an unjust legal system. And if you thought the government had the power and appetite for doing that, you might be deterred from taking that job in the first place.

Criminal punishment, as we've discussed, has two main purposes. Most good prosecutions are aimed at both. One is to reduce crime by persuading people not to break the law because the risk of punishment is too high. The other is to ensure that those who do morally bad things to others, or to society as a whole, are held responsible by receiving the punishment they deserve. The second purpose, contrary to what some might think, entails that criminal justice has both a floor *and* a ceiling. Wrongdoers deserve to be held accountable. But people also should not be punished more than they deserve. That too would be a moral wrong.

What determines the type and amount of punishment that's deserved? Philosophers of criminal law have debated this question for centuries, refining the academic answers even as Western criminal justice systems have evolved to be at least somewhat more attentive to its nuances. It will be sufficient for present purposes to observe that modern Anglo-American legal systems follow the view that bad acts are worse when they involve morally wrong thinking. This is intuitive. It's far worse to shoot someone through the heart out of spite or greed than it is to drive inattentively into a person walking on the road.

In breaking the law, awareness and choice translate into greater responsibility. Not only because deliberate choices to harm others are morally serious. Also because the exceptionally coercive government action of taking away liberty ought to be a consequence that people in a free society have the opportunity to foresee and avoid.

These principles produce friction when it comes to corporations. Corporate misconduct can be very serious. It can kill people, as in the BP or GM cases. It can wipe out massive wealth, devastating people's lives, as in the banking crisis. But the structure of large institutions, especially corporations, dilutes responsibility. Big jobs like drilling for oil, manufacturing autos, and financing the global economy are possible only by organizing people into large, complex groups with layers of hierarchy and supervision. Doing this produces efficiencies but also diffuses knowledge and control.

Consider the case of the traders at J.P. Morgan's London office that included Bruno Iksil, who became known as the "London Whale."[20] Those traders managed a profitable book of derivative securities that earned J.P. Morgan as much as $1 billion annually. Like all successful traders in the competitive investment banking industry, they were well compensated with bonuses tied to profits they generated for the bank.

When the market for their products turned against them in 2012, the traders held a large quantity of securities that had to be marked down—in an amount that eventually resulted in J.P. Morgan announcing a nearly $1 billion reduction in its earnings results. Instead of timely reporting the truth about the plummeting value of their books internally within the bank, and thus ultimately to shareholders and the public, the key players in this trading group lied—with the mentality of the fraud perpetrator that, soon enough, the market will turn back in his favor and no one will have been the wiser.

Investors in J.P. Morgan were victims of fraud because the bank gave them false information about the value of its trading portfolio. Senior managers at J.P. Morgan approved that information and its release. They also authorized a compensation system that caused the traders in London to take big risks and then lie when their risks went bad. Managers also approved reporting and compliance systems that did not prevent the traders in London from controlling how the bank valued their own trading book in its overall financials.

But, as far as the public evidence shows, the top managers at J.P. Morgan didn't know that the numbers reported from the usually profitable group in London had turned massively false. CEO Jamie Dimon initially insisted that the story of the London losses must be wrong because his bank's systems did not allow such a thing to happen. Dimon was delusional about the fraud, not a conspirator in it.[21]

Criminal Recklessness

THERE'S NO clever lawyer's maneuver for avoiding the dilemma of where to fix criminal responsibility within the bureaucracy of the big firm. There's only the decision whether to compromise commitments about legal responsibility and criminal punishment for the problem of business crime. Perhaps ironically, one answer to the complaint that the American criminal justice system mercilessly grinds the street criminal under its heel while letting the culpable businessman roam free is to make rules for business crime that would cast a wider net than even those that apply to violence, drug dealing, weapons trafficking, and alien smuggling.

Some have explicitly argued this position, with welcome candor. They've said perhaps it *should* be criminal for a bank manager to compensate her traders in a way that's practically guaranteed to make them push the legal envelope and then to look the other way, happily ignorant of the particulars of what they do. Maybe it even should be criminal for a corporate safety manager to fail badly at her job, presiding over an organization that does nothing in response to the kinds of red flags that popped up in the disasters at BP and GM. Such arguments might go as far as to suggest that criminal liability should extend to those in the corporation whose responsibility is to watch the watchers: those who sit on boards of directors.

To evaluate these important arguments, a very small bit (I promise) of introductory criminal law is needed.[22] Anglo-American criminal law has, for a long time, been organized around five or six concepts about guilty states of mind. Let's order them from more to less culpable. To act with *intent* is to do something with the conscious object of accomplishing it, like defrauding someone by trying to deceive her about the value of a product. To act with *knowledge* is to do something with awareness of a vital fact or obvious consequence, like importing a suitcase knowing it's full of heroin or detonating a bomb knowing it will kill the occupants of a building.

The legal concept of knowledge is expanded a bit by the doctrine of *willful blindness*. This is sometimes called the "ostrich principle"—inaccurately, because ostriches aren't trying to avoid anything when they dig into the sand. Under this idea, consciously avoiding knowledge of something incriminating (like the contents of the imported suitcase) in order to evade criminal responsibility is treated the same as knowledge.

To act *recklessly* is to do something with a particular kind of knowledge, that is, knowledge of a risk that is sufficiently large and serious. Recklessness is not just extreme lack of attention or care. It's the conscious disregard of serious risk, like choosing to drive way over the speed limit on a winding road full of pedestrians in spite of knowing that such driving might kill someone walking on the road.

In criminal law, to act *negligently* is to act really carelessly. Negligence is not a state of mind so much as the absence of one. It's the failure to be aware of—to think about—a serious risk that a reasonably careful person would have considered before acting. An awful example of criminal negligence that has led to some homicide prosecutions would be a person forgetting that his infant is in the back seat of the car and locking the car and walking away.

American law is full of crimes that can be committed with various of these mental states. Negligence is the most controversial and least sufficient state of mind for a criminal conviction. Some theorists of criminal law think negligence should never be enough to justify imprisonment because a person forgetting or not thinking about something is never morally bad enough to justify taking away her liberty.

It's probably fair to say that negligence, which is a common basis for private tort lawsuits in American law, usually lands people in prison only when someone is killed as a result. Even then, the matter is highly controversial and controlled by troubling amounts of prosecutorial discretion. When is it a crime, rather than a tragedy, for a football coach to drill his players too hard in summer preseason practice resulting in a kid dying from heat sickness? Which parents who fail to take their kids to the doctor when serious illness sets in are criminally responsible for the deaths that result? And so on.

Recklessness, which—to repeat—is more than really bad negligence, is a more common and less controversial basis for felony prosecutions in the United States. Often there is callousness and moral fault in a person thinking, "Someone could get hurt here but I don't care, I'm going ahead anyway," that isn't present when someone merely forgets or fails to think. And punishment has a chance of deterring reckless people because they may reflect on the consequences of risks they're thinking about taking. It depends, of course, on the social value of what the risk taker is doing. A surgeon who goes ahead with a very risky but potentially life-saving operation is not the same as a drug dealer who trains a killer dog to guard his stash house in a neighborhood full of toddlers.

Even with reckless conduct, most criminal prosecutions that lead to substantial prison terms involve homicide, as well as a few other seriously violent or dangerous crimes, such as very harmful assaults, some forms of arson, and some child abuse. For other major felonies, intent or knowledge is usually required. To imprison a person for things like transporting narcotics, possessing illegal guns, smuggling aliens across the border, taking another person's property, or defrauding a commercial partner, thinking about risk or probability is generally not enough under American law. The criminal actor must have known (or been willfully blind) that the suitcase contained heroin, that the gun was stolen, that the passengers were undocumented, that the watch on the table belonged to someone else, or that the statement about the product for sale was false.

Now we can return to the problem of criminalizing corporate managers for serious wrongdoing under their supervision. In some cases, those managers will have known exactly what was going on. That kind of knowledge (as well as intent) is what convicted the top managers in the corporate scandals of the early 2000s: Enron, Worldcom, the accounting fraud by the Rigas family at the Adelphia Corporation, Dennis Kozlowski's extravagant use of the Tyco Corporation's assets, and others. Knowledge was clear, for example, in the recent prosecution of Stewart Parnell, the owner and president of Peanut Corporation of America, whose direct written orders to employees to ship products for which safety testing had not been completed caused the deaths of nine people from salmonella poisoning. There's no problem fitting those cases, when the evidence is strong enough to win a jury trial, into long-standing criminal law. But such cases are exceptional. Most often, full knowledge at the top of the corporation is lacking.

The rule about willful blindness can help. Some critics have argued that federal prosecutors should have used that rule to bring more aggressive cases against bank managers after the financial crisis. Everyone knows, this argument goes, that the leaders of the big financial institutions knew that the bubble in the housing market, and thus the mortgage-backed securities market, was bound to burst. Actions speak loudest: many of them started shorting the market even as they continued to sell buyers securities that were long on the market and turned out to be virtually worthless.

Courts have been nervous, and often skeptical, about the concept of willful blindness.[23] If knowledge is required for criminal fraud by statute, and recklessness is not enough, then willful blindness must be equivalent to true knowledge (awareness) and not merely recklessness (disregard of risk). The criminal actor must have thought, "If I look, I'm likely going to see something that gives me guilty knowledge. I'm going to turn the other way so I can't see." To ensure that willful blindness doesn't become recklessness, courts have required the prosecutor to have evidence that the criminal defendant took steps not to acquire knowledge that she clearly wanted to avoid in order to escape criminal liability—like a CEO instructing underlings not to inform her of the daily status of the trading books in one division of the bank.

One can see why such evidence might have been lacking in instances like the London Whale affair or the mortgage-backed securities trading operations of the big Wall Street banks. A prosecutor would have had to persuade a jury, beyond a reasonable doubt, that a bank executive was lying when she asserted something like, "We were aware of the risk that the market would fall but I couldn't quantify that risk with precision or look into a crystal ball and see whether it would materialize in a month or a year. We hedged our bets, for sure. But we didn't stop betting. Our business is defined by risk and uncertainty and all of us can turn out to be wrong." To persuade a jury that this story is definitely false, the prosecutor needs something like an e-mail or a highly credible witness showing that the same executive told her deputies not to give her details about their assessments of risk in the market.

The Crime of Being Responsible

THERE'S AN alternative for the reader who thinks this tutorial on criminal law is beside the point—that existing law is the problem rather than the explanation. One could choose to criminalize, with sanctions of imprisonment, reckless management by senior corporate executives. American law could, contrary to existing criminal codes, make it sufficient for a corporate executive to have chosen to press forward despite knowing that the securities market might soon crater, that an oil well could explode, that an auto ignition switch might not be sound, that salespeople scattered around the globe could be paying bribes, that bank depositors' money might be derived from drug deals, and so on.

After reviewing its banking industry in the wake of the financial crisis, the United Kingdom took a step in this direction.²⁴ It's now a crime in England, punishable by up to *seven years* in prison, for a senior manager of a financial institution to make a decision that causes the failure of the firm, while knowing that his decision risks the company's failure. This law may deter carelessness in the banking industry. But it's vulnerable to criticism from two directions. The offense is limited since it applies only to financial institutions, not corporations generally, and it can apply only when a firm has gone completely under, a relatively unusual event outside of a major financial crisis. The law's importance thus could be mostly symbolic.

On the other hand, the UK reform is a potentially radical departure from prior criminal and regulatory law in making it a crime for a corporate manager to take too much risk. Businesses grow and die, succeed and fail, as part of the warp and woof of capitalism. To preside over a company when it fails is not a crime. Indeed, bankruptcy law and limited liability for corporations are two fundamental ways modern legal systems embrace business risk.

How is a corporate executive supposed to know, at pain of criminal punishment, how to walk the line between risk taking that is within the range of management philosophies and risk taking that is felonious? The UK law is limited to financial institutions, which we know too well have systemic importance justifying extra caution in management ("make banks boring again"). But the concern about criminalizing corporate management that is too risky, according to some undefined and debatable scale, is a serious impediment to any program of substituting recklessness for traditional requirements of knowledge and intent in criminal laws that apply to managers of corporations. (The UK statute uses the language "far below what could reasonably be expected of a person in [the manager's] position.")

Hold on, some might say, criminal law has long held people responsible for harms they cause while driving cars recklessly. How is being at the wheel of a dangerous corporation any different? The classic example of reckless driving is driving drunk. Unless someone is going to die and there's no other way to get to the ER, there's no arguable justification for getting behind the wheel drunk—or in driving way over the speed limit, blowing through red lights, drag racing in public, and the like.

It's easy to say criminalize drunk oil drilling. But under what circumstances would *aggressive* drilling exploration become reckless and therefore fairly punished criminally? Drilling for oil has immense social value, which must be accounted for along with its immense social costs. Likewise, how much leverage in a bank's trading books would be criminally reckless? These aren't the same kind of question as what makes the driver of an automobile criminally reckless. (Not to mention that corporations don't have actual steering wheels or single drivers.)

At least in the American system, risky corporate management is treated as socially beneficial.[25] To use a hypothetical, say that Sally, the manager of a massive tunnel construction project, orders that an expensive section be lowered into place immediately, before it breaks. She is told that Joe the worker, who appears trapped in the area beneath, will be crushed. Sally orders her crew to go ahead. Joe is killed.

Sally might be guilty not only of reckless homicide but of murder. She took a specific action knowing it was practically certain to cause the death of an identifiable human being. A jury would be likely to convict Sally even if she argued that she reasonably believed halting construction at that moment would have cost the public hundreds of millions of dollars.

Consider, by contrast, manager Betty. Betty authorizes starting the same tunnel construction project at its outset, after being told of a high probability that at least one worker will be killed during the project even if her safety procedures comply with the state of the art. Sure enough, halfway through the job, a section of concrete breaks free from a crane and crushes Joe the worker. Betty is probably not guilty of any crime at all, including reckless homicide. No jury would want to convict her if she indeed followed sound industry practice, especially if the tunnel project was publicly important. When it comes to corporate crime, the relevant decisions of senior managers are far more often like Betty's ("take the risk") than Sally's ("crush the worker").

American criminal law has a couple of longstanding examples of an even tougher approach toward managers—one that is based not on recklessness but on what is called "strict liability," meaning no culpability at all is required, not even negligence.[26] Under the federal Food, Drug, and Cosmetic Act and the Clean Water Act, corporate managers can face criminal liability for violations within the corporation solely on the basis that they had supervisory responsibility for the area involved. In a foundational Supreme Court case from the 1970s, the president of a national food company, Acme Markets, who worked in its Philadelphia office, was prosecuted because rat droppings were found in Acme's warehouse in Baltimore. This idea is known among lawyers as the "responsible corporate officer" doctrine.

There's a big catch. These laws impose misdemeanor liability only. The Acme Markets manager, who took his case all the way to the Supreme Court, had been given a punishment of a $50 fine on each count of conviction—less than what the federal courts now assess criminal defendants for court costs. It would be a major departure for Congress to impose felony liability, with penalties of imprisonment, on a corporate manager simply for being in the supervisory chain and having theoretical ability to prevent crime. American criminal law has resisted, for good reasons, imposing punishment on a person for failing to prevent another person from committing a crime. It's uncertain whether such a felony criminal statute could survive a constitutional challenge.

One of the most controversial cases in which the United States Supreme Court has ever affirmed a criminal conviction is its 1946 decision *In re Yamashita*.[27] The defendant was General Tomoyuki Yamashita of the Japanese Imperial Army. During the last months of the war in the Pacific, soldiers under his command committed atrocities in the Philippines. At General Douglas MacArthur's direction, American authorities prosecuted General Yamashita in a military tribunal on a charge that the Japanese general failed to prevent his troops from engaging in those atrocities. Yamashita was convicted and MacArthur had him hanged.

There was no proof that Yamashita knew of the specific criminal acts alleged in the case, much less that he ordered or condoned them. The case was based purely on a theory of "command responsibility." Military justice for commanders is a special situation. The need for rigid hierarchy and the idea that the officer must authorize his soldiers to violate core morality, including by committing murder, calls for the strictest possible legal accountability. Even given that special setting, the legal theory in the *Yamashita* case—grave legal consequences solely by virtue of rank—remains controversial and is sometimes used as an example of a point to which criminal responsibility for failure in military command should not be stretched.[28]

Our Trouble with Corporations

THE DILEMMA of how to criminalize the corporation eludes solution not because prosecutors lack enough courage or imagination, or because corporations have a chokehold on the political system. The dilemma has no artful solution. There's a choice between less than ideal approaches. The criminal justice system can continue to try to make criminals out of nonhuman legal entities, while we accept two realties. First, any form of corporate punishment will be unsatisfying because it can't include imprisonment. Second, most cases will need to be settled to reduce their impact because destroying large corporations, given our dependence on them, can mean shooting ourselves in the foot.

The law can be reformed to expand the criminal exposure of corporate managers, making it a felony to act, or authorize acts, or fail to prevent acts in the face of known risks. But we would have to bite several bullets in this painful operation of law reform: compromise of the general idea that, except for manslaughter, reckless behavior typically does not justify a substantial term of imprisonment; acceptance of a serious departure from the rule-of-law principal that a person is entitled to be able to determine and predict clearly where the line will fall between criminal and permissible behavior; and the unpredictable—perhaps beneficial but possibly uncontrollable—consequences for markets and the economy of a much greater chance of imprisonment as part of the standard job description of "C-suite" positions in American companies.

The legal dilemma reflects the quandary of our relationship to the corporation. Indeed, it's striking how common it has been in recent public debate about corporate crime for people to fail to distinguish clearly between the corporation and the person. "Did you see how the government let HSBC off with a slap on the wrist for laundering drug money? Those banks have gotten away with the financial equivalent of murder. Why isn't anyone in jail?"

It will continue to be important to say, when justified, that grievous wrongs generated by institutions are crimes. It's true as a matter of social fact, not just law. Corporate criminal liability is here to stay. But prosecuting corporations will never be a sufficient response to the problem of corporate crime. Such legal actions do not fully pierce the cloak that the corporate form places around its individual agents.

5

The White
Collar Beat

WITH ROUTINE CRIME, criminals work to avoid discovery. Police and prosecutors set themselves to the competitive task of catching the criminals and holding them in custody. Sometimes, with enough leverage, criminals can be turned against each other. Setting aside the problem of police abuse in the handling of informants, the law accepts that ugly business only because there's no good alternative for dealing with clandestine lawbreakers.

The most professional criminals of the traditional variety become expert at, and even obsessed with, evading law enforcement. They are known to resort to brutally violent tactics to elude capture. Given the nature of their crimes, one arrest can end their careers. Law enforcement, in turn, feels enormous pressure to try all available means of reaching into the redoubts of career criminals, including measures that involve heavy coercion and can stretch constitutional constraints on government power.[1]

Whitey Bulger

IN MY experiences as a prosecutor, the best example of this sort of battle in the war on crime was the pursuit of the infamous Boston mobster James "Whitey" Bulger.[2] The Bulger saga, during which my three and a half years amounted to a cameo, had barely gotten started where *Black Mass*, the Johnny Depp movie about the case, leaves off. The small band of federal prosecutors and Massachusetts State Police and DEA investigators who stubbornly saw through the project of bringing Bulger and his partners to justice gave two decades of their careers to it. That wasn't because they had slow work habits. They were dealing with an extremely hard target, in part because Bulger corrupted law enforcement, including FBI agents. Bringing Bulger to justice required a medieval siege mentality, in both patience and willingness to be heartless.[3]

Years of relentlessly grinding down a group of relative schmucks, who were mostly in the business of running illegal sports books, eventually produced an amazing thing: digging up, identifying through DNA, and returning to families the bodies of five murder victims who had been in the ground in Quincy and Dorchester for two decades (with a long stopover under a basement floor in South Boston). The skeletal remains—which included those of two young women whom Bulger's partner Stephen Flemmi had used and discarded and whom Bulger strangled with his hands—became the centerpiece of an indictment charging nineteen murders. Bulger was captured in 2011, after sixteen years as a fugitive, and convicted two years later.

The cases that led to Bulger's landmark indictment would never have gotten started without prosecutors' use of siege tactics against the Boston bookies and loan sharks whose businesses, from the late 1960s well into the 1980s, fed Bulger's enterprise. Almost all of them were victims (not naively of course) of Bulger's extortion racket. Nonetheless, to turn them into witnesses and thereby get to Bulger, prosecutors hit them with the full force of federal statutes and sentencing rules that had expanded, mostly during the 1980s war on drugs, to a point of extreme severity. Bookies saw their sentences for gambling offenses tripled or quadrupled by the addition of money laundering charges.

To put it plainly, the grand jury was used to knuckle witnesses under, including many who reasonably feared the persons whom the Boston prosecutors were after. A venerable legal institution created in England to protect persons against unfounded charges, the American grand jury has developed, especially in federal court, into an engine for criminal investigations, not just a preliminary screen on cases. Its powers—invoked and managed by prosecutors with little court supervision—include the ability to compel witnesses via subpoena to testify and produce evidence; to place witnesses under oath and on the record, at pain of prosecution for perjury or obstruction of justice; to examine witnesses in secret and without counsel present (lawyers can stand outside the room and offer advice to witnesses when breaks are requested); to ask judges to hold witnesses in contempt for refusing to testify; and to invoke the judicial power, when the Fifth Amendment privilege is asserted, to grant witnesses immunity for their testimony, thus removing the right to refuse to answer prosecutors' questions. Most of this happens in secrecy, subject to serious punishment of leakers.

In the Bulger investigation, recalcitrant witnesses were forced to testify in the grand jury with immunity orders, then prosecuted for perjury when they lied out of loyalty or fear. Those who refused to talk in spite of immunity were jailed for contempt, twice if necessary: once for civil contempt during the term of the grand jury, and again for having committed the offense of criminal contempt. (No, that's not unconstitutional.) Almost all of them eventually succumbed.

The extortion cases prosecutors built with the testimony of these low-level criminals were used to make distasteful agreements with Bulger's key partners and deputies, in order to solve nearly two dozen cold-case murders and dig up those bodies. John Martorano served only twelve years in prison after admitting to killing twenty people over the course of a long criminal career. (Martorano had turned on Bulger in anger when he learned that Bulger had been an FBI informant. The government had no case against Martorano for the murders until he disclosed them.) Kevin Weeks served five years after pleading guilty to helping Bulger commit several murders. (Weeks was the subordinate directed to carry the body bags and use the shovel, and thus the one who could show the State Police where to start digging.) Stephen Flemmi, after being convicted and sentenced to life in prison without parole, agreed to talk in order to avoid a possible death sentence in Oklahoma. (In the 1970s, Flemmi and Bulger had dispatched Martorano to kill Roger Wheeler, a Tulsa businessman whose interests in a Florida pari-mutuel business (involving the sport of jai alai) they found a nuisance; Martorano shot Wheeler in the head as Wheeler returned to his car after a round of golf).

The law enforcement tactics needed to make a singular case like the prosecution of Whitey Bulger require strong stomachs and ugly compromises. Patience and luck help too. Most of all, prosecutors need the full suite of weapons that modern federal criminal law offers—laws that are the products of efforts to address the Mafia, global drug trafficking, and terrorism. These include extremely high sentences for violent crimes and gun and drug offenses, the RICO (antiracketeering) statute, the federal wiretapping and witness protection programs, and the grand jury machine.

Catching Corporate Criminals

EVEN THOUGH it uses the same law enforcement apparatus and is controlled by the same principles of law, investigation and prosecution of corporate crime bears almost no resemblance to policing street crime. Ordinary law enforcement takes place in the binary relationship—one defined by powers and rights—between the state and the individual: search warrants for evidence, interrogations and confessions, crime scene forensics, traffic stops, surveillance, and the other games played in stories like *Law & Order*, *Breaking Bad*, and *The Wire*.

Corporate law enforcement operates along a strange triangle connecting the state, the individual, and the business firm.[4] A variety of powers and rights are spread among all three legs of this triangle. The firm sits in the oddest position, as both cop and criminal. In some instances, a firm practically pays its workers to break the law and then hides evidence of the crime. Other times, the corporation is the one that digs up the smoking gun document and elicits the confession from its miscreant employee. Sometimes a firm does both things in the same corporate scandal (sequentially, of course).

This might sound strange, perhaps even untenable. But it shouldn't be surprising. Even in punishing corporate crime, and striving to prevent it, the American legal system cannot help but rely on the powers and structure of the corporation itself.

Walmart

SUPPOSE THE American consumer were told, several years ago, that Walmart was about to be in trouble for a corporate crime and asked to guess what the company's problem might be about. A lot of people could have imagined that it was for using bribery to get stores built faster. The scandal, as we saw, was in Mexico, where representatives of the company routinely paid bribes through *gestores* (facilitators for hire) to accelerate zoning approvals and permits.[5]

Perhaps not so many would have predicted that Walmart would deepen its troubles by following a cost-cutting approach even when it came to legal services. Walmart, at least temporarily, has become emblematic of the irresponsible corporation that does not make the effort to discover and root out crime when it spots red flags. As the saying goes, you can pay me now or you can pay me later. Later almost always costs more, especially when dealing with a federal prosecutor.

Suppose the whistleblower at Walmart Mexico had never gone to the *New York Times*. He might have called the SEC or the FBI anonymously and said, "Walmart has been paying massive bribes in Mexico, you need to look into it." Assume there was something especially credible about his tip so the Justice Department decided, with nothing else to go on, to devote resources to it. If you were the prosecutor initially assigned to this, and were told by your supervisor to figure out whether Walmart violated the FCPA, the criminal prohibition against bribing foreign officials, what might you do?

Any effort to gather evidence would lead you down one of two paths. On the first path, you might try the gumshoe approach of the beat detective. Maybe you recently began handling white collar cases after many years pursuing gangsters and narcotics traffickers. So you decide to treat Walmart as you would an organized crime family or a drug cartel.

Walmart is really, really big. As in any white collar case, the evidence that will allow you to figure out what happened is going to consist of paper and electronic records and people telling you what happened at their work. And not much else. CSI tactics are out.

The best evidence in a criminal investigation is often recorded conversations of the criminals talking about the crime. There are two ways to get those: informants and wiretaps. Actually, the two are really the same. The Justice Department rarely allows a prosecutor to go to a federal judge with a wiretap application unless investigators already have a "dirty call" on the target phone. (A wiretap is a search warrant that requires, among other things, probable cause and a court order.) The government is able to get that call on the target phone only if it already has an informant who has agreed to record his own conversations.

Informants are made by charging people with crimes, or at least showing them that they are easily chargeable, and then negotiating. People don't volunteer to work undercover for law enforcement. It's dangerous and tends to make one a pariah. The work can pay: DEA and FBI guidelines, for example, include a mechanism for obtaining approval for payments that can reach hundreds of thousands of dollars. But the more the government spends on an informant, the less credible the informant becomes in the eyes of jurors and judges and, experience shows, the more likely the informant and the handler will be to engage in abuses.

Sometimes investigators and even prosecutors have hidden facts about the crimes and earnings of their informants, causing much more damage to criminal cases when such abuses are revealed. (The Bulger saga includes some prime examples.) Professional or paid informants have had a regrettable history in the federal system and make far less persuasive witnesses than actual accomplices who agree to testify only after getting caught and prosecuted.

In drug and organized crime cases, prosecutors usually make informants by catching lower-level people in possession of drugs or engaged in extortion, loan sharking, illegal gambling, bank robbery, or the like. In the Walmart investigation, there is no entry-level crime that will produce the informant who gets you to a first recorded conversation. By the time the government receives the anonymous tip, the bribery likely will be over.

Witnesses come more readily in street crime cases because the crimes are easier for the police to see and the penalties for them afford prosecutors much greater leverage. American law's war on drugs appears to have failed cost-benefit analysis. But its benefits were not zero. When I was a prosecutor in New York during the city's murder boom of the early 1990s, we used some extremely harsh legal tools to get to some of the most violent and elusive gang leaders and lock them up, probably saving lives and perhaps contributing to the remarkable drop in the city's homicide rate.

One of those tools was to take gang members who had already been prosecuted and convicted for drug dealing in state court and ask judges to order them transferred into federal custody by "writ" as potential grand jury witnesses. Then we would have the U.S. marshal bring them from the federal jail to a room in the courthouse. There we would sit down and explain that if they didn't agree to testify about crimes they had committed or witnessed, we would recharge them again for the same drug offenses in federal court and then lengthen their prison terms with federal law's much harsher sentencing rules, including the infamous rule that equated dealing a single gram of crack with selling a hundred grams of powder cocaine. This was in the midst of the crack boom of course.

More often than not, it worked. We were able to build federal racketeering cases that brought down gang leaders for dozens of murders, including ones some of them had been acquitted of in state prosecutions after threatening or killing witnesses. (The Witness Protection Program was also a key element in the strategy.) This success was at the cost of treating the gang lieutenants and underlings—sympathies for whom probably vary—with some of the most punitive and arguably unfair rules in federal law: the now partially defunct crack sentencing rules, and the not commonly understood exception to the constitutional double jeopardy rule that permits a second prosecution in federal court for a crime already prosecuted in state court, even if the state prosecution produced a conviction. It is exceedingly hard to imagine an equivalent suite of legal tools for use in corporate criminal investigations—and even harder to imagine tolerance, whether within or outside law enforcement circles, for its routine use.

Once in a while the government gets lucky in a white collar investigation and a whistleblowing employee walks in and offers to make tapes while criminal activity is still afoot. But such witnesses are rare and must be treated with caution. In the early 1990s, the government botched a huge price-fixing case against executives of the Archer Daniels Midland Company because prosecutors and agents badly mishandled the tipster Mark Whitacre—played by Matt Damon in *The Informant,* Stephen Soderbergh's movie about the case. (The lessons for law enforcement are made much clearer in Kurt Eichenwald's excellent book that was the basis for the film.[6])

More common, especially with new incentives Congress created after 2008, is the witness who says he has a whistle to blow after the crime has already occurred—in exchange for financial rewards available under the securities laws or the False Claims Act (a law against defrauding the federal government). This kind of "informant" is actually a plaintiff, usually represented by a lawyer working for a contingency fee. Laws that encourage these whistleblowers help surface cases that might otherwise have gone undiscovered. But such laws, with their lucrative potential payoffs, don't often produce credible trial witnesses on whom prosecutions can be built—in part because they don't allow awards to those involved in crimes, depriving the most knowledgeable witnesses of the monetary incentive to report wrongdoing.

In the Walmart investigation, you can pretty much forget real-time informants and tapes. Other common tactics in street crime investigations include the grand jury and search warrants. You certainly have the power to start subpoenaing documents from Walmart and calling its employees into the grand jury for questioning under oath and beyond the reach of Walmart's lawyers. You might even be able to cobble together enough facts, together with your anonymous tip, to persuade a judge to let you go into Walmart's offices in Arkansas with a search warrant and dig around in the company's documents.

But where would you even begin? Would you subpoena Walmart for every document it has about Mexico? Would you start marching its hundreds of employees who might know something about the Mexico operation into the grand jury one at a time? To review those millions of documents and handle all those witnesses will take at least months and probably years. The task will require a large team of prosecutors and investigators. All the while, you'll be playing something like the game of Battleship, blindly asking questions and groping around in the documents, trying to guess where the evidence of crime might be tucked away inside the giant company. You will get little help from Walmart's personnel, who will view you and the investigators (correctly) as adversary cops on a mission to imprison someone.

These problems stand in the way of all big corporate investigations. Volkswagen, for example, has disclosed that in its internal investigation of the company's cheating on emissions laws, its outside law firm gathered 102 terabytes (the equivalent of 50 million books) of data.[7] In the case of Walmart, you have another serious problem—one that has become more common as corporations have become more global. Much of the best evidence, both documents and witnesses, is likely in Mexico. And you have no power in Mexico. You can't even issue a subpoena there.

Mexico has a Mutual Legal Assistance Treaty (MLAT) treaty with the United States. This means the Mexican legal system is supposed to help you get what you want. But, for each document or witness you need, it requires going—no exaggeration—down the following path: a request from you the prosecutor to an office at the Justice Department that handles MLAT requests, then to the U.S. State Department, then to the Ministry of Foreign Affairs of Mexico, then to the Office of the Mexican Attorney General, and finally to the Mexican prosecutor or law enforcement officer who will (hopefully) attempt to secure the document or testimony for you.

The Department of Justice and other federal enforcement agencies could not conduct corporate criminal investigations this way unless Congress multiplied their budgets and personnel by at least ten. Even then, maybe only a dozen really big cases could be seriously pursued in any year. As long as countries in which multinational companies do business subscribe to basic principles of jurisdiction and sovereignty, legal barriers will prevent speedy international investigation of corporate crime.

Gumshoe policing doesn't work with corporate crime. Except when prosecutors get lucky. A recent example was in the crackdown on insider trading in the hedge fund industry in New York, when they got one informant who led them to one wiretap, which then led to many wiretaps on many phones and ultimately produced over eighty prosecutions.[8] It helped that prosecutors had never used wiretaps in an insider trading prosecution so that, for a time, the government's targets were not careful about conversations and did not routinely get rid of their cell phones.

Fortunately, you have an alternative in your Walmart investigation. It comes from a power discussed in the preceding chapter: corporate criminal liability. Criminalizing corporations isn't only a way to impose responsibility for harms like those in the BP and GM disasters. Nor is it just a way to deter crime by encouraging corporations to keep their employees within the confines of the law. It's also—indeed, has become mainly—a way to get corporations to help the government gather evidence of crime.[9]

If you say to Walmart's lawyers that you're likely to charge the company itself with any bribery offenses you discover by its employees unless the company helps you investigate the case, barriers around Walmart's evidence will fall away. Walmart wants to maintain a decent reputation with consumers and investors. The company's management doesn't want you holding a press conference to say Walmart is a bad corporate citizen because it refuses to help the government investigate crime. In the actual Walmart case, after it came out that Walmart didn't take that approach when it first learned of the bribery in Mexico, the company was eager to get credit for assisting the government.

Most of all, Walmart's top managers really don't want the company charged as a criminal. That would deal a blow to the company's reputation, and therefore their reputations as well. A criminal charge also might prevent Walmart from carrying on parts of its business, including selling things to the government, because of laws barring convicted felons from some industries and contracts.

Walmart's executives and lawyers control two things that will speed up your investigation. First, they have a bigger budget. They can hire lots of worker-bee lawyers to swarm Walmart and collect the relevant documents and witnesses. They can fly their Walmart Mexico employees to you to be interviewed and testify. And their tech people can digitize and search the company's documents.

Second, Walmart bosses have the power to fire Walmart's employees. That means they can require their employees, as a condition of remaining at Walmart, to "cooperate" in any criminal investigation. When directed, the employees have to sit down and answer the questions of the company's lawyers and, eventually, the government's lawyers. Or they lose their jobs.

Lying remains an option for such an employee, of course. But that too can get an employee fired. More to the point, if government agents are at the table when an employee tells a lie, she can be prosecuted for the federal crime of making a false statement in a matter "within the jurisdiction of the United States."[10] The government has occasionally turned this heat up even more, charging corporate employees for lying to the company's own lawyers—on the theory that the liars knew the company would give their statements to government agents, and thus the lies could impair a federal investigation.

Over the last twenty years, the government has come to rely heavily on corporate criminal liability for investigating corporate crime. Prosecutors trade liability for policing. The result is the routine settlement of cases against companies with those unpopular deferred prosecution and nonprosecution agreements described in chapter four.

This process has real upsides, including for corporations. Companies can use their powers to gather evidence—their capacity to see into themselves in spite of their opacity to outsiders—in trades to avoid criminal charges. Corporations also get to monitor the progress of a government investigation, so they're not blindsided as they might be in a system of search warrants, wiretaps, and taciturn FBI agents serving grand jury subpoenas. Routinizing this system also ought to have generated better deterrence of crime because corporate employees now know that if they commit a crime on the job, their powerful employer is likely to team up with the awesome forces of the federal government to make sure they're caught and prosecuted.

What's not to like about this clever program for uncovering and prosecuting crime in corporations? Quite a lot. The system's critics are legion.

Corporations: We're Not the Police

LET'S START with the objections of corporations and their lawyers. The argument starts with a complaint about the law. The *de jure* (on the books) rule for when corporations can be criminally prosecuted in federal court, is said to be far too harsh. Federal law makes a corporation eligible for prosecution anytime any employee violates the law in the course of doing her job and does so, even in part, for the company's benefit. The rule, which is ancient and used in many other areas of law, is called *respondeat superior*, or master-servant liability.[11]

The law doesn't care if the employee's violation is minor, the violator holds a low-level job in the company, the company's managers are in no way involved, the firm's policies prohibit the conduct, or the employee acted mostly to enrich herself. The idea is to give the "master" lots of good reasons to police his "servant" carefully. When this rule is applied in civil lawsuits, it also gives access to a deeper and better insured pocket for compensating injuries.

In one well-known case, Hilton Hotels was convicted of an antitrust offense when a purchasing manager in Portland, Oregon, in the face of a company directive against such conduct, participated in a cartel agreement to give discounts to favored suppliers. Another notorious example is the conviction of the Sun-Diamond agriculture company for the conduct of the lobbyist who secretly siphoned cash out of the company to help the brother of Mike Espy. The lobbyist's crime was said to be a fraud in which the company was both victim and, by imputation of its employee's crime, perpetrator. The Janus-faced theory was that the employee had harmed Sun-Diamond by using its funds to commit a crime, but also that his criminal actions were intended to help curry favor for the firm with the secretary.

This rule for criminal liability of corporations is overbroad, the argument goes, because it sweeps onto the company's legal ledger every conceivable case of crime on the job. The powerful rule becomes a weapon of prosecutorial mass destruction when combined with two other overbearing features of federal law. First, federal criminal law is stuffed with thousands of overlapping criminal offenses, particularly in areas of business subject to heavy regulation like health care products and securities dealing.[12] Second, as we have seen, federal regulatory regimes are replete with rules that can bar companies from doing business in markets or industries if they're convicted of crimes.

The collective force of these rules leaves corporations without practical ability to contest criminal cases. If a prosecutor comes along with even the notion of a criminal charge, a company has no alternative but to roll over. If the *de jure* rule makes corporations almost always guilty, then the *de facto* rule becomes that corporations must always settle with the Justice Department.

Corporations, the argument continues, also do not have the means that individuals enjoy to keep information out of the government's hands. Ordinary regulatory requirements mandate lots of ongoing, routine disclosure that is not required of private citizens. And the threat of corporate criminal liability makes it impossible for corporations to resist prosecutors' demands for further evidence. Under constitutional law, corporations have no Fifth Amendment right against self-incrimination.[13] Fourth Amendment search-and-seizure protections are of little value to corporations because those constitutional constraints don't limit duly issued subpoenas, which are the primary tool for gathering evidence in investigations of white collar crime.[14] A government subpoena occasionally can be resisted because it asks for too much or is too vague—just fishing. Otherwise, its demands must be obeyed.

This suite of laws has, in the eyes of its detractors, produced a cadre of corporate crime prosecutors who do not act in the greater public interest.[15] Over the last fifteen years, the Justice Department has developed guidelines on when to charge a corporation. These purport to limit the use of corporate criminal liability to cases in which harms are widespread and serious, management bears responsibility for the wrongdoing, or companies don't behave like good citizens by having effective compliance programs and helping discover and root out crime.[16] But individual prosecutors don't have to follow these guidelines and there's no way for a company's managers and lawyers to be sure how the Justice Department will apply them.

Therefore, corporate managers and their legal advisers say, even the mention by prosecutors of a potential charge against the corporation has to be treated as if it were a death threat. Any prospect of contesting matters through litigation vanishes. Prosecutors know this, which makes them complacent, even lazy. They can get corporations to do their work for them and they lose motivation to examine cases closely and make careful distinctions among them. It's irresistibly easy to make every corporation jump through the same evidence-collection hoops, reach the same kind of settlement, and write the same sort of check to the government in the end. Some evidence for this alleged lassitude can be found in cases in which the Justice Department settles with a corporation but never prosecutes individuals—a result that, as several critics have pointed out, seems to defy legal logic. Criminal liability can attach to a corporation *only* through the imputation of an individual employee's provable crime.[17]

The corporations' argument sounds like a variant on one we hear about other parts of the American criminal justice system. On this account, if there's such a thing as an innocent corporation, we'll never know because the government has the power to make everyone roll over. Cases are never tested at trial. (Never is an overstatement; it's more like rarely.) Prosecutors, who don't hear the views of judges and jurors about their cases, lose the ability to tell a weak case from a strong one or an important one from a minor one. Even corporate defense lawyers—who complain that they have been turned into nothing more than "deputy prosecutors" whose job is to investigate their own clients—lose the ability and desire to poke, prod, or try criminal accusations.

This line of argument extends further, beyond investigation of crime and settlement of cases. The government, viewing the problem of corporate crime as part of the general project of corporate regulation, now routinely uses criminal settlements as an entree to prevent future law violations and reform companies. A common feature of a settlement agreement is to require the corporation to change its operations in various ways—to rehabilitate itself—to reduce the chances of future similar violations of law. Part of this process typically involves the forced hiring of an expensive outside "monitor" for several years—a reputable, independent individual with an office and staff inside the company and the power to inspect, ask questions, receive complaints, report to prosecutors, and generally make sure the company is fixing itself.[18]

The problem with this practice, it is said, is that prosecutors— English majors with law degrees, in the phrase of one critic[19]—don't know how to run corporations. Just as companies shouldn't be distracted from their business mission by working as beat cops in the fight against crime, prosecutors shouldn't be playing amateur corporate manager when their training is to litigate in criminal courts.[20] This part of the argument has made hay off notable government missteps, including big bills for monitor work submitted by former prosecutors hired to do that job shortly after landing in private practice and a settlement in which Chris Christie, while the chief federal prosecutor in New Jersey, required a pharmaceutical company to fund a chair in research of corporate misconduct at Seton Hall Law School, Christie's alma mater.[21]

As the government has become more accustomed to working this way—using the blunderbuss of corporate criminal liability to compel companies to police themselves, and settling case after case with large payments and promises to reform and accept outside supervision— the feelings behind these arguments in America's corporate sector have grown intense, even impassioned. More than once I've heard this process called, not kiddingly, "extortion" and "like threatening capital punishment to get someone to plead to life in prison."

Sometimes I wonder what those who voice these complaints would prefer. Surely they would not want maximum enforcement of the law, an end to settlements, trial as a matter of routine, and much greater involvement of judges and juries in policing and punishing corporations. It's the allegedly intolerable consequences of full criminal enforcement that corporations finger as disabling them from challenging even the barest allegations of criminal wrongdoing. Business objectives take precedence over principled vindication of legal rights. Corporations, by their own accounts, exist not to realize their own liberties (whatever that could even mean) but to make money.

It also seems unlikely that corporations would welcome a system, even if one were feasible, that policed business crime like street crime. That would interfere far more than current practices with companies' ability to conduct business. And it would give corporations far less control and transparency than they enjoy over the government's gathering of information from corporate records and employees. As things stand, almost every document that goes to a prosecutor in a corporate investigation travels through a company lawyer and almost every employee who speaks to a prosecutor has already spoken to corporate counsel. Corporate violators manage criminal investigations in real time; street criminals either preempt arrest with violence and threats—or flight—or they wait and hope.

Businesses would, of course, like there to be less criminal law, at least when it comes to the kinds of things businesses do. The Chamber of Commerce has teamed up with conservative and libertarian think tanks like Cato and Heritage to decry the oppressive reach and weight of federal criminal law.[22] But these arguments are almost always pitched on behalf of the imagined citizen who must go about her life under the shadow of a bloated and intrusive state, in perpetual fear of federal arrest. Corporations hardly want to be seen as launching a vocal lobbying campaign on behalf of white collar decriminalization. (Walmart: The Let's Stop Taking Bribery So Seriously Company.)

One thing companies *would* like is for prosecutors to adopt a third alternative in corporate criminal investigations other than the overbearing settlement agreement or indictment and trial. Corporations, like anyone dealing with law enforcement, want more "declinations," that is, decisions to forgo prosecution altogether. Given current public attitudes towards corporate crime, this seems like an unrealistic ambition and one that could produce an unwelcome backlash for corporations, not to mention prosecutors.

Notice, by the way, how this last proposed solution—more declinations—relies on the thing corporations and their advocates have lamented most: the allegedly unreviewable and absolute power of the prosecutor to determine the fate of the American business firm.

The Government: Corporations Aren't People

PROSECUTORS HAVE a fundamentally different view than corporate managers of the place of the corporation in the world and, therefore, the law. (It's amazing how far that view can evolve in the mind of a lawyer who spends just a year or two on the private sector side of the revolving door.) Though they won't say it, prosecutors don't think corporations have especially convincing arguments about rights. Corporations are not people. They are particular projects chartered by the law and the state, which can produce social benefits for, but also impose costs on, the public—whom prosecutors understand themselves to represent. So, they think, there should be no objection to harnessing the corporation, when it makes sense to do so, in service of an important endeavor like the prevention and policing of crime.

Why fret about corporations' vanishing opportunities to try criminal cases, or the intrusiveness of reforms imposed by settlement agreements, when firms are simply a vehicle—one neither virtuous nor corrupt—for dealing with the problem of human beings and their tendencies to do ill? This line of thinking has affected the way prosecutors have approached issues with corporations that lawyers, even prosecutors, see very differently when it comes to individual criminal cases.

For example, the attorney-client privilege has often been called (mostly by lawyers) "sacrosanct"—essential to the fair and effective operation of the American legal system. But why must corporations enjoy a robust attorney-client privilege that is not routinely waived when the government seeks evidence of crime? After all, the purpose of the privilege—which is an exception to the general principle that, in legal process, facts should out—is to encourage people to talk to lawyers. The corporate privilege is not personal and can be waived by the corporation. Routinely it is waived, for many reasons and regardless of the wishes of officers and employees who happen to have spoken to lawyers on the company's behalf.

A compelling reason to know what a corporation's people have said to the company's lawyers, and what the lawyers have said to them, is to figure out complex issues of business and finance that almost always involve, and often turn on, legal advice. In the age of the modern regulatory state, corporations don't do anything without lawyers. The privilege's shield, meant to encourage the candor that leads to better legal advice (and maybe even better compliance with law), should not be stretched over everything that happens in office buildings. It should be noted that the attorney-client privilege is only tangentially a concern of constitutional law and is in no sense a right. It's a rule about admissibility of evidence and a confidentiality rule that governs members of the bar.[23]

Likewise, prosecutors have asked, why should corporations be permitted without scrutiny to engage in the routine practice of funding lawyers for, and even partially controlling the defenses of, individuals who work for them and might have broken the law? Why shouldn't prosecutors view a corporation that circles the wagons around its employees as akin to a mob boss who does the same with his soldiers? Remember John Gotti, New York's "Teflon don"? His lawyer was disqualified from representing him at trial because Gotti's practice of paying that lawyer to represent underlings made the lawyer himself evidence of the "Gambino family" conspiracy in which Gotti was charged.[24] Of course prosecutors think companies should be allowed, perhaps even encouraged, to assure their employees that they won't face financial ruin from involvement in the routine legal skirmishing endemic to regulated industries. But why should that idea extend to helping those who, in the view of prosecutors at least, have betrayed their employers by breaking the law?

Even asking these questions—and, beyond that, pushing corporations in criminal cases to relax their attorney-client privilege claims or limit their programs of paying for the defense of wrongdoers—has gotten prosecutors in trouble.[25] It's not often that the criminal defense bar persuades the Justice Department to change its own written policies. It's also unusual to see the Chamber of Commerce and the National Association of Criminal Defense Lawyers (the latter is a major trade association for street crime lawyers) team up in a lobbying campaign.

Both things happened with Justice Department practices in corporate crime investigations that were said to constitute a "war" on the attorney-client privilege and the right to counsel. In 2007, Congress threatened legislation to limit federal prosecutors' practices, a rare event. Congress's plan to ban prosecutors from even asking companies to share privileged material caused the Justice Department to back off. The Department changed its policies—in writing at least—about whether prosecutors could treat a company's willingness to waive attorney-client privilege or limit funding of individual defenses as evidence of the company's seriousness about cooperating.

Prosecutors would like to see a corporate sector that is enthusiastically and unreservedly on board a joint program of fighting white collar crime. Companies should want to be "responsible corporate citizens" and should seek out and enjoy the fruits of marketing themselves as such. That's the corporation that works best for its shareholders, for its employees, and for the American public. We're all against crime here, as we're all against terrorism and for apple pie. Right?

This attitude does not match the view of those who work in the executive suites and their lawyers. To them the Justice Department is an adversary, albeit their most powerful one, among many litigants and lawyers who benefit from suing corporations or threatening to do so. The Department's activities, and the laws it is chartered to enforce, are one part of a vast legal apparatus that hampers, makes more costly, and threatens to cripple growth and profits. This machinery is to be managed, priced, and accounted for like other business "risks," albeit as a grave one.

Employees: Don't We Have Rights?

POLICING CORPORATIONS requires law enforcement officers to deal with people. Corporations can't be jailed. And they can't speak—give evidence—except through their human agents and the documents those agents leave behind as they go about their work. Those people have their own reasons to dislike how the legal system manages corporate crime.

One of the more incredible stories in corporate crime is the saga of the high-end abusive tax shelters of the 1990s and early 2000s, and the lawyers and accountants who cooked them up and sold them en masse to wealthy clients. As told in a recent book—a gripping story about taxation, of all things—the practitioners of this trade exemplified a parable sometimes used to illustrate the psychology of the white collar criminal.[26] It's the one about a frog in a pot of water set on the stove to boil. The frog, it's said (inaccurately, it turns out), is unable to sense gradual increases in temperature and doesn't realize how hot the water is until it is no longer able to jump out.

What started as a practice of taking existing ideas about tax "planning" a step or two beyond legal precedents became a feeding frenzy that generated hundreds of millions of dollars in fees for a few large accounting and law firms that were willing, in rapidly changing and ruthless markets for professional services, to risk their brands. Some of the greed, especially on the part of the king of the practice, Paul Daugerdas, would have been repulsive in any context, much less the practice of law. That greed, and the exceptionally easy money the novel tax shelters produced, led practitioners to engage in contorted and bogus analysis. Barely plausible arguments became rock solid ones. Ridiculous ones became "more likely than not to succeed" (the standard for a tax lawyer to give a formal opinion).

At some stage, the professionals knew how far they had pushed the envelope, and that there could be no going back without serious consequences. Their awareness was evident in their efforts to limit distribution of records of the shelters, to control how documents were created in order to reduce risk of IRS audit, and even to mislead their own clients about transactions so that the clients would use the right language if the IRS asked questions.

The Justice Department decided the situation was bad enough to do what it hadn't done before: pursue criminal prosecutions, with the objective of imprisonment, of lawyers and accountants from prestigious national firms for the giving of professional tax advice—lawyering and accounting as crimes. And not for the sort of lawyers and accountants who service the mob or the drug cartels. The government's assault worked, at least to an extent. Some of those professionals ended up in prison and the tax shelter industry has changed.

This affair of the high-end tax shelters was also a case of corporate crime. To get the evidence to prosecute individual lawyers and accountants, the Justice Department had to penetrate the large, opaque organizations in which those professionals did their work. Those institutions included the national accounting firm BDO Seidman, the large law firm Jenkens & Gilchrist, and KPMG, one of the "Big Four" auditing and consulting firms. (Tax shelters, of course, are not auditing. They are a form of consulting, which typically pays more.)

The involvement of KPMG presented prosecutors with a particular challenge. For one, the firm is really big. The scale of its operations, as well as the seriousness of its responsibilities in financial markets, arguably made it imperative to teach KPMG a strong lesson. On the other hand, the big four had been the big five not too long before. The failure of Arthur Andersen in the Enron affair made the government nervous about a repeat that would further consolidate the accounting industry.

In the end, after brinkmanship by lawyers on both sides, the government was able to settle with KPMG and get the evidence it needed for the individual tax shelter prosecutions. But a surprising thing happened along the way. KPMG—both the firm and some of its partners—became a cause célèbre, at least among lawyers and insiders. KPMG and its tax partners got sympathy not because the government threatened to prosecute another big accounting firm but because the government was seen to have treated the individuals, not the firm, too roughly.[27]

Federal prosecutors in New York told KPMG's lawyers that the government would consider it important to KPMG's eligibility for a non-prosecution settlement to know whether the firm was (1) telling its employees that they were required to give interviews to the government and (2) limiting the legal fees the firm would pay for employees who were involved in the wrongdoing. The government had made these two points, at least subtly, in many prior corporate investigations. But the New York prosecutors were unusually bossy about it, appearing to treat KPMG almost as their own instrument. They told the firm, according to KPMG's attorneys, that payment of legal fees for employees would be looked at "under a microscope." And prosecutors directed KPMG to tell its employees in writing that they were free to meet with government investigators without counsel present.

It looked as though the prosecutors, a court later said, were mainly interested in minimizing the involvement of lawyers. Any prosecutor or investigator would prefer that a suspect, or even an ordinary witness, choose not to "lawyer up." But there's a difference between hoping to have a clear shot at someone who might naively spill the beans without a bothersome lawyer getting in the way, and actively trying to make it harder for someone uninformed about her rights to get help from a lawyer before she encounters the police.

The government indicted over a dozen KPMG partners and employees for tax evasion related to the abusive shelters. Then Lewis Kaplan, a federal judge in New York, got involved. He gave the prosecutors a severe reprimand for how they handled the investigation. Kaplan dismissed the case against a large number (but not all) of the KPMG defendants, ruling that the government violated their rights under both the Fifth and Sixth Amendments to the Constitution. It was a violation of some employees' rights against self-incrimination under the Fifth Amendment, he said, to be compelled by their employer into interviews with the government on pain of losing their jobs if they didn't answer questions. And it was a violation of their rights to counsel under the Sixth Amendment, Kaplan ruled, for the government to have encouraged KPMG to spend less money on lawyers to defend suspected and accused employees.

The government appealed Kaplan's decision and lost in a decision by the Second Circuit Court of Appeals, one of the most influential federal courts. The court declined to address the self-incrimination issue but concluded that the Sixth Amendment does prohibit prosecutors from interfering in this way with a company's private payments of attorneys' fees for its employees.

The KPMG saga produced some recognition that employees of a business have legal rights in the investigation of corporate crime. Employees might have a way to avoid getting squeezed between the combined forces of their employers and the government. If anyone has a sympathetic basis to complain about the system for policing corporate crime, wouldn't it be the salaried folk who sometimes get caught up in this stuff because they're doing their jobs? The success of these arguments in the KPMG case was unexpected because the law has been mostly indifferent to the plight of the employee in the investigation of corporate crime.

A fundamental fact about the Constitution of the United States is that it regulates the government and only the government.[28] It is, after all, the charter that created our government. That was its purpose. It has no ambition to afford us rights to complain among ourselves about how we treat each other. Other parts of law give us those kinds of rights.

Except for government workers, the relationship between employer and employee is a private one. The Bill of Rights does not speak to what corporations may do to their employees. So there is no constitutional right to remain silent at work. If your boss wants to say, more than reasonably, that it's a condition of being a worker here that you have to answer the questions we ask, she's entitled to say so. It would be hard to run a supermarket without being allowed to make the stockers say whether milk has gone missing.

Likewise, the boss can say the rules around here are the same if the police come asking questions about a milk heist. The police, of course, *are* the government. When it comes to their questions, the worker has the absolute constitutional right to refuse to answer. But the boss can still say that this store works with the police to make sure the law gets enforced. We don't employ people who refuse to help the police. Therefore, worker, you're fired. (Or would you like to reconsider whether to have that conversation with the police about the missing milk?)

The same is true of the right to counsel.[29] The Sixth Amendment prevents the government from prosecuting a person who is not represented by a lawyer, unless that person insists on going it alone (*pro se*). The Supreme Court, in its famous *Gideon v. Wainwright* decision, said that means the government has to pay for a lawyer if the accused person can't afford to hire one. A corollary of this right is that the government can't prevent people from spending their own money to defend themselves against criminal charges. For the wealthy criminal defendant, this means spend it if you've got it.

But a constitutional right to make someone else pay for your lawyer does not exist. When you go interviewing for jobs, employers can offer you all kinds of perks, like extra days off, a great health plan, dental coverage, and even—like most corporations for their top officers— payment of attorneys' fees. This is in effect law insurance, though it's not called that. Employers can also refuse to offer any of those things, including a program of paying for private lawyers. (There is an exception. Some states' laws require chartered corporations to reimburse their senior officers for certain kinds of legal expenses.[30])

If you sign a contract that includes the perk of legal fees, contract law might allow you to sue your employer for those payments if the employer reneges on the agreement. The Constitution, however, has nothing to say about the matter. In any event, most employees don't get these contractual promises. The employer, at most, might have a practice of paying fees for legal representation related to the job. That sort of employer is free to change her policy whenever she wishes, or even apply it inconsistently from one case to the next, provided she does not do so while engaging in illegal discrimination.

Think about the thicket this legal structure can place a person in. Consider the situation of, for example, a midlevel accounting employee in a big public company. Let's say she knows enough about part of a possible fraud that she's at least a witness and might also end up charged with involvement in the crime. She can't possibly know how the latter question will be resolved, even if she happens to be an amateur expert in criminal law, because it depends on what the prosecutors in her case choose to do.

At some point in the investigation, maybe before the government becomes involved, our accounting employee will have to make a choice. One alternative, when the company's lawyers come to speak to her, is to tell those lawyers everything she knows. That choice likely means eventually having to tell the government, too. If she does talk to the company's lawyers, she probably will keep her job, at least for the time being. The company might fire her anyway at some point if it decides she broke the law or should have reported sooner what she knew. If she agrees to talk, she also might get the help of a lawyer paid for by the company in what promises to be a drawn out and expensive legal process that, if worse comes to worst, could include a criminal trial defense.

The accounting employee's other option is to refuse to talk. She could try to protect herself by making it more difficult for the company, and thus the government, to get the proof that could deliver a fate much worse than loss of employment. If she takes that path, she almost certainly will be fired immediately. She also won't get a company-funded lawyer. She will be on her own and probably dangling for a long time with uncertain fate. In the end, she might be charged with a crime anyway and, depending on what savings she managed to salt away, could have to live with representation by a second-rate lawyer.

The employee's situation is dark. One could even call it nightmarish. It's easy to say that she shouldn't have gotten involved in this in the first place, or let it fester without doing something about it. The criminal justice system deals grim consequences of all sorts to those who fall into its path, some much worse than those facing this corporate accountant. (Remember the bookies and the loan sharks in the Whitey Bulger investigation.) But that's cold comfort. She'll likely be wishing dearly that she'd never taken that thankless job.

In the KPMG prosecutions, Judge Kaplan appeared to be trying to find a way to lessen the plight of the employee. That's hard to do, for two reasons. Because the Constitution does not control private conduct, Kaplan had to stretch his legal analysis implausibly to say that when KPMG told its employees they would lose their jobs if they refused to talk, that was really the government speaking because the prosecutors had, in turn, threatened to punish KPMG if the firm didn't help the investigation.[31]

Kaplan had to stretch on the same style of reasoning to say that it was really the government that cut off KPMG's checks to the employees' lawyers. He had to stretch even more to say that the KPMG partners had a constitutional right to that money—that it was really their money, not someone else's—just because KPMG had followed a practice of paying fees. (Only one of the tax shelter defendants had an express promise of legal fees written into his employment contract.) The appeals court upheld Kaplan's ruling. But one wonders whether the same result would have been reachable, even in a stretch, without the aggressive micromanaging of KPMG's behavior by prosecutors on the case.

A second obstacle to changing the situation for the corporate employee is practical rather than constitutional. The investigation of corporate crime would be more difficult, or at the least vastly more expensive, if the legal rules weren't as they are. As we've seen, leveraging corporate criminal liability to get the employer to compel the employee-witness to answer questions is the linchpin of policing business crime. That power is the lubricant of large, difficult investigations of complex business matters, some of which would never get moving without it.

This investigative tool is roughly equivalent to the legally permissible coercion used to get workaday bookies and loan sharks to talk in mob cases. Most corporate employees have not been caught making sports book or extending usurious loans, or laundering the proceeds of such crimes. The government must find its leverage elsewhere. The employment relationship happens to provide some. Our legal system has a way of discovering the means to accomplish what it needs to accomplish.

Altering the law of employee rights could produce further problems for the policing of corporate crime. Suppose, for example, the rule were that prosecutors could not pursue a corporate employee— or at least that prosecutors faced constitutional obstacles to doing so—once that employee gave a statement under pain of her employer's threat to fire her. With such a rule, corporations (not to mention employees) might have a perverse incentive to dip everyone into an "immunity bath" every time an investigation appeared on the horizon. Threaten to fire the employees, take their statements, then widely share those statements with all potential witnesses and their lawyers, tainting the whole affair. Some will remember that Oliver North, of Iran-Contra fame, got his criminal conviction overturned because his immunized—and televised—congressional testimony was found to have tainted the entire case even though the prosecutors in his case used none of North's actual testimony before Congress.[32]

This account of the corporate employee in criminal investigations should not be mistaken for a claim that his or her situation is especially tragic among America's many recipients of criminal justice. The point is that the system for policing corporate crime is defined by the relationship between the government and the corporation. The general problem of how to control and regulate the activities of corporations prevails over the particular concerns of the employee who may become a witness, a potential informant, an accomplice, or even a full perpetrator of a major business crime.

The Public: Corporate Crime and Street Crime

THE MOST vocal line of complaint about this system of policing is also the most widespread. More and more Americans are convinced that our criminal justice system—the product of a forty-year War on Crime that has included a thirty-year War on Drugs—is an embarrassment. A good measure of that feeling has to do with matters of process: police shootings, stop-and-frisk programs, "broken windows" policing, weak constitutional rights against intrusive searches, lack of privacy in information technology, and abuses of asset forfeiture laws. But most of the feeling—especially in its strongest and bipartisan forms—has to do with outcomes, mainly the state of America's prison system. Liberals and libertarians agree: locking up vast numbers of people is un-American.

Our "incarceration nation" (or "carceral state," in the academic language) has the world's largest prison population and, more to the point, by far the highest rate of imprisonment per person. China and Russia, controlled by famously illiberal governments and legal systems, are America's only serious challengers among large nations.

The brunt of mass imprisonment has fallen on poor and minority populations, which are vastly overrepresented in institutions of confinement. Most infamously, a man in the United States who is African-American is over six times more likely to be imprisoned than his white counterpart. At present rates, he stands a one-in-three chance of being in the custody of the state at some point in his lifetime. These facts constitute both a failure and a disgrace for the American legal system. (Though it doesn't change anything about this book's subject, it turns out—perhaps discouragingly—that drug criminalization does not provide the simple explanation for this disaster; the causes are more elusive and complex.[33])

In this accounting of American justice white collar crime is a rounding error. Of the over 1.3 million state prisoners in 2009, about 33,000 were locked up for fraud; of the nearly 200,000 federal prisoners in 2010, about 8,000 were in custody for white collar crimes.[34]

Still, America's prisons and their inhabitants glower in the background of any examination of how the legal system treats business crime. It's salt in this wound of injustice when businesspersons, who generally have financial resources, have access to a concierge level in the criminal justice system, which is what the enforcement system for corporate crime can look like. When skirmishing over corporate investigations, prosecutors and defense lawyers can appear to be playing a polite game of cricket while cops and street criminals are engaged in a grim blood sport.

This contrast is especially stark for corporations themselves, which, as we've seen, are given the option (indeed are encouraged) to "partner" with the government in the fight against crime and to avoid criminal prosecution altogether by undertaking elaborate programs of rehabilitation. Nothing could make a less attractive comparison to a single poor citizen destroyed by the state because of one bad decision and the color of his skin than a nonhuman machine for spewing profits that has run an oil tanker aground, filled pharmacies with a drug that hurts people, or scammed the Pentagon by selling it defective equipment for America's soldiers. That's putting the point clinically. Full-throated expressions of this point have gone much further.[35]

Those who voice this line of complaint rarely specify what an alternative system of corporate policing might look like. They have no obligation to do so, especially if they are aiming at the problem of mass imprisonment, using the treatment of business crime as a foil or aggravating fact in a case for decriminalization and "decarceration."

But to think critically about corporate crime in America, which is the task here, we must carry out the thought experiment. What might a legal system look like that did not treat corporate crime differently— not as a special problem of crime in corporations but as a problem of crime like any other? As the argument so often goes, "Treat 'em like common criminals, I say."

Let's imagine that we could afford the cost of saturating with cops large corporations in major industries like banking, energy, pharma, and auto manufacturing. Perhaps we could figure out, whether by legislation or even constitutional amendment, a workaround for legal rules that do not permit police to walk corporate hallways and drive corporate campuses the way they do the streets of America's cities.

What would these cops look for? Accounting fraud, insider trading, disregard of health and safety regulations, failure to report defects in industrial processes, and the like are not easily observable crimes.

There is no office-level equivalent to the street crimes that give law enforcement an entry point into problems of group crime like mob rackets, international trafficking in humans and narcotics, or sex crime enterprises. Some have suggested, in part for the point's rhetorical value, that locking up loads of bankers for consumption of drugs and prostitution services might crack open some fraud cases. The occasional investigation might get a break this way, but I'm skeptical of it as a sustained strategy.

Many successful corporate prosecutions have relied on the up-the-ladder strategy of charging key players with crimes and using that leverage to turn them into prosecution witnesses against more senior executives. The Enron prosecution succeeded, in part, by securing the testimony of CFO Andrew Fastow. The case against Fastow was developed from cases against members of his own staff, and even his wife. But all of those cases were made possible because Fastow and others had looted Enron in a series of flagrant self-dealing transactions.[36] These transactions were provable through corporate records the government obtained mainly from Enron and several banks.

Without the extra greed of Fastow's embezzlement from the company, and the postbankruptcy cooperation of Enron in investigating itself and surfacing the key records, the government's already steep path to the end point of the Enron prosecutions would have been longer and harder. Critics often say that to get at top corporate executives, prosecutors need to work their way up the ladder. Unfortunately, the first rung of that ladder is often out of reach.

The greater reason that a vision of blanket corporate policing is unrealistic is the prospect of massive law enforcement intrusion into daily business activity. Entrepreneurs, professionals, and business institutions that depend on confidentiality and teamwork would struggle to function under omnipresent and overbearing official surveillance. Imagine the lawyers who would be needed to shadow employees and police officers in the workplace and mediate their constant interactions.

The rejoinder here is obvious: The constant and intrusive presence of policing in poor, urban neighborhoods in America is a real nightmare, not a thought experiment, and it can crush the efforts of those communities and their inhabitants to generate economic value and better their own lot.[37] However, short of envisioning a different society altogether—a social order not simply more just but unrecognizably novel—this kind of goose-gander logic is not helpful. The maladies of the urban policing–poverty axis must be treated. Radically enhancing corporate policing won't do anything to advance that urgent project of reform.

Detecting and punishing law violations in corporations are very different projects than policing street crime because the two types of crime are different. *That* fact could itself be changed. But only if we decide to rethink the basic moral architecture of criminal law—what sends one to prison and what does not—by, for example, legalizing drugs and criminalizing the sale of securities.

Short of wholesale adjustment, we have to deal with the fact that corporate crime, as we have explored, requires line drawing that criminalization of entire markets or social practices does not. Corporate crime is embedded within activities that can be dangerous and harmful but are for the most part entirely acceptable. It cannot be policed, even remotely, the way governments have attempted to manage (with mixed success, to say the least) drug trafficking or immigration offenses.

In the corporate sector there is a vast apparatus for enforcing law that has no equivalent in the realm of street crime: the regulatory state. Almost every important industry in the United States *does* have a kind of constant police presence, in the form of Washington's alphabet soup: the EPA, SEC, FCC, CPSC, FDA, FAA, DOD, FDIC, DHS, HHS, and on and on. Law and legal institutions do not intervene in the problem of corporate crime only when prosecutors and FBI agents get involved. In theory, the regulatory system addresses these problems before matters escalate to criminal prosecution. This system has many mechanisms of surveillance, evidence gathering, and sanctions short of criminal punishment. Many agencies have sharp teeth, including the power to banish companies from industries and hobble them with large financial penalties.

Critics charge, often rightly, that American industrial regulations and regulators are too soft. The laws aren't tough enough, regulators don't enforce them vigorously enough, and officials are captive to industry. Fair enough. But these systems exist and they take a different form from police departments. Their charter is not to eliminate the scourge of factories, oil rigs, prescription drugs, and investment products. It's to make those things safe enough to buy, use, and live around.

Americans could certainly enjoy a better system of corporate regulation, as well as a more robust apparatus for enforcing laws against white collar crimes. So too, the inhabitants of America's regions of poverty should experience more tolerable policing—policing that involves fewer guns and handcuffs and looks more like the regulatory systems that govern American business.[38] But these objectives cannot be achieved through a brute trade that transplants street policing into the corporate sector.

So we have the current situation, arrived at over twenty years or so, in a kind of ad hoc development of practices by prosecutors, corporate defense lawyers, and companies. The law treats the corporation as both criminal and cop, and uses the corporation as a vehicle for detecting, proving, and punishing business crime.

Policing Crime in the Corporate Century

THE MAIN point in saying that a nation has "the rule of law" is that it's run by rules, not the officials who apply and are controlled by those rules: a government of laws, not men. The Netherlands has ample rule of law. North Korea has none. The rule of law, in all its component parts, constrains the behavior of the people who operate the powerful and dangerous machinery of the state.

That's not all there is to the rule of law. The idea not only harnesses government power but also demands its use. A society without law enforcement also lacks the rule of law. The United States has a lot of rule of law but also more prisoners than any other nation. Somalia desperately lacks the rule of law, but in a very different sense than

North Korea. Liberty, after all, means freedom from the intrusions of not only the state but also other human beings, especially those bent on harm. A legal system that fails to reach crime committed within corporations, especially in a society pervaded by the activities of large businesses, would not comport with the rule of law.

Consider the escalating problem of cybercrime. The American legal system (or perhaps an international body that will have to substitute for it in the future) will fail to measure up to the rule of law if it cannot prevent an individual with a laptop and code-writing skills from executing an algorithm that pilfers ten million credit card accounts, or empties the bank accounts of thousands of small businesses. Legal solutions to this problem are not at hand, and perhaps not even imaginable at present. But a government that gives up on the problem would not be tolerable.

Likewise, corporate crime cannot exceed the reach of American investigators, prosecutors, judges, and juries for the reason that it's too innovative, arcane, or complex; or too global; or too deeply buried under the opaque surface of the giant firm. As long as we charter the large corporation and license and encourage it to innovate and grow, we'll need tools to penetrate and police it. Having access to those tools will require accepting compromise with companies as the state responds, case by case, to widespread harms and other byproducts of corporations' social and economic projects.

If you were that prosecutor tasked with getting to the bottom of the Walmart Mexico bribery scandal, you thus would need to understand something else. As we saw, a path is available to you to get your evidence. It leads straight through Walmart and requires Walmart's participation in your investigation. If you're thorough and keep a close watch on the company and its lawyers, that path can get you what you need to prosecute the most responsible individuals and ensure that they're punished for their crimes.

Along the way, you'll be able to extract significant things from Walmart, including a large financial penalty and changes in the corporation that, in the end, only Walmart is going to be able to accomplish anyway—whether you put a corporate monitor in their offices or not.

Who, after all, really had the resources to clean up the environmental disasters in the Gulf of Mexico and Prince William Sound other than BP and Exxon? Who has the knowledge and control to make GM's cars safer other than GM itself?

But no one will like what you do. Walmart and its lawyers are going to view you, or at least your powers over them, as tyrannical. The public is going to think you sold them out, letting one of the wealthiest criminals in America off the hook. And Walmart's employees, like most people subject to the hard blows of criminal justice, are going to believe that, in your efforts to get to the bottom of the matter and sort witness from defendant, you treated them coercively and without mercy, in many cases with the connivance of an employer that turned on them. Nobody will be pleased with the compromises the American justice system has had to make in policing crime in corporations.

6

Criminal Defense
That Pays

L AWYERS HAVE LONG been blamed for many of America's discontents with politics, business, and law. (Our relative stock might have risen in recent years. Thank you, bankers and Congress.) If only the prosecutors would act more like prosecutors and the defense lawyers would stop defending everything. Then there might be progress on all this corporate malfeasance. In this chapter we'll look at the unique, and perhaps misunderstood, functions that criminal lawyers who practice in the corporate field perform in the American legal system.

Wrongful Convictions

TWO GENRES of story occupy the American imagination when it alights on the subject of crime. One is the epic of the renowned criminal career, with its diverse protagonists, real and fictional. The casting call includes John Gotti and Tony Soprano; Bonnie and Clyde and Butch Cassidy and the Sundance Kid; Jeffrey Dahmer and Hannibal Lecter;

Al Capone and Nucky Thompson; Whitey Bulger and Walter White; and Bernard Madoff and Jordan Belfort (the Wolf of Wall Street).

The other story is the tragedy of the innocent person wrongly imprisoned. In popular culture, the narrative is typically one of triumph over adversity, focusing on the heroic lawyer who rights injustice by obtaining her beleaguered client's freedom. Think Matthew McConaughey or, in the world of real lawyers, Barry Scheck and Peter Neufeld's famous Innocence Project or my colleagues Theresa Newman and Jim Coleman, whose Wrongful Convictions Clinic with law students at Duke University has delivered exoneration to men locked up for decades in North Carolina for crimes they did not commit.

The full story of the wrongful conviction in America is the far less entertaining, and not at all uplifting, tale the data tell.[1] The very subject of data is discouraging in this context: there is no way to determine the number of wrongfully convicted persons in America's prisons. Because DNA technology now allows for decisive proof of some cases of innocence, we know that hundreds of people at least have been imprisoned for acts they did not commit. Analysis of those cases has developed a picture of a deeply flawed system of investigation and adjudication in which many jurisdictions have allowed coerced confessions, mistaken eyewitness identifications, and botched or falsified forensic work to send innocent persons to prison.

How many white collar crime defendants have figured in these narratives of innocence—whether the gripping individual story of the wrong righted, or the systemic account of chronic errors that produce mistaken verdicts? The answer approaches, if not arrives at, zero. This fact is rarely discussed in conversations about criminal justice. It should be noticed.

Perhaps the first explanation that leaps to mind is that white collar offenders get better justice than others because most of them have money and are white not only in shirt but also skin. Later in this chapter we'll see whether this intuition proves true. For now, this most obvious explanation for what we might call the puzzle of the missing wrongful conviction doesn't help. Nobody who studies law thinks the American criminal justice system is infallible, or that the country could afford the costs, not least sacrifices in security, necessary to build a nearly perfect system. It's fantasy to think that we don't know of any wrongfully convicted white collar criminals because those cases don't exist. The jury trial is like democracy: the most flawed system known to humankind, except for all the others.

There's a more plausible explanation for the puzzle of the missing wrongful conviction. Think about the causes of most known cases of legal guilt in spite of factual innocence: eyewitnesses who identify the wrong person in error or because of police manipulation; confessions extracted from people who didn't commit the crime (research has made it abundantly clear that innocent people can be led to "confess"[2]); lab work fouled up or tampered with; expert witnesses peddling junk science; and police perjury. Rarely, if ever, are business crime cases botched in these ways. White collar crimes do not lend themselves to these forms of proof in the first place.

If there are indeed innocent white collar defendants in America's prisons, the likely cause is errors made by prosecutors and jurors when they must figure out, in court and after the fact, what went on in other people's heads. Remember the nature of white collar crimes. Fraud and other major offenses in business crime turn on questions of line drawing that the law often handles by examining thought processes. The typical defense in a corporate fraud case is not "I wasn't there," "You've got the wrong man," "This e-mail is a fake," or "The police are lying about what they found in my office." It's "I didn't intend to deceive anyone," "This sort of transaction is not deceptive in the market we work in," "No one told me the key fact that the prosecutor says made this deal shady," "I relied on the advice of lawyers that this was permissible," or "The government doesn't understand how this industry works; they are trying to criminalize ordinary legitimate business."

Even though the litigation in a white collar case concentrates on the facts of business transactions, often the prosecutor and the defendant are fighting over a question of law: Does this particular set of facts count as a crime?[3] Does it belong in a broad category such as "fraud," "obstruction of justice," or "tax evasion"? The contest is over what the defendant was thinking and whether what the defendant did, given what the defendant was thinking, ought to be treated as criminal.

In the vast majority of street crime cases, there's no equivalent dispute. Murders, assaults, possession of contraband, and most theft offenses rarely require courts to grapple with the fundamental question of criminality, that is, the first-order question of law. That question has been settled offstage, prior to the trial, and often a long time ago. What remain in dispute are questions about what happened, which are usually susceptible to forensic methods and eyewitness testimony, however prone to error those forms of evidence can be.

The special nature of uncertainty in white collar cases has at least two implications. First, a wrongful conviction will be hard, if not impossible, to discover. Once legal guilt attaches at a trial, the criminal justice system quickly reverses its orientation, on appeal and beyond, so that the burden of proof effectively shifts to the defendant. How is a white collar convict or her lawyer to establish that the jury made a mistake and that she did not in fact commit the crime? In any modestly complex case, no single ascertainable fact (such as identity) will settle the question of guilt. Indeed, since part of the question in the litigation of many fraud and other white collar cases—whether lawyers and judges admit this or not—is whether the defendant's conduct counted as criminal, a jury's decision on that question would seem, by nature, almost impossible to challenge.

Second, defense lawyers play a special role in this arena of crime. While lawyers are no more or less important to ensuring accurate outcomes, the value they contribute is different and comes earlier.

Prosecutors in a business crime case, like the judge and jury that may eventually hear it, have to decide whether a particular instance of business conduct constitutes a crime. Think of the debate, for example, over whether the Justice Department should have treated some of those mortgage-backed securities deals that led to the 2008 financial crisis as criminal fraud.[4] In doing this—again, in spite of the legal system's reluctance to say so—prosecutors are in effect making law.[5] They're acting like judges except that they don't have the insulation of life tenure, they report to political appointees, and they're adversarial lawyers tasked with winning their cases.

The system for prosecuting business crime, perhaps inevitably, has developed a check on prosecutors as they do this quasi-judicial job. That check is the defense bar. In contrast to most cases of street crime, the criminal defense lawyer who handles business cases shows up long before her client has been taken to the police station.[6] Most of the time, she's heavily involved in the case during the government's investigation, at a time when many targets of illegal drug investigations, for example, don't have a lawyer and don't even know that government agents are looking at them.

This early intervention by the lawyer might seem like a leg up for the business criminal. Her attorney has an idea what the government knows and where it's going, a head start in planning her defense. But the lawyer in the corporate case is also doing something during the investigation that would be irrelevant for the typical street crime defendant: trying to persuade the prosecutor that what the client did was not a crime. In order to do that, she has to know the facts. She must have the documents—which she normally will because those documents belong to the client's employer, which has little reason to withhold them from her. And she needs access to what witnesses are telling the government—which she normally will have because lawyers for the company and its employees will want to help each other do their jobs better by sharing what each witness has told the government. This sharing of information, called a joint defense agreement, is rare in street crime cases but routine in business crime defense.

As we try to understand what lawyers have to do with the present situation of business crime in America, it's essential to understand the particular role of the defense lawyer in the white collar case. These aren't lawyers for people who have more money—though good money is surely needed to hire them. They're lawyers for people who need lawyers to do a special job.

White Shoes in Criminal Court

THE "WHITE shoe" after which the fancy Wall Street law firms (nearly all of which have moved to midtown) were named is that men's pale buckskin with the brick-red soles. The shoes were popular among the Ivy League set during a middle stretch of the twentieth century, repeatedly coming back in fashion as things tend to among that crowd. They were sometimes worn around the office. Pat Boone liked them too. The "white shoe firm" thus was one populated by Ivy League graduates. In that era, this meant a firm that was white, male, and Protestant (meaning not too Catholic and not at all Jewish).

For a long time, the white shoe firms comfortably occupied the elite tier of New York practice, representing corporations and very wealthy individuals in their business transactions. Lawyers at these firms had what they called an "office practice." They rarely went to court. (Picture the crowd from early seasons of *Mad Men*, with stuffier offices and less profligate drinking.) Certainly these lawyers did not practice anything remotely involving criminal law, which was viewed as a sordid business to be handled by the "downtown" (i.e., Jewish) lawyers who graduated from law schools like NYU (then seen as a "night" school) and hung their shingles along lower Broadway.

As in many realms of American life, something changed around the late 1960s. For one thing, large firms founded by Jews, who had not gained access to the white shoe world, came of age. Those firms started to make high-end New York law practice a more competitive affair, eventually shaking the white shoe firms out of their complacency (and into hiring Jewish lawyers). Then the government started prosecuting more white collar crime and focusing its enforcement efforts on major Wall Street firms, like Drexel Burnham Lambert, where Michael Milken plied his trade in the heady takeover days of the 1980s.

The practice of corporate and white collar criminal defense became a major business. Naturally the established firms wanted in. Over the next couple of decades, those firms' clients found themselves needing these kinds of services more often as the government increased the volume of its investigations, often overlapping, in both civil and criminal enforcement. When the American Bar Association held a first national meeting of white collar defense lawyers in 1986, the small group's booking at a resort in Boca Raton was canceled at the last minute because the hotel did not want to be associated with a meeting about crime.[7] In 2013, the same meeting attracted over 1,200 lawyers for a week's gathering at a resort in Las Vegas. (That figure is probably a low measurement of the practice. I know lawyers who've stopped attending because the meeting produces more hangovers than referrals and insights.)

A recent study of America's most profitable law firms found that the higher one looks in the ranking, the higher the percentage one will find of a firm's partners who work in the investigation and defense of corporate crime.[8] That practice is now one of the pillars of large law firm earnings, along with mergers and acquisitions, corporate financing, and litigation disputes among companies. The study's authors surmised that clients are now willing to spend whatever it takes to get large public corporations beyond problems of business crime that often constitute major scandals. Fees are not the issue. These are "bet the company" cases. Or at least cases of stop the company until this problem is resolved.

At the high end of the scale is the Siemens bribery scandal. The company spent over a *billion* dollars in fees for lawyers, auditors, and their staffs to dig the company out from under its mess in the early 2000s.[9] This wasn't a case of dumb managers throwing money at lawyers for no reason. At Siemens, new wised-up management was trying to fix a broken company. It was extremely expensive for a company of Siemens's size to investigate bribery in every corner of its operations and construct a comprehensive new system for internal reporting, monitoring, and compliance.

When it came time for Siemens to be sentenced, the *prosecutors* argued that the court should treat the company's huge expenses to reform itself, especially the legal and auditing fees, as a form of fine for the criminal conduct, to be credited against Siemens' total penalty.

The prosecutors' argument is debatable of course. (Lawyers arguing that the larger the legal bill, the lower the fine? Hmm.) But there is some sense to the position in a case like Siemens. The expensive legal work Siemens bought was essential to rehabilitating a corrupt institution. The lawyers weren't only defending the corporation. They were repairing it.

Walmart's bribery scandal will be another case of huge resources devoted to cleaning house. The company's dismissiveness toward the initial allegations in Mexico later resulted in an army of lawyers hired to inspect every part of the company for evidence of bribery in order to satisfy prosecutors, who will be skeptical of Walmart's commitment to global compliance given the early cover-up.[10] Walmart has disclosed having spent over $400 million so far in the investigation and defense of the matter.

While we don't know the total bill, the costs to BP for professional assistance in responding to its myriad legal problems, criminal and civil, from the Gulf spill has to have run into the hundreds of millions at least.[11] The company's guilty plea settlement with federal prosecutors involved a complicated program of over $4 billion in payments to entities including victims, the Gulf of Mexico Research Initiative, the National Academy of Sciences, and the National Fish and Wildlife Foundation, as well as the appointment and staffing of offices within BP for a process safety monitor and an ethics monitor.[12] Such a complex deal could not have been structured and carried out without the work of BP's lawyers, whose ranks dwarfed the staffing that the Justice Department and other government agencies had available to manage legal and remedial aspects of the Gulf spill.

The defense lawyer in the business crime case is far more than a well-paid version of the courtroom advocate who populates the sets of *Law and Order* and *The Good Wife*. Except in the few simpler cases that make it all the way to trial, her work involves a completely different intervention in criminal justice. She mediates how business conduct is criminalized (or not), as a first-order question of legal policy. And she mediates how the government responds as both punisher and regulator to institutional breakdowns in large companies.

The AUSAs

THE PHENOMENON of the modern Assistant United States Attorney (AUSA) is a remarkable thing in the American legal system. The government takes smart people in their late twenties and early thirties and recently out of law school—many of them from privileged backgrounds insulated from the subcultures of crime they will confront—and gives them the task of dealing with problems like the Mafia, international narcotics cartels, corruption in state and municipal governments, corporate fraud, jihadist terrorism, serial gang murders, and environmental disasters.[13]

Amazingly this works, at least most of the time. In the era in which federal law enforcement has exploded relative to its historical role (roughly since the early 1980s), the Mafia has been practically crushed, the prosecution of major corporate crimes has gone from rarity to commonplace, quasi-military adversaries like Al Qaeda have been brought (when we've wanted to do so) under the heel of the federal judicial system, and major drug cartels have been largely dismantled (only to be replaced elsewhere, alas).

Fred Wyshak, one of these AUSAs, is a rare bird.[14] Fred started work as a prosecutor in Brooklyn in the 1970s, fresh out of law school at St. John's University. He's never left the trade. Fred grew up in Boston, where he delivered the *Herald American* in the afternoons as a kid and saw a run of headlines about grisly, unsolved mob killings. In the late 1980s, Fred took an opportunity to move back to Boston with his family and work in the federal prosecutor's office there. He soon learned from the law enforcement grapevine that Whitey Bulger had run rackets in Boston untouched for decades and was probably behind many, if not most, of the city's unsolved mob hits going back to the late 1960s. Trained in the New York approach to things, Fred decided to do something about it.

Fred has the patience, and unyielding demeanor, of an elephant. That's what it took to make the Bulger case. To get to Bulger, Fred and his group started putting witnesses in the grand jury in about 1989. In

2013, Fred and some of the same crew were in a Boston federal court-room when a jury reported its verdicts against Bulger for racketeering and murders. That's nearly a quarter of a century, during which the case ebbed and flowed, victories were followed by defeats, bodies were exhumed and fugitives went on the lam, presidents were elected and appointed one chief prosecutor after the next to run the Boston office, lawyers with less patience (like me) came and went on the case, and some families paid heavy prices. In federal law enforcement, the biggest, most important prosecutions require relentlessness.

Leslie Caldwell's career has been a bit more typical than Fred Wyshak's, but with no less impact. She grew up in Steelers country and went to college at Penn State. Just out of law school at George Washington University, Leslie spent a short time at one of those white shoe corporate firms in Manhattan. Then she discovered a place to which a remarkable group of young lawyers were lured in the late 1980s and early 1990s: the federal courthouse in Brooklyn, home of the United States Attorney's Office for the Eastern District of New York. A funny and street smart man, Andy Maloney, who seemed to play the part of the old school New York Irish pol, was in charge in those days; Maloney had an eye for a certain kind of fearlessness. Leslie, like Fred, was looking for something to do as a prosecutor that would matter. In those days, Leslie has said, the roofs of buildings in Brooklyn were for dead bodies, not chicken coops and kale gardens.

Leslie helped pioneer the use of the federal racketeering statute (RICO)—a law Congress designed in the late 1960s to stop organized crime infiltration of labor unions and help take down the Mafia—as a tool for dealing with murderous gangs that were proving beyond the reach of criminal justice. Her cases included the prosecutions of Lorenzo "Fat Cat" Nichols and Howard "Pappy" Mason. From behind bars, Mason ordered the signature crime of that era, the murder of New York City police officer Edward Byrne, who was executed by gunshot to the head while he sat in his patrol car guarding a witness's house.

Leslie's cohort in those days included Cathy Palmer, a diminutive and outspoken product of Worcester, Massachusetts, Holy Cross, and Catholic Law School. Palmer earned the nickname "The Dragon Lady" among narco-militants in the Golden Triangle of Burma because of her efforts to prosecute international heroin trafficking from her little office in Brooklyn Heights. And John Gleeson, the prosecutor who finally prevailed over John Gotti. And Beth Wilkinson, who prosecuted a hit man in Pablo Escobar's operation for exploding an Avianca jet in midair to kill an individual passenger on board, and who later prosecuted Timothy McVeigh for the Oklahoma City bombing. And Loretta Lynch, from Greensboro, North Carolina, the first African-American woman to serve as attorney general of the United States.

Amazing things happened almost every day in that courthouse. One of Caldwell's cases was the prosecution of a man who attempted to kill Palmer by delivering to the office a pizza box rigged with a .22 caliber spring gun. A gang case I prosecuted there included an attempted murder in which one of the defendants threw a grenade into a bodega, then opened fire on those fleeing the explosion; another included a firebombing of a store in which an old man playing cards in the back room was burned alive. Neither trial even warranted a story in the New York tabloids. One of our colleagues who happened to be assigned intake duty one day ended up with the prosecution of ten drownings caused when the Golden Venture, a shaky boat carrying nearly three hundred smuggled immigrants, was grounded off of Rockaway Beach in Queens and its passengers were ordered to swim ashore.

After the wild days of 1990s Brooklyn, Leslie went on to innovate the prosecution of securities fraud cases in Silicon Valley during the first tech boom. When Enron imploded in 2001, the Justice Department quickly assembled a prosecution task force and put Leslie in charge. She relished the challenge of the most complex accounting fraud case ever. Two years later, indictments were returned against the company's top executives, who were ultimately convicted. Leslie then spent almost a decade as a partner at a big New York law firm, doing the kind of corporate defense work we've examined in this book, before returning in 2014 to run the Justice Department's Criminal Division as assistant attorney general, supervising initiatives to prosecute fraud, corruption, and international cybercrime.

The big, important cases require enormous work and commitment, not to mention ingenuity and teamwork, and there are some prosecutors who never make the effort. When the targets are hard and the resources limited, there are always reasons to give in, or not try hard enough in the first place. As the saying goes, "Big cases, big problems. Little cases, little problems. No cases, no problems."

The lawyers who become AUSAs are human, of course. They have material desires, limited energy, and often families. Like most expensively educated American professionals, they want to live comfortably, send their kids to good colleges, and maybe have a vacation home. Most of them eventually leave the government. And most who leave take the opportunity that the profession makes available: the business crime defense lawyer—advocate for and adviser to both the corporation and the executive.

This job is one that most of these lawyers are suited for. It requires intimate knowledge of the peculiar legal subculture of a modern federal law enforcement system dominated by prosecutors. Beyond the law firms, companies have taken to hiring former federal prosecutors as in-house counsel, in part to improve their efforts at legal compliance and crisis management.

What I'm describing, of course, is the infamous revolving door. These days, especially in the wake of the 2008 financial crisis, critics of the Justice Department—as well as other federal regulatory agencies such as the SEC—have charged that the prosecution and defense of business misconduct is too clubby. The lawyers in this club, on this account, are not so much adversaries as brethren in a guild meant to enrich everyone in perpetuity, including the lawyers, the corporations, and the corporate managers.

The jaundiced version of the revolving door story goes like this.[15] Prosecutors are people. People care about material rewards and effort—getting the most benefit for the least work. It's human nature. Since government jobs aren't lucrative, especially relative to the cost of living in big cities, the material rewards from prosecution are the private sector salaries for which prosecution experience can be cashed in. To reduce workload in the meantime, there is the dominant institution of the plea bargain. Happily for the prosecutor, the plea bargain has double benefits in business crime cases: offering reductions in punishment in negotiations with individual and corporate defendants not only avoids the work of trial but also ingratiates the prosecutor with the corporate defense bar and its clientele, who control access to the spoils of post–government employment.

The result, it is said, is a profession that poorly serves the public. Business crime cases are churned by a cadre pursuing their own enrichment. The merits involved in questions of corporate wrongdoing are ignored or forgotten and suitable punishments are rarely imposed. The account of the classically minded economist focused on incentives and rational choice lines up here with the story favored by the left-leaning journalist preoccupied with abuses of power.[16]

It's true that prosecutors regularly trade their government credentials for high-paying jobs as defense lawyers in the corporate sector. It's also true that plea bargains are a tempting way for prosecutors to avoid the ordeal of trial and that, in the great majority of cases, defense lawyers are in the business of cajoling prosecutors to favorably exercise their extensive discretion. These truths do not mean, however, that federal prosecutors pull their punches when they confront business crime. And they certainly do not mean that insidious corruption is afoot in the federal criminal justice system.

To stay with self-interest for the moment, which lawyer is more likely to translate prosecution experience into top-flight work in the private sector: the dullard who runs a plea bargaining mill and catches the 5:15 home every day, or the star who makes a name for herself winning a string of trials against well-financed executives defended by the best lawyers in town? Which lawyer would *you* be more likely to hire if you were the general counsel of a big corporation and cost were no object?

Preet Bharara, as we saw, is the U.S. Attorney in Manhattan whose work landed him on the cover of *Time* magazine. He is known for his campaign that produced over eighty convictions for insider trading within elite circles of New York's hedge fund industry. Bharara, of course, would not be so well known if he decided, as many defense lawyers undoubtedly urged him to, that there were too many gray areas in the hedge fund business for clear legal theories of insider trading to work. (They had a point. A few of his convictions have been reversed on appeal.[17])

At times, material incentives might point the other way for the same prosecutor. Bharara is also known for not bringing significant prosecutions for securities fraud against executives of the major banks for their involvement in the creation and collapse of the mortgage-backed securities market.[18] Although he has not said so explicitly, it's clear Bharara avoided those cases because he didn't think he could win them. Maybe he was wrong about that. Some have argued that Bharara, or some prosecutor somewhere, should have been willing to roll the dice on those cases.

But no rational, ambitious lawyer—whether she plans to leave the government sooner, later, or never—wants to be known as the Captain Ahab of prosecutors, the one who foolishly went after the biggest quarry but failed to land it. That prosecutor will be viewed as lacking judgment, competence, ethical principles, or all of the above. To put the point slightly differently, a defense lawyer saying to a prosecutor, "You're going to lose this one and here's why" or "You're going to be seen as reckless and irresponsible if you go forward on this one" is far more persuasive than saying, "At our firm we really value the judicious lawyer who holds back and knows when not to bring the case, if you know what I mean."

Understanding how prosecutors think, and why the revolving door is not so sinister in the practice of criminal law, requires going beyond simplistic models of material incentive. This ought to be uncontroversial any time we want to fully understand human behavior. It's especially not a stretch in this instance because we're looking at a group of people who self-select as interested in more than maximizing their bank accounts.

Federal prosecutors, at least in the big offices that handle most corporate crime—New York, Chicago, Los Angeles, San Francisco, Boston, Washington, main Justice—are mostly drawn from a select tier of relatively new lawyers who excelled at elite law schools and then landed prestigious first jobs, such as clerkships with federal judges and associate positions at top-shelf law firms. Those young lawyers are the sort who went to law school because they thought, perhaps vaguely, that the law might be a way to make a difference. During law school or shortly after, they came to the understanding that federal prosecutors have a huge amount of power and influence in the legal system and that these lawyers deal with important and interesting problems of public policy, like organized crime, terrorism, public corruption, and financial crime.

There are many other ways, some of them more helpful, for young, driven lawyers to contribute to society. But becoming a federal prosecutor is one route. It pays better than starving nonprofit work. And it comes with resume value that serves as insurance for the anxious new professional who is unsure where her longer-term future lies.

In any event, this career path is not the most profitable one available to this lawyer. At a big corporate firm, even as a brand-new attorney, she can make more money, and her salary there will rise quickly. Government service is one route to an eventual law partnership or a good in-house counsel position but it's not the only path to those jobs and, in most fields of law practice, not the most reliable one.

Naturally, when she takes up the position of federal prosecutor, this lawyer will be hungry for big cases, big challenges, jury trials, victories, and tangible results. Perhaps in her development as a prosecutor, especially as she makes the common transition from dealing with violent criminals to handling business crime or corruption, her outlook might change. Bureaucratic inertia, office culture, industry and professional norms, and an eye that has begun to wander toward the exits can change the appetites of the young idealist.

Simultaneously, something else happens in the maturation of the prosecutor, something welcome and essential in our system. As she sees more cases, both her own and those of her colleagues, she acquires that essential feature of professionalization in which judgment solidifies. Crimes and criminals begin to arrange themselves along a spectrum rather than in a dichotomy. She begins to appreciate the extent of her powers and how they can be exercised to good effect both when she wields them and when she does not. She develops the ability to listen— to witnesses, victims, judges, defense lawyers, colleagues, supervisors, and law enforcement officers—and to recognize when she's hearing the stock argument or criticism that comes with the territory versus the considered point that deserves attention.

The United States has constructed a criminal justice system that reposes in the prosecutor a disproportionate role in determining outcomes. The prosecutor's decisions about whom to charge and whom to release or leave unmolested, about what to do in the grand jury, about who will receive the generous plea bargain and who will face trial, about who will testify and who will be testified against, and even about the precise sentences judges are likely to give those who are convicted, are essentially beyond review. Fortunately, ethical, professional, and bureaucratic constraints, when they work as designed, control the prosecutor's behavior. But law, at least of the sort that those who are prosecuted can invoke, has little to say on the matter.[19]

The federal white collar crime prosecutor is the paradigm of the discretionary prosecutor. There's no pipeline to her from patrol officers and their arrests. She has no cases other than the ones she chooses to make. A finer line than many people imagine separates the prosecutor whose decisions are compromised, some would even say corrupted, by the revolving door from the prosecutor who uses skillful judgment.

You Have the Right to (Some Sort of) Lawyer

NOW WE can widen our view on the subject of American criminal lawyers. Let's get something on the table that is outrageous, with a little legal background necessary first. The Sixth Amendment to the U.S. Constitution guarantees that a person cannot be prosecuted without the help of his lawyer. In *Gideon v. Wainwright*, one of the most important cases in American law, the Supreme Court (belatedly) recognized what this constitutional guarantee entails: if a person cannot afford to hire a lawyer to defend her in a criminal case, the public must pay for one.[20]

A less famous case about lawyers is *Strickland v. Washington*.[21] That case seems to say something equally important: the guarantee of a lawyer means not simply someone with a pulse and a law license, but an *effective* criminal defender. Alas, *Strickland* has been a bad case for criminal defendants. It has turned out to mean that ineffective lawyering is only that which falls below a low bar of minimal competence and, even then, only if the convicted person can prove that a competent lawyer would have won her a different result. The reason courts have been so stingy with the Sixth Amendment right is that real review, after the fact, of the performance of every counsel for every convicted defendant would be extremely costly and burdensome, in part because attorney quality is hard to measure.

The combination of *Gideon* and *Strickland* has produced the infamy of the American system of publicly funded criminal defense. While most public defenders deliver excellent performance under difficult conditions, the frequent failures of the system are unacceptable. The legal literature is full of stories of drunk, sleeping, ethically compromised defense attorneys who failed to cross-examine prosecution witnesses or investigate potential alibis.[22] These stories include defenses in death penalty cases. More common, and equally damaging, are the strapped and underfunded lawyers who lack the time or the financing to hold the prosecution to its burden by retesting forensic materials, hiring experts to analyze key items of proof, or even paying investigators to do basic shoe-leather work in preparation for trial. Often we learn of these stories when they turn up as explanations for how errors were made when wrongful convictions are discovered years later through DNA work.

We're not at the outrage yet. There is another, parallel line of logic that flows out of the Sixth Amendment right to counsel. The amendment may have a (low) floor but it has no ceiling. The wealthy criminal defendant has an absolute right to spend his every last cent on lawyers. On a use-it-or-lose-it logic, emptying the coffers for counsel can be rational, especially if potential punishments include a long term of imprisonment and financial penalties likely to reach deep into the defendant's pockets. Jeffrey Skilling is reported to have spent over $70 million on lawyers in the Enron case.[23] Raj Rajaratnam, the Galleon hedge fund boss, likely spent over $40 million defending himself against insider trading.[24] To go to trial with a top-tier lawyer in a business crime case of any complexity requires, at a minimum, a retainer of a million dollars. More lawyers and more effort will multiply the bill from there.

And still we've not gotten to the outrage. Remember that companies routinely pay the costs of lawyers for their executives and employees who face regulatory inquiries, lawsuits, and even prosecutions for conduct on the job. This means that most persons investigated and charged in cases involving crimes within large corporations have a sort of legal insurance that the average American does not enjoy.[25] Payment of legal fees is usually a matter of business practice even if not promised by contract.

A typical company won't be willing to buy every employee the Skilling or Rajaratnam level criminal defense. But large corporations routinely spend hundreds of thousands and even millions of dollars on lawyers hired to represent executives in legal trouble. Sometimes these funds are advanced on the condition that they can be "clawed back" if the executive is convicted of a crime. But recovering these monies can be difficult and companies commonly forgo the effort.[26]

Now we get to the real outrage. In the KPMG tax shelter affair, discussed earlier, a leading federal appellate court ruled that corporate funding of defense lawyers is more than a perk. It's a constitutional right—not one enforceable against the employer but one the government cannot interfere with as it did by questioning payments to lawyers in the KPMG prosecutions.[27] This ruling stands even though the Supreme Court has long said that the Sixth Amendment does not give a person the right to spend someone else's money on her criminal defense.[28]

To take stock, the Constitution apparently guarantees one kind of criminal defendant nothing more than the solo effort of a threadbare lawyer who is not too drunk. For another kind of defendant, or even potential defendant, the Constitution promises—or at least shields private access to—the expensive, Harvard-trained shark who is a partner at a big New York or Washington firm.

The dissonance extends further. As we saw with John Gotti, courts have ruled that the attorney for a mob boss can be kicked off a case because of his conflict of interest in having represented underlings in the past, as "house counsel" on the boss's dime. This makes the attorney himself evidence of the criminal organization and a potential witness in the case.[29] Meanwhile, the idea of a corporation paying the lawyers who represent its employees is viewed as commonplace and no necessary problem of conflict of interest. Surely this all adds up to yet another instance of how the American legal system is engineered to oppress poor people, especially poor people of color.

Nonetheless, there's an explanation for what I've been calling the outrage. It's one that shows, again, how the project of criminal justice in the corporation requires us to confront our ambivalence about what corporations do. Businesses need to be able to hire talented people so firms can produce the wealth that they're generally chartered to create. Human talent is a problem, maybe the most important one, for any sophisticated social institution. The imperative of talent becomes stronger as institutions grow in scale and modern social endeavors become less industrial and more based on the production and exchange of information. Even nonprofits face stiff competition for the best managers and employees.

Though matters vary by industry, corporate employees are constantly subject to the risk of legal action, both civil and criminal. Few of us would want to devote our precious hours and unique human capital to an institution at which we expected a reasonable likelihood of being sued or even prosecuted. Especially if that prospect, regardless of outcome, might mean personal bankruptcy. Business cases are, after all, typically complicated and require a lot of legal resources. The lazy or overwhelmed court-appointed lawyer is even more likely to incompetently defend a corporate crime case than fumble the defense in an eyewitness murder case.

A company thus needs to be able to tell its employees and recruits that it will pay for lawyers for problems related to work. One might think that need is understandable only up to, and not further than, the point at which an employee breaks the law. But that's what the lawyers are there for: to represent the employee in the process of determining whether in fact she broke the law. The question is not simply whether the employee was the perpetrator. The question is whether what she did was a crime in the first place.

A prominent exception to what I'm saying proves the rule. The government is a very large institution in which people commonly get in trouble with the law. The government does not pay attorneys' fees for its employees. Yet talented people who command big salaries in the private sector take government jobs, especially top political appointments. (As to congressional seats, I make no general comment.) Think Larry Summers, Robert Rubin, Madeleine Albright, Condoleeza Rice, Elena Kagan, Hank Paulson, Timothy Geithner, Richard Daley, Ben Bernanke, Peter Orszag, and on through a long list.

Two things keep the elite Washington job market running. The first is a legal doctrine called sovereign immunity, which makes it hard for a plaintiff to recover damages in a lawsuit against an individual government actor for conduct on the job.[30] The reason, or at least a modern one, for this very old legal doctrine (the word "sovereign" used to apply literally) is to allow people to take government jobs and do something with those jobs without being crippled by fear of personal liability. This legal rule is a big reason why the less famous members of the federal bureaucracy, including thousands of political appointees, are willing to board DC's Metro for work each morning.

Sovereign immunity is not the whole story, though. The rule does not protect against the potentially ruinous financial consequences of a criminal prosecution or even a serious congressional inquiry. In the Washington of fill-in-the-blank-gate, those are real risks for those who toil in the media spotlight. Consider the likely legal fees of Oliver North or Scooter Libby or Web Hubbell, or even White House intern Monica Lewinsky.

Why do people still take these jobs? One answer is that the prospect of the lucrative future in law, finance, or lobbying—or perhaps the book deal—gives some assurance against the risk of personal bankruptcy. Another explanation might be the uncertain prospect that one's status as a political football might spur one team or the other to raise a "defense fund" from partisans to cover legal bills. An additional answer, of course, is that lots of people decline these jobs to avoid even the ordeal of vetting, much less potential later consequences in burnout, reputational damage, and legal risk.

Washington is a special case. State government institutions, where the potential payoffs (at least of the legitimate kind) are much lower, struggle to attract premier talent in adequate numbers. Big corporate headquarters could look more like America's statehouses. The law could be structured to deny corporate managers and employees any more comfort with regard to legal risks at work than they have in their daily activities at home, on the public thoroughfares, and in their social circles. It's hard to say how such a change in incentives might affect employment markets and performance on the job. A natural prediction would be to expect brain drain in the most legally risky industries. Maybe that would be acceptable. In a column, Michael Lewis argued, tongue in cheek, that Wall Street would work better for America if we banned all the math geniuses and staffed the trading desks with female senior citizens asked to exercise their common sense.[31]

For a long time, America's law and economy have chosen a different approach. We've wanted talented innovators to manage large corporations and we've wanted them to be willing to take risks. So the law takes with one hand and gives back, at least a little, with the other. It says that severe punishments may be imposed on individual corporate actors for illegal conduct but that the costs of defending against the government's efforts to impose those punishments may be borne by the corporation. This stance might be especially defensible for criminal prosecutions. In civil and regulatory lawsuits, the ultimate sanctions too rarely fall on individual corporate managers. There's no way, on the other hand, for a corporation to serve an executive's term of imprisonment in her place.

For the court in the KPMG prosecutions to have taken this point to the level of constitutional law is debatable. The problem in that case, which has remained a one-off, was that the prosecutors acted as if they had the right to rescind the basic bargain American law has struck with corporate employees on the subject of legal risk. The prosecutors' unusually explicit statements to KPMG about cutting off attorneys' fees for the firm's partners evidenced a view that the costs of lawyers should be part of the punishment for corporate wrongdoing—that the prospect of financial ruin in having to defend oneself might even be a welcome boost to the deterrence of corporation crime.

Imagine, for the sake of argument, how we might correct for the inequality in legal services. One option would be to limit by law the amount of money that can be spent on a criminal defense, whether by an individual or a company on her behalf. That would require a constitutional amendment. The idea that a person has the absolute right to defend herself against prosecution to the limit of all resources she can lawfully acquire and deploy is basic to the American concept of the individual's relationship to the state.

The inverse approach would be to boost indigent defense to the level of lawyering in business cases. Give every street criminal a KPMG defense. In a fanciful world, Congress could legislate and fund such a thing. Or the Supreme Court could force Congress to fund it (or compel the executive branch to stop prosecuting people) by revising Sixth Amendment law from the *Strickland* case to say that constitutionally "effective" counsel is well-funded counsel.

This of course is a dream. Most in Congress probably do not share this vision as a matter of political preference. Virtually all of them lack the will to take the required funds from somewhere else in the budget. The Supreme Court will never go down this constitutional road. Managing national institutions of lawyer funding through judicial doctrine and case-by-case decisions is a project for which this Court, perhaps any court, would have no appetite.

A third approach might be to take from one pocket to fill the other. The government could tax private criminal defense to increase funding for public defense. A tax on wealthy criminal defendants—hey, Ken Lay or Bernard Madoff, for every dollar you want to spend on your lawyers above say $100,000, fifty cents goes to the public defender— probably would require the same kind of constitutional amendment we just discussed. Taxing the private lawyers, either directly or by making them do more pro bono cases, might be possible through regimes of attorney licensing without implicating the Constitution (with the emphasis on "might"). One would want to be careful not to create mass flight from criminal practice altogether among lawyers at elite law firms. In any event, we're still taking about pie in the sky.

Winning the Conference Room

WHAT DOES all this work by the lawyers who administer corporate criminal justice add up to? Does America's criminal justice system afford not just white privilege but also white collar privilege? To some extent, the obvious answer is yes. Wealth matters. But the advantage to the defendant with the hired lawyer is not as clear as people commonly think.[32]

Let's focus on federal court because that's where the clearest data are available and it's where most serious white collar crime is prosecuted in the United States. Start with the point in the process where most people would think better-paid, and thus likely more skilled, lawyers would deliver better outcomes for their clients: actual criminal litigation, namely trials and appeals.

In federal court, where substantially less than ten percent of criminal cases go to trial, the acquittal rate in white collar cases is not significantly higher than in others.[33] Permit me to repeat. Among the relatively small group of federal criminal defendants who contest a prosecution at trial, white collar defendants do *not* have higher chances of acquittal. For all persons charged with criminal offenses in the federal system, the prospects are equally grim. About one half of one percent of all such persons will go all the way to trial and prevail over the government. Between 2005 and 2014, white collar defendants fared better than all defendants by a margin of *twelve one hundredths of one percent.*

What about the second bite at the apple? Are appellate courts more likely to toss out the convictions of business crime defendants than drug dealers? When I was prosecuting cases in New York City in the 1990s, we used to think so. There was a running gallows-humor joke about the "country club test" applied by the federal appellate court in New York: the only defendants to get their convictions reversed on appeal were the ones who looked like they could be members of the judges' clubs.

Anecdotal evidence seemed to validate the cynicism. My eight-murder racketeering case with wiretaps and a two-month trial would be affirmed by summary order without a published opinion, while a colleague's complex case involving insurance fraud by a big corporation would be overturned for failure to have proved that the prosecution was brought ("venued") in the proper geographic courthouse. In recent years, this appellate court has upset convictions for a major accounting fraud in the insurance industry because the trial judge made a mistake in allowing prosecutors to use a particular chart; and tossed out insider trading convictions in the hedge fund industry because, the court said, a jury was wrong to conclude that the defendants knew that tipped information about corporate earnings came from a corrupt source.[34]

Again, the data are surprising.[35] The annual reversal rate for all federal criminal appeals is usually about eight percent. The reversal rate in fraud cases has been only slightly higher, ranging between nine and twelve percent. In 2010, for example, nine percent of fraud defendants won reversal on appeal, while six percent of drug defendants and ten percent of violent crime defendants obtained the same result. (It's not possible to say whether the rate of appellate wins is higher in high-profile or large business crime cases, as data are not separated on that score.)

Lawyers do not appear to deliver a huge benefit to their clients in litigation before trial either. Less than ten percent of federal cases are dismissed before trial, with fraud cases falling out pretrial about eight percent of the time versus a seven percent overall dismissal rate.[36]

All right, then, if so few federal criminal defendants win at any stage, and those who do win prevail at about the same low rates, what about sentences? Surely the skilled lawyers hired by white collar defendants deliver lower punishments for their clients.

Whether business crime is punished properly in relation to other crime—a value-laden matter nearly impossible to quantify—is a question that will occupy the next chapter. For now, suffice it to say that if paid advocates were delivering decisively for their clients before sentencing judges, the data on sentencing would be moving opposite from the actual trend.[37] Between 1996 and 2015, the mean federal punishment for fraud convicts rose from thirteen months to twenty-seven months; the mean bribery sentence increased from thirteen to twenty-one months. Meanwhile, the mean federal drug sentence fell from eighty-three to sixty-eight months and the mean federal robbery sentence fell from a hundred and eleven to seventy-eight months. These trends developed during a time when changes in the law gave federal judges increased leeway in sentencing, thus affording defense lawyers only more opportunity to capitalize on advocacy skills at sentencing hearings.[38]

Now consider the prosecutor's decision to charge. The number of criminal violations in the United States vastly outnumbers the (albeit embarrassingly large) number of criminal cases in our courts. Thus the most important inflection point in any criminal case, by a wide margin, is the decision whether to prosecute it in the first place.

The charging decisions of prosecutors take place in what scholars who study criminal justice have called a black box.[39] Prosecutors' decisions are so multifaceted that they would be exceptionally hard to measure even if there were data. And there are no data, at least not for the federal system. Federal prosecutors don't accurately and completely record their decisions and the Justice Department doesn't share data on prosecutorial discretion. In white collar cases, most arrests come only after a prosecutor decides that a long investigation has produced sufficient evidence to give agents a warrant to bring in the defendant—or to make a call to the lawyer to ask the defendant to surrender. Prosecutors' decisions are perhaps somewhat easier to measure in state systems dominated by street crime; but there the problem is pushed back a step, to measuring how and why police decide to arrest the defendants they bring to the prosecutors' offices.

There's no way to know whether white collar defense lawyers deliver an advantage to their clients in the federal system by more often winning the best result of all: no prosecution. We do know, without question, that the federal system for prosecuting business crime includes a virtual right to something that almost no street crime defendant enjoys: the opportunity to retain counsel to, in effect, litigate one's case with the government before it becomes a case.[40]

That process of "conference room litigation" includes, at least, the opportunity to meet with the prosecutor at some point in the investigation and attempt to persuade her that the documents and witnesses will not make a case—that the client is innocent or, more commonly, that the case is "really" or "at most" one for civil litigation and not criminal prosecution. Defense lawyers often can appeal to the prosecutor's supervisors and sometimes—in a novel, controversial, or high profile case—even to the overlords at main Justice in Washington.

This sounds like a huge leg up, an opportunity amply justifying spending money on a skilled lawyer. But remember the question with which we started: whether the business crime defendant's privilege in type and quality of lawyer cashes out to unjust inequalities in criminal process. That's harder to say than it might have seemed at first blush, because of the question that opened this chapter: how would a prosecutor know when she's about to bring a case against an innocent white collar defendant? Given that the crimes in corporate cases so often involve fuzzy boundaries between legal and illegal, and between civil and criminal wrongs, critical questions about guilt and innocence are apt to *require* the responsible prosecutor to give the potential defendant the opportunity to litigate in the conference room.

Consider the case of Lauren Stevens.[41] She was a midlevel in-house lawyer for the big pharma company GlaxoSmithKline. The FDA began looking at whether GSK had been unlawfully marketing Wellbutrin, a drug approved for treatment of depression, as a weight loss drug, a use for which Wellbutrin had not been approved. In a standard move, the FDA sent GSK a request for documents and information, which Stevens was assigned to handle. In responding to the FDA, Stevens enlisted the help of lawyers at one of the law firms GSK regularly used. With that firm's guidance, GSK produced documents and information to the FDA.

The next thing Stevens knew, the Justice Department was examining her for the crime of obstruction of justice. The prosecution theory was that GSK's responses to the FDA's requests, which went out with her signature, had falsely denied that GSK marketed Wellbutrin for weight loss. Then prosecutors got a grand jury to indict Stevens. She had gone from pharma lawyer drafting letters to the FDA to federal criminal defendant, possibly on her way to prison.

The judge in Stevens's case was skeptical. First he dismissed the indictment because, it turned out, prosecutors had given the grand jury a wrong instruction about the law. Then the government went back to the grand jury and got a second indictment, this time free from legal error. The prosecution of Stevens went on to trial. The judge, after hearing all of the government's evidence, was no more impressed. He dismissed the case before it went to the jury, calling the prosecution a "miscarriage of justice" and concluding that no reasonable juror could reach any conclusion other than that Stevens had acted as a law-abiding attorney, working in good faith and relying on the advice of other lawyers.

Lauren Stevens's defense lawyers apparently failed to persuade the prosecutors to use their discretion not to charge her. She had to litigate all the way to trial and nearly to a jury verdict. But she had the benefit of one of Washington's best white collar defenders, presumably at GSK's expense. And that might well have made all the difference in the world to the rest of her life.

Or consider the case of Prabhat Goyal, who was the CFO of the software company Network Associates (the company that used to be McAfee).[42] Goyal was indicted and convicted for securities fraud. He avoided prison only when a federal appellate court reversed his conviction, with one of the judges writing, "This is not the way criminal law is supposed to work." Goyal's crime, according to the government, was causing Network Associates to recognize certain revenue in its financial reports to investors. The revenue itself was perfectly valid. But the company recorded the funds sooner than it should have by using "sell-in" accounting (book as revenue when distributed to retailers) on some software sales when it should have followed "sell-through" accounting (book as revenue only when end-consumers buy).

Lying about financial performance is securities fraud, of course. Playing games with accounting rules, as we've seen, can be one way to lie. But Goyal's conduct didn't exactly scream "crime" on its face. And the government, it turned out, never clearly proved that the use of sell-in accounting on these deals was wrong. Nor, more importantly, did the government prove that the accounting made a sufficient difference to Network Associates' earnings results that investors would have cared enough to be defrauded by it.

Goyal, like Stevens, had to litigate a long way to prevail. He was able to do so with the benefit of top-flight counsel paid for by the company that employed him. We know about cases like Stevens and Goyal because they are the rare ones that surface in reported litigation in the federal courts. We can't know how many potential Stevenses and Goyals never see a courtroom because defense counsel "won" the case in conference-room litigation. And we cannot know how many of the cases that never make it out of the prosecutor's office die there because the potential defendant didn't commit a crime, versus how many falter because a skilled lawyer for a guilty client has outfoxed the government.

The extent to which differences in advocacy, and access to legal services, constitute injustices are difficult to measure in this context— as we'll see in the next chapter, it's even harder to say which sorts of differences in punishment are wrong. The point has not been to minimize the grave problem of inadequate indigent criminal defense, or to reach any conclusion at all about that problem. It's been to explain why the American approach to crime in the business world—mainly to the very question of how to define what is criminal—has produced a specialized cadre of prosecutors and defense lawyers whose work makes this part of the legal machine run.

7

Judges and
Their Sentences

PRISON IS THE common denominator of American criminal justice. It is a bitter irony that one way America affirms its status as
the nation of liberty and equality is to insist that most wrongdoers be
subject to the penalty of liberty deprivation—with the result that we
have more persons with their physical freedom revoked than any other
nation.

This uniform currency of human time measured in days, months,
and years is also a fixed point to quantify and compare crimes. Here,
perhaps, we can trade off the murderer or the drug dealer against the
corporate fraudster and hope to measure whether America treats business crime too softly, too harshly, or just right. This is why the public's
attention fixes so closely on the actions of sentencing judges when a
notable case of business crime reaches that moment when it will be
given a number.

Readers are far enough along in this book to expect that the common denominator will disappoint. Sentencing in numbers is a neat
tool for measuring business crime. But the denominator of punish-

ment is not really common. Different crimes don't become the same simply because a judge has affixed similar numbers to them. Numerical sentences cannot resolve hard questions about how to think about the differences between street crimes and white collar crimes.

The judges who sentence corporate criminals enact a ceaseless conflict about how to view white collar crime, generally and in relation to other kinds of crime. Their decisions do not resolve America's unstable relationship with business crime. They bring it into clearer view.

To see this, let's begin with two cases. Neither was part of a major crime that spread through the ranks of a large corporation. But each required a court to explicitly confront difficult conflicts about punishment that arise in sentencing business criminals.

Rajat Gupta

THE FIRST, which we saw when discussing insider trading, is a high-profile case.[1] It's an incomprehensible story about the long fall of a good man. As told in Anita Raghavan's book *The Billionaire's Apprentice*, Rajat Gupta was the embodiment of the postwar Indian-American immigrant success story—an avatar in a generation of exemplary leaders. Gupta grew up in New Delhi, the son of a schoolteacher mother and a journalist father who, in the 1940s, was imprisoned and severely beaten for his participation in India's fight for independence. Gupta excelled in school and came to the United States to complete his education. He rose within the corporate world to become, in the 1990s, the chief executive officer of the McKinsey consulting firm, the world's most trusted adviser to corporate managers. Gupta won the tournament of the American meritocracy. He built his success on prolific work and assiduous cultivation of a gold-plated reputation for judgment and trustworthiness.

All along the way, Gupta gave back. His charitable work was extraordinary, entrepreneurial, and life-changing for others.[2] Major endeavors included service on the board of the Global Fund to Fight AIDS, TB, and Malaria, a highly effective health organization that would not have succeeded without the work of Gupta—as attested to by the likes of Bill Gates and Kofi Annan. Gupta created the Public Health Foundation of India, which has established a string of public health institutes across a sprawling country that previously lacked such institutions. He founded the Indian School of Business, the first MBA-type program in Asia and one that quickly achieved an international reputation as one of the top business programs in the world. And Gupta worked with Bill Clinton to raise tens of millions of dollars in relief for victims of the massive 2001 Indian earthquake.

Then came the fall.[3] Gupta's work at McKinsey had forged ties with the elite of corporate leadership. When he retired from the consulting firm, he was invited to join the boards of blue-chip companies, including Goldman Sachs and Procter & Gamble. This was in the early 2000s, when the hedge fund was ascendant on Wall Street. Gupta saw friends and associates making sums off their own investment ideas that dwarfed the salaries and bonuses available to most managers, board members, and advisers of public companies. Those investors included Raj Rajaratnam, who operated a large hedge fund called Galleon and had partnered with Gupta in some investment activity.

Gupta soon made a decision that confounds the observer. On September 23, 2008, a week after the pivotal collapse of Lehman Brothers, the board of Goldman Sachs met hurriedly to consider an offer that might help the firm avoid the fates that its competitors were suffering as securities books plummeted in value. Warren Buffett was offering to give Goldman a cash infusion by buying a $5 billion ownership position in the firm, on terms highly favorable to Buffett.

As soon as the Goldman board discussed Buffett's offer and decided to accept it, Gupta picked up the phone and called Rajaratnam at Galleon. Immediately after getting off the phone with Gupta, Rajaratnam started telling his people to "buy Goldman Sachs, buy Goldman Sachs," and to do it fast before the market closed for the day. When the Buffett news hit the market the next day, Goldman's stock went up and the value of Galleon's stake in the firm increased by a hefty $1.2 million.

Gupta of course had no idea that Rajaratnam had by then become a lead target in an investigation of insider trading on Wall Street that had already produced numerous witnesses and leads, as well as wiretaps. The government had been listening to some of Rajaratman's phone calls. While that wiretap did not cover the call with Gupta after the board meeting, it caught Rajaratnam telling another person, "I got a call at 3:58 right? . . . Saying something good might happen to Goldman. Right?" A $1.2 million phone call.

A month later, the pattern repeated. This time Gupta let Rajaratnam know that Goldman was about to announce poor earnings results so Galleon could dump Goldman stock. Again Rajaratnam was recorded, this time telling someone, "I heard yesterday from someone who's on the board of Goldman Sachs, that they are going to lose $2 per share." Rajaratnam avoided almost $4 million in losses by unloading Galleon's Goldman positions in advance of this bad earnings news. Another quick and very lucrative phone call, courtesy of Rajat Gupta.

This was a clear and egregious case of insider trading. The jurors at Gupta's trial in 2012, who said they had looked for but could not find a way to acquit him, understood that their decision would destroy a great American success story.[4] Gupta—betraying the principles of trust and confidence on which he had built his career and grown the McKinsey firm—listened to blockbuster market news in his capacity as a board member at Goldman and then passed those secrets along to a wealthy man in the hedge fund business so that man could get a bit wealthier.[5]

Even more incredibly, Gupta did not profit by a penny from his corporate betrayal. The prosecution's theory was that Gupta had been cultivating his relationship with Rajaratnam as part of a push to break into the highest reaches of the hedge fund and private equity world—to ascend into the domain of the billionaires.

Judge Jed Rakoff, no stranger to the world of white collar crime, had the job of imposing sentence on Rajat Gupta. Rakoff used to prosecute business crime in Manhattan. He also defended corporations and their managers as a partner at a big New York firm. And he has written and spoken a great deal on the subject. Indeed, it was Rakoff who made waves with a cutting essay in the *New York Review of Books*, while sitting as a federal judge, questioning why the Justice Department had not prosecuted more bankers following the 2008 financial crisis.[6] Rakoff is a product of what we examined in the last two chapters: the American legal profession's corporate crime industry.

As we'll discuss, all criminal sentences in federal court since 1987 have been subject to a set of laws called the United States Sentencing Guidelines. For a long time, the guidelines were mandatory in almost every federal case. Since 2006, they have been advisory only. But these rules provide the starting point for every federal criminal sentence. The guidelines in Gupta's insider trading case called for a sentence of between 97 and 121 months imprisonment—eight to ten years—largely based on the amount of money that Rajaratnam's fund made from trading in Goldman stock around Gupta's leaks. There is no parole in the federal system; a ten-year sentence translates into at least eight and a half years served, even for the inmate who earns every possible credit for good behavior.

The prosecutors argued that Gupta held "extraordinary positions of privilege and prestige," including his Goldman board seat, and therefore should be punished severely. A crime like this committed by a person of Gupta's station, they said, "fuels cynicism among the investing public that Wall Street is rigged."[7] A punitive sentence, they contended, can help defuse that cynicism. Gupta's leaking of inside information to Rajaratnam was aggravated, the prosecutors said, by the leverage it potentially created in the market given the size of the Galleon fund. The prosecutors also described insider trading as difficult to detect and highly lucrative. Therefore, they contended, a long sentence in Gupta's case was necessary to deter others who might be tempted to commit similar offenses.

Any good lawyer for a white collar defendant will put forward, at sentencing time, a robust story about the defendant's charitable works, reputation in the community, and family and social ties. These presentations commonly include dozens or even hundreds of letters from reputable, caring, and prominent people—everyone from orphans, schoolteachers, and grandmothers to clergy, mayors, and law enforcement officers. The experienced judge can grow weary of such presentations.

Rajat Gupta's sentencing materials were extraordinary, even by the over-the-top norm for this style of litigation. They included dozens of stories about people's lives Gupta had saved or helped through unsolicited and largely quiet or even anonymous financial and emotional support. Gupta's lawyers were able to write to Judge Rakoff, without risk of hyperbole, "We have not found any case comparable to this one, in which the defendant can point not only to a significant expenditure of time and effort [on charitable works], but further, that he or she was involved in founding and helping to sustain major initiatives improving and in some cases saving millions of lives." The defense lawyers asked the court to treat this insider trading case as extraordinary and to disregard the severe imprisonment recommendation of the sentencing guidelines. They suggested that the court place Gupta on probation with a requirement that he live in rural Rwanda and devote himself to a program to combat HIV and malaria for which Rwandan government and public health officials had requested Gupta's time and manual labor.

Judge Rakoff said he had the difficult job of balancing "polar extremes" in Gupta's case. Real prison was in store for Gupta, with no creative endeavors to work on global health projects in Africa. But it would be a lot less prison than the law recommended and the prosecutors sought. Instead of nearly a decade behind bars, Gupta would serve less than two years. Judge Rakoff said he had "never encountered a defendant whose prior history suggests such an extraordinary devotion, not only to humanity writ large, but also to individual human beings in their times of need." Still, Rakoff said, Gupta's crimes were "disgusting" and "a terrible breach of trust." The main purpose of a prison sentence for Gupta, Judge Rakoff said, was to make others "understand that when you get caught, you will go to jail," a message that no program of charitable-works probation—no matter how onerous and virtuous—could send.

We should think more about the decision that Judge Rakoff faced in sentencing Rajat Gupta. The case sharply presents some of the most fundamental conflicts in how to punish white collar crime. But it's also an exceptional case, in both the crime and the criminal. Let's add a more routine sort of case.

Michael Tomko

IN THE 1990s, Michael Tomko owned a plumbing contracting business in western Pennsylvania.[8] Mike the Plumber, as we might call him, worked mostly on construction projects and employed about three hundred people. His business was doing well.

Mike was not a fan of the federal income tax. When he got around to supervising the construction of a new home for himself in the mid-1990s, Mike decided to illegally treat the costs of the project as deductible on his tax returns. He had his subcontractors invoice their work on his home as if they were doing work on one of the job sites for Mike's plumbing business. Then he deducted those payments as expenses of his plumbing company. Mike evaded about $228,000 in taxes this way—a lot more than the vast majority of Americans pay annually in income tax but small potatoes by the standards of Wall Street crime. (There was also testimony that Mike had on occasion blurted out that his vacation home in Maryland "was a gift from Uncle Sam," but prosecutors were unable to document this further tax evasion.)

The IRS does not work quickly, not even (perhaps especially not) in criminal cases. Mike the Plumber, after pleading guilty to one count of tax evasion, came before a federal judge for sentencing in September of 2005. For his amount of tax cheating, and with credit for his guilty plea, the sentencing guidelines called for a sentence of between twelve and eighteen months in prison, with a fine of between $3,000 and $30,000. The judge did not send Mike to prison. Instead the court placed Mike on three years' probation, with the first year to be spent in home detention—the bracelet—in Mike's Pennsylvania house. The judge also ordered Mike to do 250 hours of service work in the form of post-Katrina rebuilding in New Orleans for Habitat for Humanity, and to pay a fine of $250,000, the highest financial penalty the court could legally impose above the amount recommended by the guidelines.

The judge explained that prison was not necessary in Mike's case because his crime was aberrant (Mike's only prior run-in with the law was for operating a boat while intoxicated) and victimless. He had a solid record of charitable work including building houses for Habitat. He showed remorse. And placing him in prison could put Mike's many employees out of work.

The prosecutors had not seen Mike's case this way. They rather extravagantly contrasted Mike's conduct to the patriotism of American soldiers serving abroad and, more pointedly, argued that detaining Mike in the home he built with his tax cheating would be to imprison him in a gilded cage.

The government appealed the judge's decision in Mike's case, arguing that the sentence was unreasonably lenient. And then something unusual happened in this ordinary case. After an initial decision rejecting the government's appeal, the federal court of appeals in Philadelphia, which is responsible for the federal trial courts in Delaware, New Jersey, and Pennsylvania, decided to redo Mike's case as an *en banc*, that is, as a decision of all of the judges on the court. Federal appeals courts do this only when they think they have a matter of high importance, and usually serious disagreement, before them. They rarely bother with an onerous *en banc* hearing when the issue is simply whether one judge got one criminal defendant's sentence right.

The facts of Mike's case seemed mundane: a prosecution of a plumber for using his contracting business to build himself a fancy house without paying the taxes on what was in effect personal income from his business. Garden-variety tax evasion. White collar crime but not corporate crime, or even business crime of any large scale. This federal appeals court—the Third Circuit—is no Podunk jurisdiction. It routinely deals with major cases of fraud, public corruption, organized crime, and violence that come from the federal trial courts in Philadelphia, Pittsburgh, Newark, Trenton, and Camden.

When they looked at the case, the appellate judges discovered that they couldn't agree on the most fundamental questions about punishing white collar criminals. The *en banc* court ultimately upheld the trial judge's probationary sentence. But the appeals judges sharply split. Their disagreement produced nearly eighty pages of published opinions.

The eight judges who voted to affirm the sentence said the trial judge acted within his rights and duty to make the judgment call of eliminating imprisonment and raising the fine. The federal sentencing guidelines are no longer binding law. And the law requires no more than that a judge's sentence be "reasonable," meaning, the appellate majority said, based on serious thought, not a whim or caprice.

They also agreed with the trial judge. Mike had no criminal record. He had done lots of charitable work for many organizations, including Habitat, and could do more such service as part of his sentence. He was wealthy enough to pay, and thus be hurt by, a large fine. And his many employees would lose their jobs if he went to prison.

Five judges dissented and would have made the trial judge impose a harsher sentence. The dissenters included Anthony Scirica and Dolores Sloviter, the court's two most seasoned judges, each of whom has served as chief judge of the court. The dissenting judges agreed with the prosecutors that home detention in this instance was particularly unseemly given that Mike's house kind of *was* his crime—a home, the judges noted resentfully, consisting of "an 8,000-square-foot house on approximately eight acres, with a home theater, an outdoor pool and sauna, a full bar, $1,843,500 in household furnishings, and $81,000 in fine art." Further, the maximum fine coupled with no incarceration created the appearance, they said, that Mike had bought his way out of prison.

This was, the dissenters said, the sort of case for which the federal sentencing guidelines were designed—motivated as they were to eliminate the punishment disparities and unjustified breaks for which white collar sentences were once notorious. Mike's employment record, his charitable work, the potential business losses that could follow his imprisonment, and his ability to pay a large fine were all facts, the dissenters said, that made Mike's case not different from those of most criminals, but the same as those of most criminal tax evaders.

Prison, Money, and White Collar Criminals

MOST YEARS when we talk about sentencing in my introductory criminal law course, I give my seventy-five or so students the facts of a Gupta or a Tomko case, with no law. Then I ask them to write on a piece of paper what punishment they would give. When I read through the pile of slips at the front of the room, the breadth of the range impresses me and, I expect, the students as well. "Probation." "Twenty years in prison." "Take all his money and ban him from Wall Street, plus six months in prison." "Life in prison." "Ten years." "Five years." "A huge fine and make him pick up trash on the interstate." And someone always writes, remembering that we read *United States v. Shawn Gementera*, a controversial case about the punishment of a mail thief in San Francisco, "Make him stand on the street wearing a sandwich board saying 'I committed insider trading' (or 'I cheated on my taxes')."[9]

Of course writing down a notional punishment on a slip of paper is not the same as being the judge who actually had to decide the future of Rajat Gupta or Michael Tomko. But I think my students' opinions reflect a reality about American attitudes toward white collar criminals. Our lack of consensus reflects our own internal ambivalence about the question.

It's easy for the guy on the barstool to say that Gupta and Tomko are clear cases and that both ought to be sent up the river. Damn those white collar criminals. They get away with so much and they have such advantages. It's high time we treated them like ordinary thieves and murderers. But then along comes a Gupta or a Tomko for sentencing, when all the reality of their lives and situations are put before the court in painstaking detail, and feelings get cloudier. Or even before that, at trial, where Gupta's jurors, a group of average New Yorkers not typically sympathetic to rich people who break the law, wished they could have acquitted him once they saw the fullness of his story. Ambivalence about punishment of white collar crime is unavoidable.

As we say in academic discussions of criminal law, punishment requires justification, especially the harshest form of punishment short of death, namely prison.[10] Punishment is not something a society ought to do unless it must. It's costly and it visits suffering on its objects: those who receive the state's penalties. In America—the twenty-first century's incarceration nation—we ought to appreciate that more keenly than anywhere else. This conclusion follows whether one is thinking in the utilitarian tradition of Jeremy Bentham—in which the threatened pain of punishment is meant to persuade people to refrain from crime—or in terms of the moral imperatives of Immanuel Kant—in which punishment of criminals is meant to impose on wrongdoers their just deserts.

Three basic arguments are available to justify imprisonment of the white collar offender, both as a general social project and in any particular instance, like Gupta or Tomko. Doing so might reduce the incidence of such crime at an acceptable cost. It might be necessary because those sent to prison deserve to be punished that way. Or it might be required by our commitments to equality under law. Let's consider each of these three kinds of arguments in turn.

The utilitarian case for imprisoning white collar offenders gets complicated. One might think that no kind of crime could be more congenial to arguments about deterrence. After all, this is truly economic crime. If the point of the crime is to make money and nothing more, then law should be able prevent the crime simply by pricing it high enough. A man like Gupta or Tomko, unlike many who fall into a life of street crime, has acquired social capital and therefore has a lot to lose if he goes to prison. The prospect of even a little prison might be enough to dissuade him.

But remember that prison must be justified because it is costly. The question is not whether prison deters white collar crime but whether it does so at acceptable cost—at marginally lower cost than the crime itself. In other words, is prison effective and *necessary*? Here we encounter Gary Becker, the University of Chicago economist who won the Nobel Prize in 1992, in part for having formalized with math what seems like a simple point: a fine is far cheaper to impose than a term of imprisonment, so a fine should always be preferred to prison when a fine is sufficient to deter crime.[11]

An implication from Becker's argument—one that his colleague Richard Posner, and others who write about law from an economic perspective, have argued—is that fines, not prison, ought to be the default punishment in white collar cases. Offenders like Gupta and Tomko generally have enough money to be fined.[12] The flip side of this point, some economists would contend, is that America's bursting-at-the-seams prisons are a natural result of the law's inability to deter street crime through fines. Most street criminals have nothing to levy a fine against: they are, in the economic jargon, "insolvent in relation to the optimal sanction."

There are, of course, several retorts to the Becker argument, even if we hold for the moment to the utilitarian method of reasoning that's concerned simply with deterrence and social costs. The idea that money is a universal, straightforward, and easily measurable instrument of deterrence—a clean common denominator for pricing crime—is an illusion. Consider Gupta and Tomko. A hundred thousand dollars is not the same for Tomko, the plumber, as it is for Gupta, the former McKinsey CEO and Wall Street investor. Becker's formula didn't account sufficiently for the *relative* utility of money to different people.[13] We all know the stories about how Wall Streeters ruthlessly compete over astronomical salaries and bonuses not so much for what that compensation can buy them but for how the numbers measure their standing relative to each other.

Then there is the house money point. If the wealth stake of the offender is the fruit of his big career play in the corporate world, whether directly traceable to crime or not, what does threatening to take it away do other than present him with the challenge of having to make the great American fresh start? Given a less than one hundred percent probability of being caught, the game of engaging in corporate crime would appear to be worth the candle if the highest price is simply getting wiped out. That's especially likely to be the corporate offender's thinking if the crime he's contemplating is the familiar one of committing fraud to conceal from investors and the public that his business has gone sour.

Finally there are the insights from psychology that qualify the story about rational economic decision making on which the arguments of the Beckers and Posners rest.[14] Let's use a simple example. Suppose, unrealistically, that the Justice Department and the SEC could set things up to ensure that out of all those who engage in acts of insider trading netting $1 million, one in five persons is punished. Thus there is a twenty percent chance of getting caught and convicted. Becker's theory, which formalized Bentham's classical insights, would say we can deter these acts of insider trading by setting the penalty for a $1 million offense at a fine of $5,000,001. This is really cheap to do because all it requires is that the government write something down about the law and make it publicly known. No need to build more prison cells or hire more guards.

But deterrence is a question of prevention. It turns not on what actually happens in the legal system but on what the inside trader *thinks* will happen. If he's a bullish, risk-taking kind of guy—not a strained assumption when it comes to this crime—he might think that the probability of being caught is much less than twenty percent. If so, the law has to set the fine much higher. If he thinks he has a one percent chance of being caught, the fine must be $100 million plus a dollar, and he must have that much in the bank. At a certain point, the necessary fine will reach a level at which even our Wall Streeter can no longer pay and thus the fine will run out of deterrent bite. You can't fear losing what you don't have.

Of course, in the real world the SEC and Justice Department cannot calibrate a twenty percent probability of punishment. No one actually knows the chance of getting caught. Remember that while we can count the number of insider trading prosecutions, we don't have any idea how many instances of insider trading there are in the world. There is no denominator for a probability calculus.

We could keep going on this line of reasoning. (The academic literature certainly has.) The point is that basic social welfare analysis resolves neither the case for, nor the case against, using prison as the usual sanction for the white collar criminal. The case against has a good point about the costs of prison, the handiness of fines as a deterrent, and the idea of this being all about money anyway. No doubt that's a big part of what Mike the Plumber's judge was thinking when he chose probation but then set Mike's fine at the maximum allowable amount. But the case in favor of prison also does a good job of complicating whether fines are ordinarily, or ever, scary enough to dissuade the business criminal.

Alas, the matter of prison does not get simpler if we set aside the methods of utilitarian analysis—whether by our own tastes or out of frustration with its limitations—in favor of thinking about just deserts. In other words, we might be tempted to think that if a business criminal like Gupta or Tomko deserves to suffer the pain of imprisonment, then that imperative of justice could moot the difficult question of whether prison is necessary to deter the next Gupta or Tomko. (Much less the vastly more difficult question of *how much* prison might be sufficient to get that message across.)

Arguments about blame for wrongs have a kind of sharpness that can make them alluring. That's because these arguments are hard to deconstruct—though scholars have for centuries tried—beyond the moral intuitions from which they spring.[15] "It's just not right that Tomko gets to stay in his house and doesn't have to go to prison." "His tax cheating was wrong and he deserves to suffer more for it than that." "I pay my taxes but he didn't; that's not fair." And so on.

When we say someone deserves punishment for a crime, usually a mix of two things motivates us: what she did and what she was thinking while she did it. All else equal, crimes are worse the more tangibly they hurt other people. The drunk driver who kills is more blameworthy than the one who is pulled over and has his license yanked before any accident occurs. Also, all else equal, crimes are worse the more the offender displays morally abhorrent thinking in committing the offense. Between two (plenty guilty!) drunk drivers caught in a police dragnet, the recidivist who pounded half a case of beer and said "I love to drive wasted" before grabbing his keys is more blameworthy than the one who didn't say no to a second bottle of wine at dinner and mistakenly judged himself as below the legal limit. Assessments of moral desert for our wrongs to each other turn on how the wrongdoer's conduct does, or could, *affect* other people—*and* on how the wrongdoer *thought* about the effects of his behavior on other people.

The trouble, of course, is that crimes and the people who commit them present a limitless diversity of facts. Most cases involve complicated mixtures of harm to others and wrongdoer thinking that point in varied directions on the question of just deserts.

Take a chestnut of a problem presented in many introductory courses in criminal law. It involves two unrelated killers, Ronnie Midgett of Arkansas and Clyde Forrest of North Carolina.[16] Both killed family members, as is sadly the case in a great portion of America's homicides.

The three-hundred-pound Midgett (real name) beat his own helpless forty-pound child, over and over, until the child was at death's door. The boy's ten-year-old sister testified as the state's chief witness in the prosecution of her father for killing her brother. In these serial beatings, the coroner said, one of Midgett's many blows eventually precipitated the child's death.

Forrest's father was dying in a hospital and Forrest couldn't bear to see him suffer anymore. Forrest got his handgun, loaded it, brought it to the hospital, walked past the nurses into the room, and shot his father four times in the head, killing him. He then dropped the gun and waited for the police to arrive. "You can't do anything now. He's out of his suffering," Forrest said.

Pretty much everyone agrees, when they read this pair of cases, that Midgett is morally worse than Forrest. Under the law in these cases, as in many states, however, Forrest was guilty of the more serious form of homicide. In states that distinguish between first- and second-degree murder, the law says that it's morally worse to plan to kill someone (to "premeditate and deliberate") than to do it in the moment. Forrest planned. Midgett did not. Grotesquely, Midgett might have preferred that his victim go on living. Forrest thought long and hard, however misguidedly, about how he might ensure that his victim would no longer suffer.

In white collar crime, questions about harm to others and about morally faulty thinking are more complicated—whether we're trying to assess the blameworthiness of a business crime standing alone, or are trying to compare it on the same dimensions to other forms of crime. Let's go back to Gupta and Tomko.

With Gupta's crime, as with most insider trading, it's hard to specify the harm. There are no victims to name or even a discrete class of victims to describe. In the huge, liquid, faceless market for Goldman Sachs stock, people who bought or sold shares on the same days Rajaratnam bought or sold got nothing more or less than that day's market price. That price, which was a product of abundant public information and opinions about Goldman Sachs's prospects, would have been about the same, maybe exactly the same, had Rajaratnam stayed out of the market. The way modern securities markets work, one might have a hard time even tracing Rajaratnam's transactions to identifiable human counterparties.

Insider trading harms others by eroding confidence in markets, discouraging capital from entering the market, and ultimately making capital markets less efficient and productive. We all do better, in theory, when these markets are robust. No one wants to venture his money in a rigged game. A market with insider trading, or enough of it, starts to look fixed. Seen this way, the harm from Gupta's crime is impossible to measure, at least in numbers. The few trades he helped Rajaratnam with were a drop in an ocean. But the participation in any amount of insider trading in Goldman Sachs stock by a member of Goldman's own board could be highly corrosive to investor confidence.

So much for harm as a clear measure of moral blameworthiness. On the dimension of thinking, Gupta's case remains a puzzle. Greed, in some form, must be the explanation. There is no other discernible reason for Gupta to have wanted to help Rajaratnam pad Galleon's profits. Though Gupta made nothing from Rajaratnam's trades,

Gupta perhaps hoped his tips would curry favor with a man who could help him attain entry into higher levels of the hedge fund business. Or so the prosecutors argued.

The moral fault in Gupta's thinking, while still opaque, can probably be described as a willingness to violate important trusts placed in him by virtue of his high position in the corporate world, all for the selfish purpose of improving the prospects of his own portfolio. Helping someone else cheat the market is blameworthy. It displays a refusal to be bound by the rules for getting along and trusting one another that the majority who play by those rules have agreed to follow. Indulging in that exceptionalism is especially blameworthy for a man in Gupta's position. So most people (though far from everyone) would agree that Gupta's case warrants at least some prison.

In Mike the Plumber's case, the harm his tax evasion caused can be measured two ways. One measure is the loss of revenue to the government and the costs that loss, and the job of chasing it down, imposes on the public. We all collectively bear the federal budget. Of course, the cost in a little case like Mike's is so minute in the vast American taxation system that it is hard to say Mike's tax evasion hurts us much. Perhaps the real harm from what Mike did is an erosion of confidence in the fairness of taxation and the willingness of others to play fair. It is, after all, a fact that even though the IRS is ridiculed and despised, most Americans voluntarily pay their taxes in spite of the low risk of audit and penalty for shirking.[17] (Most of us W-2 wage earners have little opportunity to cheat, of course.)

Collective belief in the reasonable effectiveness of the tax system would seem to be critically important. Yet the government pursues so few cases like the prosecution of Mike that one can question whether unprosecuted tax evasion does anything to undermine general compliance with tax law. Some researchers have pointed to the irony that the government might want to keep the number of tax prosecutions— which, unlike the total amount of tax *cheating*, are observable—fairly low, lest the public conclude that tax evasion is rampant.[18] This has been described as avoiding the "chump effect": people who wouldn't otherwise cheat will do so to avoid feeling like a chump.

The argument for retribution against Mike the Plumber is stronger when concerned less with harm to others and more with the thought process of the offender. Mike did a really selfish, greedy, and underhanded thing. He chose to exempt himself from the general rules about taxes that all of us hate but most of us dutifully follow. He hid what he was doing behind false invoices so his bad behavior wouldn't be discovered. And he did it so he could live in a bigger house with more bling. All the while, he knew he was committing a crime. How else than imprisonment, one might ask, can we send Mike the right message about how wrong he was?

Even if one agrees with this view, the question, as with Gupta, remains how much prison is necessary to deliver the required amount of retribution. And it's inevitable that, once we begin to ask this more precise and fraught question about measuring punishment (what lawyers call the question of proportionality in punishment), we reach for comparisons that might help us get a better fix on things. Those comparisons include not only other inside traders and tax evaders, as well as perpetrators of other white collar crimes, but also violent and other forms of street crime. The question of *relative* desert of punishment ends up pivotal in deliberating how long, if at all, a Rajat Gupta or a Michael Tomko must spend in prison.

Now we run into a paradox. There's no good way to talk about the relative blameworthiness of business crimes without comparing them to street crimes. But there is no algorithm or even theory to fix the relative blameworthiness of these different forms of crime, at least not at the interesting margins. Would it have been worse for Tomko to murder his wife than cheat on his taxes? Certainly yes, even if Tomko had a horrible story in which he had long been a victim of physical and emotional abuse. That's the easy case.

Would it have been worse for Tomko to have dealt drugs, or beat a man for fun outside a bar one night, or run a prostitution ring out of his plumbing business, than cheat on his taxes? I have no idea. And thus I, at least, can't say, from the standpoint of retributive argument, much more than that Tomko should not be punished like a murderer.

Gupta's case is even harder. As bad as murder, or perhaps some murders? Most people would say no way, though a few hard-liners might disagree. The prevailing view likely holds that if Wall Street fraud ever approximates the moral seriousness of taking human life, it is only in an extreme case like Bernard Madoff's, which included both callous thinking and devastating financial harm to a huge number of victims. Is Gupta more deserving of punishment for stealing secrets from the Goldman Sachs boardroom than he would have been for importing a few kilos of heroin on a corporate jet or seriously injuring someone while driving drunk? Again, these questions can be answered (for sentencing judges, of course, they must be), but I don't see a path to those answers other than through the gut.

Some white collar defendants do end up with murder-like sentences. Madoff received a sentence longer than the natural term of any human life. Bernard Ebbers of Worldcom and Jeffrey Skilling of Enron each received sentences in excess of twenty years without the possibility of parole, which is equivalent to a murder sentence in many states. Other offenders in business crime cases of all kinds, including insider trading, accounting fraud, obstruction of justice, embezzlement, health care fraud, bribery, and Ponzi schemes, have commonly received sentences of twenty, fifteen, ten, eight, five, three, two, one, and zero years in prison, and everything in between. That array of numbers is also routinely attached to cases of rape, assault, robbery, arson, theft, drug dealing, and extortion in the United States.

Martha Stewart served five months in prison, followed by five months of home confinement, for lying to the FBI to cover up possible insider trading.[19] Somebody who committed a relatively low-level drug offense almost certainly got the same sentence yesterday in some courthouse somewhere in America. The judges who select these sentences have no standard-issue slide rule on the bench that allows them to take a business crime defendant and find the equivalent arsonist or cocaine dealer against whom to measure the case.

The question of how to punish business crime proportionately isn't really, or at least not ultimately, a question about tweaking formulas to achieve optimal deterrence as a matter of social welfare, or precise retribution for those who deserve it. It is a question not so much about specific crimes and criminals as about crime in general: whether the American justice system treats people equally before law when it engages in its most coercive and powerful act, the imposition of criminal punishment. When we talk about the fair, right, or proportionate sentence for a business crime, we're often talking about equality.

A Fruitless Quest for Equality in Sentencing

PUNISHMENTS FOR white collar crime have been at the center of a four-decade-long conversation about American sentencing law. Before sentencing guidelines, the federal courts and most states had "indeterminate" sentencing laws.[20] That meant that punishments were flexible in one or both of two ways. Judges could select sentences from wide ranges, subject to almost no rules. And individual sentences could be expressed in ranges that deferred the question of the ultimate prison term to a parole board examining the case years later.

A federal law against robbery might have provided that the punishment be "up to twenty years in prison." Depending on her view of the particular offender and crime, a judge could impose probation, or twenty years imprisonment, or anything in between. A common sentence might have been five to ten years imprisonment, meaning that the defendant would serve at least five years and then the parole process would determine how many more he would serve after that.

In the 1970s and early 1980s—not coincidentally, in the wake of the civil rights movement and the overhaul of criminal procedure rights by Earl Warren's Supreme Court—a movement arose against indeterminate sentencing.[21] The primary argument against indeterminate sentencing was from equality. "Equal justice under law," the engraving on the Supreme Court, must require, at the least, that the severity of a convicted person's punishment not turn on the identity of the judge who drew his case, the location of the courthouse in which the prosecutor chose to file the charge, or the person's race, national origin, gender, or social and economic circumstances.

When reformers began to look harder at American sentencing,

primarily in the federal courts, the data were alarming. The same crime could receive different sentences depending on whether the offender was sentenced in Boston or Beaumont, by Judge Staunch or Judge Grace, or even before or after the holiday season. The difference between probation and prison for economic offenses in particular seemed to turn first and most on who imposed the sentence, where it was imposed, and on what day.

Two other ideas motivated the push to reform sentencing law. Again, white collar crime was central to both arguments.[22] Some people believed that sentences had become too lenient. Probation and community service were perceived as the default American punishments for better-heeled defendants. That perception was corrosive to the legitimacy of the justice system. Greater toughness was in order, and Republicans and Democrats agreed on that. Another important idea was that criminal justice scholars in the 1960s and 1970s came to agreement that the programs twentieth-century governments had deployed to rehabilitate criminals hadn't worked. In a related vein, some argued that parole systems damaged legitimacy because observers would conclude that the punishments judges announced at criminal sentencing hearings were never the "real" ones that offenders served.

This movement culminated in a wholesale reform of the law of federal sentencing, and the pursuit of similar reforms in many states. New elaborate guideline systems for sentencing were severely *determinate*.[23] Their algorithmic calculations and detailed punishment grids virtually dictated to judges the sentences they were required to impose in most cases. The federal parole system was abolished. From now on, there would be "truth in sentencing." It would be mechanical, predictable, and *legalized*, to an extent only American law could aspire toward. The big value judgments about relative punishments would be made by an administrative agency (the United States Sentencing Commission), not case by case among hundreds of judges who couldn't agree on anything.

This was a progressive reformer's project about equality in the administration of justice. The work product emanated from Ted Kennedy's Judiciary Committee staff, including a lawyer working for Kennedy named Stephen Breyer. The vision was for an elegant body of law that would treat like cases alike. The drafters disavowed any agenda to decide value questions about degree of punishment for specific offenses. They set up the system so it would derive its results from baselines derived by averaging federal judges' actual past sentences.

But frustration with the appearance of leniency, especially for white collar crimes, and especially in relation to street crimes, was always a major motivation for reforming American criminal sentencing. After all, this movement came to fruition in the 1980s—precisely when the great American crackdown on the crime boom of the 1960s and 1970s was gaining momentum.

Whether with foresight or not, the federal reformers had built a system that could ratchet up punishment: a powerful Sentencing Commission, the specificity of the rules, the absolute bindingness of the system on judges, and more power to appellate courts to reverse trial judges' sentencing decisions. For the next three decades, between the early 1980s and the early 2010s, the ratchet turned and the federal prison population grew, by a factor of nearly *ten*. The actual sentences judges imposed got longer. And because potential sentences on the books were both longer and more predictable, plea bargaining dominated over trials.[24]

Nowhere in federal criminal law did the ratchet turn more than in drug and white collar cases.[25] Increased harshness in drug cases (and later in immigration cases) explains much of the growth in the federal prison population. Depending on which offenses one includes, defendants in white collar cases still represent only about ten percent of the federal prison population. But both notional and actual sentences for serious cases of business crime have increased exponentially since the 1970s.

Some of this was the inevitable, and intended, result of adopting legally binding sentencing guidelines. More of it came when Congress repeatedly instructed the sentencing commission to toughen punishments for business crimes in the wake of financial scandals.[26] Both the post-Enron Sarbanes-Oxley bill and the post-2008 Dodd-Frank law included measures designed to punish corporate criminals more severely.

Whether one looks at examples or the overall picture, sentencing of business offenders in the federal courts has become a far harsher affair. Consider the case of James Olis, who became an emblem for arguments that things had gone too far.[27] Around the time of the Enron affair, Olis worked as a salaried tax manager at Dynegy, another Houston-based energy company with a lot of natural gas interests. Olis helped structure a financing deal in which Dynegy was able to borrow about $300 million but for accounting purposes treat the money as operating income, thereby improving its financial health in the eyes of investors. The prosecutors established at trial that Olis and others at Dynegy hid key facts about the deal structure from Dynegy's auditors at Arthur Andersen—facts that the auditors said would have led them to refuse to approve Dynegy's recording of this $300 million as business income rather than debt. When the facts came out, Dynegy had to "restate" its earnings, that is, file a document with the SEC showing worse financial results than it had originally disclosed to the market. Its stock then went down, as almost always happens with such earnings restatements.

Olis, a thirty-three-year-old professional with no criminal record, broke the law to help his company. No benefits went to Olis from this one deal other than the maintenance of his existing position (and thus salary) and perhaps better prospect of promotion down the line. Applying the sentencing guidelines, a federal judge in Houston sentenced Olis to 292 months in prison. Twenty-four years! The main fact driving the sentence was the amount by which Dynegy's stock declined when the bad news came out. Multiplied by the large number of shares outstanding in such a big company, the "loss" to victims from Olis's fraud, in the form of Dynegy's reduced market capitalization, was easily over $100 million.

The designers of the sentencing guidelines chose dollar loss as the common denominator to get to equality in punishments for all economic crimes in federal court. Over time, legislators and administrators had increased the number of points assigned for various levels of monetary loss in order to stiffen sentences for financial crimes. The predictable result was sentences in cases like that of James Olis: murder-like punishments for first-time offender tax accountants who stepped over the line trying to please their bosses.

Under the guidelines as written at the time of Olis's case, a reasonable application of the rules could arrive at a sentence of *life imprisonment without parole* for a senior executive of a Fortune 500 company in which revelation of accounting fraud caused a substantial drop in the market capitalization of the company.[28] In ten years as a federal prosecutor, the only defendants I saw sent to federal prison never to return were men who killed multiple human beings in order to promote extensive narcotics businesses or organized crime empires. Come to think of it, there *was* one nonmurderer: a notorious Brooklyn criminal whom we subjected to the life sentence of the federal "three strikes" law when he brutally raped a witness's girlfriend to discourage the witness from testifying against him; his many prior convictions included the armed robberies of an entire New York City transit bus and of the congregation at his mother's church.

Not surprisingly, federal judges often found ways to avoid imposing on white collar defendants the kind of sentence that James Olis received. Indeed, Olis's lawyers persuaded an appellate court to send his case back for resentencing because the judge had not considered carefully enough arguments that other market forces depressed Dynegy's stock price along with revelation of the fraud. Olis was resentenced to a still stiff six years in prison, although in the interim the law also had changed in his favor and allowed the judge to depart from the sentencing guidelines. I know of no corporate fraud case (as opposed, say, to a Ponzi scheme like Bernie Madoff's) in which a court has actually imposed a sentence of life without parole.

Meanwhile, as federal sentences went from lenient and higgledy piggledy to harsh and wooden, a counterrevolution against the sentencing guidelines, again based on arguments about both drug and white collar cases, gained momentum. The movement started among federal trial judges, especially the more senior ones, almost as soon as

Congress enacted the guidelines in 1987.[29] From their perspective, the value of individualized judgment far outweighed the benefits of rigid equity in sentencing. They hated being forced to impose long punishments on people who, prior to the guidelines, they would have been permitted to treat as candidates for mercy. The mom who smuggled drugs to support her kids or avoid abuse at the hands of a partner. The kid who stupidly agreed to courier a small amount of drugs for a network that turned out to be much bigger than he had thought. And, yes, the accountant without a criminal record who fell under the sway of corporate peer pressure.

This counterrevolution strengthened as the cumulative results of federal sentencing reform became apparent. Academics, some appellate judges (including some Supreme Court justices), people worried about booming prison populations, and even some members of Congress began to see the trial judges' point.[30] The success of the sentencing guidelines in rigorously imposing equal prison on federal defendants was becoming the project's greatest weakness.

Then, in the space of a few decisions over about six years—more or less out of the blue as constitutional law goes—the Supreme Court struck the whole thing down.[31] The constitutional law of this has to do with the Sixth Amendment right to jury trial. The Supreme Court politics of it—shifting alliances among reform-minded liberal justices and the originalist theories of Justices Scalia and Thomas—are inside baseball. Neither subject need divert us.

Whatever the legal rationale, it was clear that the justices had heard their lower-court colleagues. The Court's decision, in form at least, returned to the trial judges the sentencing discretion that Congress had taken away. The "guidelines," which had been strictly binding law, would henceforth be "advisory" only—thus bringing them into conformity with the Pirate's Code which, as Geoffrey Rush's character in *Pirates of the Caribbean* explained, "is more what you would call guidelines than actual rules."

So is 1970s sentencing back in style? Are we headed back to the old days of routine probation and community service for white collar offenders in federal court? It should not be surprising that the answer is no. The judiciary may have succeeded in throwing off the shackles of overly determinate sentencing laws. But, along the way, federal judges appear to have been persuaded that Americans were right to think that the lenient white collar sentences of the mid-twentieth century don't belong in a justice system for the twenty-first-century corporate world.

Anyone who maintains that individual business criminals today are routinely getting off with the clichéd slap on the wrist is misinformed.[32] While white collar crimes still draw lower sentences overall than violent and drug crimes, the directional arrows have been moving opposite to common beliefs. Between 1996 and 2011, the mean fraud sentence in federal court (that includes every fraud from Enron to the fellow in Dubuque who passed a bad check) nearly doubled, from over a year in prison to nearly two years in prison. During the same period the mean sentence for all federal crimes *dropped* from fifty to forty-three months. Federal drug trafficking sentences have declined by thirteen percent since 1996.

Here is a more vivid way to look at punishment for business crime— an unscientific but more telling view. Every two weeks, Bloomberg publishes a thorough online trade journal called the *White Collar Crime Report.* It includes blurbs and stories about almost all major white collar investigations and prosecutions. A law student and I selected an arbitrary eighteen-month period in 2011 and 2012 and counted the serious sentences for business crime. During that year and a half, federal judges imposed 187 criminal sentences on white collar offenders that included five years or more of prison time. The mean term of imprisonment in those 187 cases was twelve years in prison. A term of ten years or more in prison was imposed in nearly half (84) of the 187 cases. The mandates of the sentencing guidelines may be gone, but judges are sentencing dozens and dozens of financial offenders to a decade or more in prison.

After the long effort to prosecute Enron's CFO, Andrew Fastow, he agreed to plead guilty and testify for the prosecution. Fastow's plea agreement called for him to serve ten years in prison, no matter what he did or how his testimony went at trial. Not long ago, that sort of sentence would have been unthinkable for a senior executive of a Fortune

10 company, even *without* credit for cooperation and testimony. We the prosecutors knew that we'd be criticized for "cutting a deal" with the "mastermind" of the Enron fraud and that the trial defendants would attempt to lay the whole crime at Fastow's feet. His punishment had to be serious and certain. The stiff guidelines and the harsh trends in federal white collar sentencing at the time empowered us to persuade Fastow's lawyers to recommend that he take the onerous plea agreement. (It was bad for the Enron victims and for future prosecutions that, long after the Enron trial, a federal judge in Houston reduced Fastow's actual sentence to five years, in part because of the acquiescence of a successor prosecutor.)

Where judges are pushing back against the trends of the last few decades in white collar sentencing is on the idea that all frauds are alike and can be measured simply by dollar loss to victims. Consider the case of Richard Adelson, who was the chief operating officer of Impath, a cancer diagnosis company.[33] Adelson was convicted of participating, as a relatively minor player late to the game, in a scheme to boost Impath's stock price by overstating the company's earnings. The sentencing guidelines called for the forty-year-old Adelson to spend the rest of his life in prison with no chance of parole, in part because prosecutors calculated Impath's loss in market capitalization, after it corrected its reported earnings, at $260 million. Although the prosecutors wouldn't come right out and say it, even they signaled to the judge that enforcing the guidelines in Adelson's case would be, as the judge said, absurd (if not also barbaric). The judge set the guidelines aside and sentenced Adelson to three and a half years in prison.

Or there is the pair of cases another New York trial judge wrote about in 2010.[34] Fraud defendants Aisha Hall and Isaac Ovid, whose cases were unrelated, came before Judge John Gleeson for sentencing on consecutive days. In each case, the guidelines called for very stiff sentences, based primarily on the dollar loss involved in the two cases: between twelve and fifteen years in prison for Hall and between seventeen and twenty-one years for Ovid. In the end, Judge Gleeson sentenced Hall to ten years in prison but Ovid to only five. He wrote at length to explain how the texture of the wrongdoing differed greatly in the two cases, in ways that had nothing to do with the roughly equivalent dollar amounts. Hall's scheme, which involved phony "proof of funds" letters and bribes paid to bank employees, was brazen and "one hundred percent fraudulent" from the start. Ovid's fraud stemmed from his creation of a legitimate investment fund to help the minister and congregants of his church. When the fund began to fail, Ovid had compounded the damage to everyone by resorting to fraud in a doomed effort to prop it up.

Even the United States Sentencing Commission has recognized that its guidelines for financial crime cases need more flexibility. Recent proposed reforms would stop treating the loss in market capitalization as the primary measure of the seriousness in frauds involving publicly traded companies.[35] The American Bar Association has drafted a detailed proposal for reforms to the guidelines in which dollar loss would be only one of several measures in cases of economic crime.[36]

The sentencing of white collar crimes in the federal courts is by no means back where the debate started in the 1960s and 1970s. But the quest for rigid equity in punishment, as with many other areas of crime including drug cases, now appears to have been a failure. Aside from what it can teach about law reform projects, the guidelines experience is powerful evidence for the claim that the principal question of how much punishment business criminals deserve may be exceedingly difficult if not impossible to settle. Largely that's because we are, for good reasons, ambivalent between "a lot" and "not too much," and especially on how to translate those feelings into the hard currency of days, months, and years.

Doubling Down on America's Incarceration Binge

SOME PEOPLE think that business crime isn't as serious a thing as street crime and that white collar offenders generally shouldn't go to prison. Fines, professional debarment, and social censure are enough to deal with this sort of thing. For some, the line of thinking extends to questioning whether a lot of this stuff—insider trading, playing games with accounting rules, using bribery to get business done in corrupt countries—ought to be criminal in the first place.

I doubt such beliefs are widely shared. They're mostly confined to the economics departments and management schools of certain universities, libertarian and right-leaning think tanks like Cato and Heritage, lobbying groups like the U.S. Chamber of Commerce, and perhaps hushed executive dining rooms, jet cabins, and golf club locker rooms. Not even the lawyers who defend corporations and their executives really think this, even if they might occasionally say it when working for clients.

As much of this book has set out to establish, Americans take corporate crime seriously because corporations—and the harms people do with the powers and influence those institutions confer—are a matter of genuine social and political concern, even urgency. In this chapter, however, we've seen that when it comes to punishing those who have been judged guilty of business crimes, something else is also motivating the American justice system. It's a motivation that, when pursued, inevitably leads to ambivalence.

That something is equality. The United States, like every large nation in history, remains full of divisions and troubles along the dimensions of class, race, and wealth. But the United States also takes its principles and ideals seriously and, when at its best, tries hard to get public institutions to follow them, nowhere more than in law. Equality and liberty are America's two primary ideals. So when we take away liberty, we very much want to think we do it equally.[37] Of course, we haven't done so. Not at all. The signature fact of America's criminal justice system in the early twenty-first century is massive and persistent inequality, especially on the dimension of race.[38]

However natural the desire is to punish harshly in circumstances where otherwise privileged people have been convicted of criminal offenses, application of law is supposed to be based on more than tit-for-tat reasoning. As we've seen in this chapter, when a judge, or even a jury, has to confront an actual person and an actual white collar crime, it gets much trickier to work out an argument about the justness of a given punishment. Moreover, a line of thinking that leads from the virtue of equality to "what's good for the goose is good for the gander" leads, in the end, to a perverse result: the cure for America's incarceration binge is more incarceration.

Mine is definitely *not* an argument for sparing corporate criminals from the jail cell. My objective has been to demonstrate why punishment of business crime offenders is genuinely, and necessarily, an inconclusive project. If you think that the cure for America's anxieties about the problem of corporate crime is to administer more prison, down a rabbit hole you'll fall. Finding the right punishments for business offenders is a much harder job than commonly believed. And getting harsher is not going to change the problem of business crime. We've already tried that, with gusto. From available evidence, it hasn't changed much at all.

8

Washington and Wall Street

Visiting the chairman of the Federal Reserve is a bit like going to see the Wizard of Oz. When I went, on official business in 2002, the physical surroundings were what brought the Emerald City to mind. In those early days after the booming Clinton years, the chairman's job had not fully taken on the sense of the man behind a curtain. A walk through a hushed and Delphic building led to a huge conference room where we were seated for a few minutes before the chairman, all by himself, shuffled in through a side door. That man, of course, was Alan Greenspan. He was still at the height of his powers, holding forth engagingly with that glint in his eye and genuine Brooklyn accent.

My Justice Department colleagues and I were there to ask Greenspan about Enron. It was a few months after the company's stunning and historic collapse. We weren't looking for his economist's expertise on the question of how America's seventh largest corporation could have disappeared in a matter of weeks. We wanted to know whether one of the most powerful men in Washington—who happened to have recently accepted something called the Enron Prize from Rice University's James A. Baker III Institute for Public Policy—had taken a call from Kenneth Lay.

Greenspan could not have been more straightforward. (The man knows how to handle a question.) Lay had called him in late 2001, as Enron's troubles had exploded onto the front pages and the company was desperately trying to stave off bankruptcy. Lay talked about his company's problems and their potential impact on the markets. Greenspan listened, his job being basically to listen to the American economy. And he waited to see if Lay would come around to an "ask."

Lay never did. But Greenspan knew "to a moral certainty," he told us, that Lay called that day hoping that the chairman of the Fed would offer to help Enron, if for no other reason than a sense of obligation to the economy as a whole. Greenspan made no such offer, remaining impassive and letting Lay talk. With that, their call, and this Washington minuet, came to a close. Enron was permitted to go on collapsing. Greenspan could have had no idea that day (we should hope) that his overall body of work would make it immeasurably harder for his successor Ben Bernanke to cut short the frantic calls he received from CEOs six years later.

Early in the Enron investigation, this parlay with Alan Greenspan was repeated, less entertainingly, with a string of Washington players. We interviewed Donald Evans, who was George W. Bush's secretary of commerce (and former campaign chair), Tom DeLay, Senator Don Nickles of Oklahoma, Karl Rove, and even Dick Cheney. The statements of each painted a single picture, and the documents and subsequent investigation backed them up: when Enron hit the press as a scandal, Republicans in Washington weren't going to touch Ken Lay—who had been a sort of pre-*Citizens United* version of the Koch Brothers—with a ten-foot pole. As fast as his company went from adored to mocked, Lay went from Bush's "Kenny Boy," the favorite Republican fundraiser in Texas and one of the top nationally, to "Ken who?"

Only DeLay (R-TX, specifically Houston) showed some humor about being interviewed. Evans and Nickles in particular gave the impression that having to answer questions from prosecutors was downright odoriferous, despite our being employees of John Ashcroft's Justice Department. Ashcroft, by the way, had recused himself from oversight of the Enron investigation because he had taken contributions for a Senate campaign from Lay.

DeLay was hale and hearty when we arrived at his office on the Hill, only too happy to offer with a chuckle, "You know what they call me don't you?" The answer was, "DeReg." DeLay proudly explained how he championed deregulatory legislation that, it turned out, enabled Enron to steer its business out onto a financial and accounting limb. But, when Enron was failing, why would DeLay have helped a guy who was headed for obvious trouble with the criminal law? There was nothing for him in that. After all (he didn't come right out and say this, of course), what would Ken Lay be able to do for those in Washington now that Lay's reputation and his company were in ruins and his foreseeable future was nothing but lawsuits and maybe prison?

When Enron's collapse first saturated the national press over the holiday season of 2001 to 2002, the scandal gave off more than a whiff of being a Washington "gate." Maybe no one had committed a burglary or illegally traded arms for hostages. But the president of the United States' biggest fundraiser's company suddenly looked like a fraud. Then, on the night of January 25, 2002, one of Enron's top executives, who had been subpoenaed to testify before Congress, was found in his Mercedes in Houston, having shot himself dead. It's worth remembering that, before September 11 eclipsed everything and changed the president's political fate, Bush 43 was a barely elected and vulnerable president whose chief liability was public perception that he was corporate America's, and especially the energy industry's, man in Washington.

In the end, Enron was not a "gate." Despite years of effort from a team of career prosecutors and federal agents, no evidence surfaced of any improper help, or even contacts, going from Washington to Enron during the company's crisis. There was nothing to see other than the usual dispiriting story of legal campaign contributions, corporate lobbying, and deregulation. When Enron fell, Washington's power brokers wanted nothing to do with the Houston crowd. That sentiment was strongest in the White House, where the lawyers who opened the doors for career prosecutors to talk to anyone and everyone included some of the same people who had chased Bill Clinton over Whitewater and Monica Lewinsky.

In a sprawling investigation like this, a group of determined prosecutors with decades of combined experience from peeling apart organized crime, international narcotics trafficking, and fraud conspiracies are eventually going to catch people who are lying and covering up. (Consider, for example, the later pursuit by Patrick Fitzgerald, the Bush Administration's U.S. Attorney from Chicago, of Scooter Libby—and Dick Cheney's apoplexy about that investigation.) The truth almost always outs in these big cases. People get prosecuted, make deals, and testify, regardless of how intense and long-standing their loyalties may have been to friends and allies. As many have said, nothing focuses the mind like the prospect of a jail cell.

We were given extra resources, told to hire the best people, and encouraged to prosecute those responsible. The word was "let the career prosecutors do their thing." Dozens of Enron executives and employees were convicted of crimes, many of them "flipped" and testified for the government, and the most senior executives of the corporation were held to account in the end.[1] Meanwhile, the Bush Justice Department prosecuted top managers of numerous other large American corporations caught up in accounting and financial scandals, including Worldcom, Adelphia, Global Crossing, AOL, and Healthsouth.

Even with its flaws, missteps, and failings, the Justice Department is one of the strongest and most professional institutions of American government. The corporate cases of the early 2000s got made because career prosecutors usually follow the law and the facts and keep politics out of it. I would like to think—and I'm far from alone in the legal profession in this—that politicians, whether in the White House or anywhere else, will have a very hard time stopping a serious criminal case in the Justice Department simply because it doesn't serve their interests.

Of course politics rules Washington. The fact of the matter in the Enron affair is that no one *tried* to stop anything we were doing because, whether they could have succeeded or not, they had no reason to want to do so.

By contrast, later in the Bush Administration when Alberto Gonzalez was attorney general, the administration created a small scandal for itself when it appeared to interfere with the autonomy of some local U.S. Attorneys in the prosecution of political corruption cases.[2] Bush eventually brought in a former federal judge from New York, Michael Mukasey, to replace Gonzalez as attorney general and repair the damage to the Department's reputation for independence.

Bush's administration prosecuting Enron administered a strong shot of inoculation. I once noted to a colleague the irony of how the group assigned to investigate some of the Republican party's top fundraisers for corporate fraud could be referred to as the committee to reelect the president. (It was a further irony that most us were Democrats.) The comment was sardonic, of course. It seemed that any political benefit to anyone in Washington from the Enron prosecutions was a byproduct of what had to be done: don't stand in the way of law enforcement when really bad crimes have been committed, especially by your rich friends.

The Salve of Punishment

MANY PEOPLE who think about business crime in the United States see it as a matter of politics all the way down. Money buys influence and influence controls government. The Justice Department is no different than any other part of the executive or legislative branches. It responds to the agenda of its political and fiscal overlords in the White House and Congress. That agenda is set by a class of donors, fundraisers, and lobbyists who overwhelmingly represent the interests of corporations and corporate managers, especially in the financial services industry.[3]

Because the prosecution of business crime is bad for corporate managers, who are at risk of being on the wrong end of legal actions that can destroy reputations and careers, the argument goes, the Justice Department can be expected to go easy on corporate crime relative to other kinds of cases. Events of the last half decade or so are held up as evidence for this account.

Anecdotally, exhibit A is the lack of prosecutions of senior managers of financial institutions after the crisis of 2008. In terms of more granular data in recent years, Congress and the executive branch have devoted proportionally less funding to the prosecution of business crime, and more to the prophylactic effort against terrorism, than before.[4] The Obama administration created no major task force to prosecute cases in the banking industry and, following the collapse of the national housing market, brought far fewer cases than one might have expected for even garden-variety mortgage fraud. The Justice Department has continued, in both the Bush and Obama administrations, to settle the lion's share of corporate prosecutions with deferred prosecution and nonprosecution agreements rather than guilty pleas.

The argument is familiar in the public square, having been advanced strenuously, and occasionally angrily, by writers such as Matt Taibbi, Charles Ferguson, Gretchen Morgenson, Jeff Connaughton, Joe Nocera, Jesse Eisinger, and others who contribute to the pages of the *New York Times*, *New Yorker*, *Atlantic*, *Huffpo*, *New York Review of Books*, *Vanity Fair*, and other organs of the Acela corridor's center left.

It took getting Enron in the rearview mirror and years more of observation, especially the years around the 2008 crisis, for me to realize that the politics of prosecuting corporate crime involve more than worrying dynamics—they include interesting ironies and perverse incentives. As with many of the issues we've discussed, the relationship between politics and corporate crime is less simple and more revealing than many believe.

The focus on the banking industry and the years after 2008 has been myopic. There are of course the counterexamples of the Enron-era prosecutions and, as the Justice Department's recent critics so often note, the criminal cases following the crisis in the savings and loan industry in the late 1980s and early 1990s. There are also the many cases of business crime the government has prosecuted outside the banking industry over the same period, as well as significant post-crisis cases within the industry—including, as we've seen, ones involving banks' manipulation of interest rate and currency benchmarks and violations of international sanctions. It's not convincing to portray the criminal prosecution offices of the Justice Department over the last several administrations as soft on corporate crime, much less politically beholden to corporate criminals, especially if you compare prosecution activity in the business sector prior to 1980.

As explained in the second chapter, I think the lack of senior-level banking prosecutions after 2008 is principally a result of the legal and factual difficulties in treating those cases as criminal frauds and winning them at trials. Based on what we know about those cases, they lacked the straightforward and intentional deceptions that were found after investigators dug into cases like Enron and Worldcom. Of course, smoking guns might have been found if the government had pursued a limitless approach to finding them. But the search might also have come up dry, leaving a trail of failed cases, recriminations, charges of incompetence and overreaching, and howls about mistreatment.

The cataclysm of 2008 caused people to forget that between 2004 and 2007 the dominant narrative in the business press was of damaging and ill-conceived regulatory and prosecutorial overreach in the wake of Enron's collapse.[5] Any reopening or reversal of a prosecution on appeal, no matter what the legal ground, was held up as proof of this line of argument.

The Obama administration's approach to the banks was complicated, to say the least. And it absolutely was political. No doubt the prosecution of one of the surviving big banks itself, in the immediate aftermath of bailouts, would have been unthinkable to both the White House and the Justice Department, not to mention nonsensical, as we saw earlier.

Some have said the government shied away from investigating bankers for the same reason. But how could an individual prosecution of a bank official destabilize an industry? CEOs are replaceable, and are constantly replaced. More to the point, two narratives cannot both have been true: that Obama steered prosecutors away from bankers because he was beholden to the industry, and that Obama alienated the industry with his tame public criticisms (he made one reference in the heat of 2009 to "fat cat bankers") and jeopardized his reelection by causing a massive drop in the contributions he was able to extract from Wall Street.

There's a more complete, durable, and convincing explanation for Washington's relationship to the prosecution of corporate crime. It's also a simpler one. Corporate America prefers being prosecuted to being regulated. Companies and their managers would of course like the government to do neither. But they also recognize that public sentiment about corporate wrongdoing and corporate harms is a powerful, lasting force in American politics. While this sentiment ebbs and flows, it has been influential since at least the late 1800s and it persists today even if the modern system of campaign finance has grown, as some argue, to essentially corrupt Washington.[6]

When it comes time for American industries to pick their poison, criminal prosecution is to be preferred to regulation. That might seem counterintuitive. Prison is more serious than regulatory requirements and the fines for violating them. But the net effect of prosecutions on business, even if the government brought many more of them than it does, will remain far less costly to business than major programs of regulation. And, for corporations, the benefit of prosecutions is that they *displace* regulation. Punishing companies and people in the wake of a big corporate scandal—whether it be Enron, BP, GM, Exxon, Tylenol, the Ford Pinto, or any other—is an immediate, highly visible, and direct salve to the public's outrage at both corporations and the government.[7]

What could the populace want more than the harshest response law can deliver? The effect is to direct attention away from structural changes, including effective regulatory reform, and onto the project of punishment. Focus eyes backward and people won't look forward. Sacrifice a group of executives, maybe even a company or two, so that business can continue more or less as usual. In terms discussed in the first chapter, capitalize on the fundamental attribution error to divert attention from the institutional setting.

Consider again the example of Enron. The company's demise was a bolt from the blue that upended established assumptions. Before the sudden fall of Enron, the American accounting and financial systems—the institutional arrangements involving regulators, investors, lawyers, auditors, credit raters, and other stakeholders in the market for public corporations—were believed basically reliable. Or at least reliable enough that a top-ten corporation could not evaporate upon revelation that the firm fundamentally was not what even Wall Street experts believed it to be.

Such a crisis predictably leads to introspection and debate about law and institutional arrangements. Planes get safer after one crashes. Drugs get pulled from the market when they make people sick. Weapon regulations get debated (with little result, alas) when children are shot at a school. This is the predictable cycle of regulatory response in American politics and government.

Enron prompted similar discussion, in the popular media, in the corridors of Washington and Manhattan, and in universities and think tanks. One result was the Sarbanes-Oxley legislation, an important but eclectic set of reforms that still has abundant critics. The bill's legal reforms probably helped to at least slow a weakening of controls in the system of corporate accounting and financial reporting. Even the Sarbanes-Oxley bill, though, once looked to be doomed in Congress. The legislation was revived only when Worldcom imploded in even more spectacular fashion than Enron.[8]

In the reckoning over Enron and Worldcom, a story about bad apples crowded out one about systemic arrangements that had at least as much explanatory power as the frauds committed by senior corporate managers. The space left for discussion of reforms like Sarbanes-Oxley wasn't sufficient to keep that conversation going. The corporate auditing system needed to be brought back in line. But more fundamental questions about the stability of the American system of corporate finance were left unaddressed—with contagion and wider disaster lying less than a decade ahead.

The Enron cases contributed to this problem. Prosecuting Enron's executives made the case about a company victimized by craven managers who took advantage of opportunities to exploit, for personal gain, an institution that gave them access to massive flows of capital. They were greedy. And they did commit frauds. But lawful practices supported large parts of Enron's financing and were used to present a speculative company desperately short on solid assets as a strong reliable performer. Lax systems of regulatory and accounting controls, ones that Enron's own management helped shape through transparent and lawful political influence, made those financial practices available to Enron's executives.

The use of manipulable "mark to market" accounting—booking assets at the price for which the company believes they would sell—for energy trading products and other assets that had no objectively reliable prices was something Enron persuaded the SEC to permit. Such accounting practices continued to allow financial manipulations in the banking sector after Enron's demise.[9] Splurging on "off balance sheet" (i.e., largely invisible) financing by creating "special purpose entities" that had only tiny amounts of real equity in them was a practice that auditing firms like Enron's Arthur Andersen, doing the bidding of their clients, pressured regulators to allow.[10] Using huge prepaid forward (that is, circular) transactions with the megabanks Citi and Chase to transform ordinary borrowing, as we saw, into something the accountants could treat as operating income was a strategy the banks cooked up and sold to Enron, in return for fees.[11] These prepaid forward deals were one new financial product among many created during the 1990s, when the largest investment houses, turned from partnerships into public corporations, rushed into new areas of finance and created new ways to churn money to generate profits for their shareholders.[12]

These aspects of Enron's era—more than the temptation of executives to lie, conceal, cover up, or divert funds—metastasized inside the banking industry during the ensuing eight years and then decimated world GDP. As some observers (admiringly!) remarked at the height of Enron's reign in Houston, if you looked at the company's big move into new trading markets under the leadership of Jeffrey Skilling, a former McKinsey consultant, and Andrew Fastow, a former Chicago banker, Enron was really an investment bank, not a natural gas company.

It's too soon to say whether the post-2008 push for reregulation will repeat this story. Dodd-Frank is a more far-reaching legislative program than was Sarbanes-Oxley. A bigger crisis got a bigger bill. But the latest wave of reforms has faced abundant criticism for failing to address structural causes of the Great Recession and for setting up new regulatory fences that Wall Street will simply find ways to tunnel under or circle around.[13] Washington, it's said, didn't do anything about the American economy's systemic vulnerability due to dependence on a few bloated and still weak financial institutions. Another catastrophe is inevitable. Even as some critics have pressed that argument, others have contended that Dodd-Frank is a "job killer" and that some of the efforts to control banks' use of novel securities products should be scrapped.[14]

Notoriously, no wave of criminal prosecutions of corporate executives followed the 2008 financial crisis. I'm as outraged as the next person about what the banks, and their accomplice institutions, did with the housing and MBS markets. I only want to add two considerations to that discussion, both important and commonly overlooked.

First, it is undeniable that the exceedingly punitive and highly visible Enron-era prosecutions did not deter Wall Street managers from pursuing the excessively risky financing stratagems that Enron and its peers had used just a few years earlier. (Perhaps prosecutions even helped bank executives understand how to avoid the sort of direct involvement in transactions that can lead to criminal convictions.) Thus the caucus that insists that more Wall Street prosecutions would have made our economy safer needs to answer a question it rarely takes up: if the likes of Richard Fuld, Angelo Mozilo, or Maurice Greenberg were in prison right now, how exactly would today's Wall Street be different?

Second, the American political space does not have a limitless capacity to absorb debate about how to manage our economy and financial industry. A big criminal roundup of Wall Streeters involved in the massive MBS market might have made it *harder* to mobilize the American political system to reform financial regulation, at both the large institutional and consumer levels. Dodd-Frank gave us something on both scores, even if it's legislative sausage.

Yes, there were bad apples in the 2008 financial crisis. But the crisis was a problem of systemic not individual scale. The notion, whether explicit or subconscious, that our problems with huge profit-driven institutions would be solved if only those who manage said firms would stop being such bad people is quite misguided.

This understandable tendency to reach for punishment as an answer is a coping method that Americans have developed—one that legal scholars have called pathological—for our most intractable social problems. We keep looking to the criminal justice system to provide the knockout punch that other forms of legal and nonlegal control seem incapable of delivering.[15]

When the quantity of narcotics imported into and consumed within the United States keeps going up, we pour billions into a criminal law "war on drugs." At present, about 100,000 people—half the federal prison population—are in Bureau of Prisons custody for drug offenses. In 1980, albeit when there were thirty percent fewer Americans, the *total* federal prison population was less than 25,000 people, about the same as in 1940.[16]

When illegal immigration feels out of control, we use criminal prosecutions to bring it to heel. Over the decade between 2004 and 2014, the number of federal criminal immigration cases tripled, to nearly 100,000 per year. In 1993, there were fewer than 3,000 immigration prosecutions.[17]

Since the 1970s, America has deployed its criminal justice system in a huge and unprecedented program of social management. Major prosecution programs have failed to fix our problems. We've ended up with an embarrassing prison system, one without parallel in modern history. Now, on top of the problems we tried to fix with prisons, we have another serious problem: what do we do about the prisons? Naively, we stare at the numbers and wonder how we got here.

Small numbers of high-impact corporate prosecutions don't have anything to do with the great American incarceration problem. But becoming obsessed with the prosecution of business crime *is* a version of the American impulse to criminalize. While this preoccupation does not threaten to stuff our prisons, it does divert us from comprehensive policy efforts—in which criminal prosecutions would be an important but limited element—that we have also failed to pursue in areas such as drugs, immigration, guns, and domestic violence, to name a few.

Washington and the U.S. Department of Justice

THE POINT I've been developing doesn't only lead to a call for deeper and more sustainable legal reforms. We'll get to that. The point is *evidence* for the claim that the federal criminal justice machinery is not captured by political interests when it comes to business crime, at least not in the manner that cynics suppose. And the relative modesty of new regulations that are not criminal in nature, as well as the severe political resistance that comprehensive regulatory efforts encounter, show that economically influential forces in Washington see the Justice Department's role in the corporate economy as the lesser evil. The possibility of the occasional call from the prosecutor is preferred to the annoyingly persistent visits of the inspector.

Good politics for the corporate lobby in Washington is to be pro-growth and anticrime. When a big bill like Sarbanes-Oxley or Dodd-Frank comes onto the congressional agenda, the fight is about whether changes in regulation of corporate auditing, or executive compensation, or derivatives trading is going to "cripple" industry. Rarely does the business lobby attempt to push back on provisions in legislation that create new white collar criminal offenses or increase punishments for business crimes. Members of Congress are offered an appealing package: go ahead and be vocally supportive of tough laws and strict prosecution of crime in the business sector while remaining fully opposed to lasting programs of industry regulation. These twin stances give legislators a win-win with the public and the corporate lobby.[18]

The only recent exception that comes to mind is the fight in 2006 over what we discussed as outrage about the Justice Department's approach to the attorney-client privilege in corporate investigations like the KPMG case. That issue had nothing to do with industrial regulation. It had little to do, in the end, with the quantity or success of criminal investigations in the corporate sector. The strength of the corporate attorney-client privilege mattered most to the corporate lawyers. The *bar* was the one lobby that nearly, but still not quite, got Congress to pass a law about business crime that the Justice Department did not want.[19]

Now I would like to adopt—with one caveat—the arguments of the "fix campaign finance" caucus, whose most effective spokespersons include my fellow law professors Lawrence Lessig of Harvard and Zephyr Teachout of Fordham.[20] Washington is indeed bought and paid for. It is *legally* bought, by virtue of the American system of elections and private campaign finance. Money in American politics may well be, as scholars such as Lessig have argued, the key to unlocking nearly all intractable problems of social policy.

The overwhelming majority of that money, of course, flows into the political system from large industries, whether indirectly from firms and their lobbying operations or directly from individuals whose economic, and therefore political, interests are closely aligned with the agendas of large businesses. It's not complicated. New regulatory programs that make it more expensive to do business—and serious controls on industrial risk cost money—are very hard to carry over Washington's legislative and administrative hurdles. Meantime, rearguard actions must be fought to protect past regulatory programs, including some once seen as sacrosanct, from campaigns to dismantle them.

In recent years, I've watched a parade of my academic colleagues—some of the best experts in areas like environmental law, telecommunications law, intellectual property, constitutional law, and corporate regulation—wearily return to universities from inside the Beltway reporting that entrenchment, stasis, and cynicism are much worse than imagined. Some of them served tours of duty in previous decades. The ones who can see the comparative picture come home the most discouraged.

Our government must be capable of controlling the social costs that come with the benefits of an economy built around the large profit-seeking firm. If not, we may be doomed—to more economic crises or, given our problems in the area of energy and the environment, to worse fates. The institutions responsible for regulating industry—from the White House to the Congress to the state houses to the administrative state's EPA, FDA, FCC, SEC, and on through its alphabet soup—must function for the public good. At present, dysfunction is commonplace.

The problem is less evident in the criminal law offices of the Department of Justice. Prosecutors, especially federal prosecutors, have long enjoyed a degree of insulation from overt political interference that few institutions in Washington have. The Justice Department's mission is almost entirely to apply the laws, not to make them. The president's relationship to the Department is more like his job as civilian commander in chief than his role as political boss. That said, prosecutors are political. The attorney general and the United States Attorneys are, after all, presidential appointees subject to Senate confirmation. But the Justice Department is political more in the way that the Supreme Court is political than in the way that the Departments of Commerce or Agriculture are.

The American people are fortunate to have a "nation's law firm" that's still protected from politics, and from the vast monies that slosh around Washington, by norms of independence and professionalism that have endured since the early Republic and carry over from one administration to the next. When federal prosecutors, in the export controls case we discussed in an earlier chapter, told the French bank that the company must accept an onerous criminal settlement, French president François Hollande intervened to try to persuade the U.S. government to back off. BNP is France's most important financial institution. I imagine it might have been difficult for President Obama to explain to Hollande why, in our system, he couldn't exactly pick up the phone to Eric Holder and say, "I need you to stand down on the BNP prosecution. President Hollande is angry at me for not showing up at the *Je suis Charlie* rally and we owe him a favor."

No paid hand for an industry group is going to walk into a meeting about a potential criminal prosecution of a bank, for example, and say that Senator So-and-so is going to be angry and will give the president problems on something else if this case goes forward. My evidence is anecdotal, of course. But in ten years in some of the largest offices of the criminal prosecution components of the Justice Department, not once did I see or hear of a prosecution being quashed, at any level, by a word from politicians on high. An attempt to do so would be considered scandalous.

Of course money and influence still matter, and sometimes make a big difference, at the margins of this process. As we saw two chapters back, corporations and their managers have access to the best defense lawyers at top-shelf Washington law firms. That gives them an advantage in negotiations with Justice Department lawyers about how a criminal case will be resolved. The revolving door is real and contributes to a clubby atmosphere in this part of the bar, where federal prosecutors are viewed as aberrant if they approach a corporate case as ruthlessly as they might a prosecution of the Gambino family or an Al Qaeda cell. These dynamics, however, are far milder than the naked (and legal) arm-twisting that happens when, for example, the White House contemplates a new regime for regulating coal-fired power plants or Internet service providers.

Justice Department prosecutors are, to put it too cynically, among the few officials in Washington who still cannot be bought. That partly explains the impulse to criminalize and prosecute in response to intractable problems of corporate regulation. These are elite lawyers, by nature ambitious and creative, with a taste for big problems. They are drawn to cases that appear to have been left behind or allowed to fester by the inactions, inefficiencies, or incompetence of the regulatory state. If regulation of oil wells fails, prosecute the spiller when disaster strikes. If coal mines are not safe, prosecute for manslaughter when miners are killed. If Medicare and Medicaid regularly waste billions, prosecute the doctors who commit fraud. Use the tools you have at hand. Prosecutors don't have the formal authority or the political juice to initiate programs of law reform. All they can do is bring cases.

Here is the caveat about money in politics. The Lessig-Teachout school of argument insists that we must understand the entirety of what has become of campaign money and politics as a single problem of "corruption." They cast the problem in these terms because corruption is the word the Supreme Court has chosen as the pivot point for its First Amendment rulings in this area. To simplify, the Court has said the First Amendment protects all but criminal bribes of politicians: the government can prosecute bribery but it can't prohibit campaign contributions. Corruption, therefore, is the idea that Lessig and Teachout want the finance reform movement to redefine.

But criminal corruption is not the same thing as a political system that has been "bought" by money. We can't prosecute people for making legal campaign contributions. And people should not go to prison except for breaking clearly defined criminal laws. Whether or not efforts to reform the American system of campaign finance (and the constitutional law thereof) ultimately succeed, we'll always need limited and clear definitions of what counts as criminal corruption. The idea that the word "corruption," because of its etymology, includes anything that distorts good government is not an idea that can be used to draw a line between imprisonment and liberty. The difference between the activities of the Koch brothers and those of recently indicted Senator Robert Menendez of New Jersey is that the former can rhetorically be called corruption but only the latter can fairly be called criminal. This basic distinction must outlive even the most ambitious reshaping of how American law regulates the flow of money into politics.

America and its Corporations:
The Responsibility Deficit

THERE'S NOW an organized legal campaign to persuade American courts that, in a variety of contexts, corporations have the same legal standing and rights as people. These include the constitutional rights to free speech (including funding political campaigns) and even free exercise of religion.[21] The public discussion around this campaign reflects our uncertainty about how to relate to the corporation and the conflict between its legal structure, designed to separate it from its owners, and the reality that the corporation dominates American life. It's ironic that some of the same people who lambaste the Justice Department for failing to hold big corporations seriously accountable and the like are horrified that the Supreme Court has said that corporations have rights to speak and exercise religious faith.

Corporations are not people but they are the products of human ingenuity and enterprise. We created them as a vehicle for accomplishing things together that were harder to do alone or in small groups. We designed the corporation to encourage people to lend their financial and human capital to social and economic endeavors without having to fear ruin if a project goes bad. This was a brilliant innovation. It worked so well that we kept on encouraging it, with the result that corporations have now reached a scale and pervasiveness that place them in competition with the state for the position of dominant social institution.

The triumph of the corporate institution has given us much, including the miracle of humanity having produced a once unimaginable portfolio of technologies in less than two centuries. But the corporate age has left us with many problems. These include a problem of responsibility—of how to hold one another accountable for harms and wrongs—when they're committed within, and seriously enabled by, large nonhuman institutions that are designed to limit responsibility. The contemporary pattern of corporate crime prosecutions is evidence for the responsibility deficit, not its cure.

Our anxieties about the massive corporate sector, and the huge individual institutions within it, should lead our gaze away from the criminal justice system and towards broader and deeper perspectives on the corporation, including those first principles that created it. In 2013, the total revenues of the Fortune 500 companies were seventy-three percent of U.S. GDP. In 1994, that number was fifty-eight percent. Of 2013's seventy-three percent of GDP, sixty-three percent went to the Fortune 100 companies. Something's going on. Whatever the cause, the very large corporation is becoming a more, not less, powerful force among the institutions that comprise contemporary America. "Too big to fail" is too mild a way of describing the present state of corporate affairs.

Institutions, including corporations, are technologies. We make them. No natural order of things, not even the Constitution, requires us to live forever with any particular set of arrangements. In 1906, when the federal government was in the midst of its first efforts to regulate large national firms, the Supreme Court explained this in a plain manner that would look alien in the opinions in business cases of today's Court: "[T]he corporation is a creature of the state. It is presumed to be incorporated for the benefit of the public. It receives special privileges and franchises, and holds them subject to the laws of the state and limitations of its charter."[22] The Court said this while explaining why a corporation has no privilege under the Constitution, against self-incrimination or otherwise, to object to the state's demands that it produce evidence in aid of enforcing state or federal law.

To say that better regulation of corporations and financial markets is the real answer to corporate wrongs and harms borders on platitude, especially after a major national conversation about reregulating the finance industry after the collapse of 2008. It's not so much better regulation that we need—though we would benefit from that—as it is rethinking of the first principles of law and theory that apply to the largest and most influential sectors of our economy. At the least, better regulation will remain out of reach if better thinking does not come first.

For the last century or so, two ideas have occupied American law when it comes to dealing with the ill effects of otherwise lawful and beneficial industries. The first is the idea of "agency costs": that the managers of firms (primarily large public corporations) that are owned by others will tend to act against the interests of the owners when it is in managers' self-interest to do so. Managers, on this line of thinking, must be given ample legal and economic incentives to do what is good for the shareholders (the owners).[23] This idea gave us, among other things, modern stock option compensation and the institution of Delaware corporate law, the state that dominates the market for charters of incorporation.

The second idea is that, in the famous words of Louis Brandeis, "sunlight is said to be the best of disinfectants."[24] Information is seen as a cure-all in a capitalist economy. If people know what they're dealing with, they will vote with their feet and wallets. If corporate managers can't find shadowy spaces in which to work, they will be less likely to think they can get away with shadowy things. The forces of the marketplace will drive out undesirable or harmful products and practices. Regulation, on this line of thinking, should be designed to force information into the open. This idea is what gave us, among other things, the landmark securities regulations of Roosevelt's New Deal.

Today, the problem of agency costs extends far beyond the protection of the interests of corporate shareholders, to encompass all persons who live in economies arranged about the large corporation. Indeed, the scale of the modern limited liability corporation may make the control of agency costs a fantasy.

Disclosure regulation may also be losing influence. The activities of the modern firm have become so complex that more information produces less understanding. Most of us are entirely dependent on experts and intermediaries to tell us what might really be going on. And that gives us another agency cost problem: The experts and intermediaries, it turns out, aren't always working for us.[25]

It's hard to avoid the conclusion that it's the structure of the corporate institution that produces the responsibility deficit. In particular, the "separation of ownership and control" in the corporation, made famous long ago by legal scholar Adolf Berle and economist Gardiner Means—in today's vernacular, the problem of not enough skin in the game—and, even more, the phenomenon of scale have made fiascos like BP, GM, J.P. Morgan, Enron, and all the others inevitable. Great power and momentous decisions are in the hands of people who don't have enough good incentives or real control.

Especially in the case of big publicly traded companies, growing evidence shows that managers—subject to relentless short-term pressure from the markets to produce quarterly profits—do not have good incentives to invest in the long-term growth that most benefits retail investors and the economy, much less to invest in efforts to ensure that laws are not broken along the way.[26]

The corporation's strengths are also its weaknesses. In gradual steps over roughly a century and a half, the law created a tremendous engine for growth and innovation. It did this mostly through three moves. First, investors in businesses that constituted themselves as corporations (and a few other forms of entity) were guaranteed limited liability. Second, corporations were permitted to charter themselves for virtually unlimited lawful purposes; the state remained mostly agnostic as to what corporate managers chose to do with the capital they raised from investors. Third, capital markets were left unfettered by what we might call qualitative regulation: transparency, not the soundness, safety, or wisdom of financial products, was made the first principle of market rules.

Limited liability, by design, tends to relax owners of the corporation about whether managers might be up to something disastrous. Not so much if an investor is one of a handful of owners and has staked her nest egg, or a lot of it, on the firm. The problem arises when the investor enjoys access to a deep, wide, and diverse market for investing in corporations—when she can choose among thousands of investments, while basic economics, in both theory and evidence, tells her that she must diversify her portfolio.

Arguments for diversification are especially compelling if she, like so many of us, is the "average" investor who needs to save gradually over the course of a career to guarantee retirement security in a country with limited safety nets. Now she, and millions like her, will sink small amounts into very many firms. It will then be irrational for her to waste time worrying about what any one corporation's managers might be up to. Some have argued that this sort of investor should be indifferent even to *fraud*, because gains and losses from corporate fraud will net out over time in the well-diversified, patient portfolio.

The liberal corporate charter makes a lot of sense too. Ideas and innovation are our lifeblood. When it comes to the creation of economic enterprises, we should let a thousand flowers bloom and see which ones turn out to be beauties. But perhaps the strong appeal of this idea makes us forget that corporate institutions are not in fact natural phenomena that grow on their own unless law gets in the way. Law *creates* the corporation. The corporation is quite literally a license from the state: to have one, one must go (or click) somewhere, file a document, and pay a fee. The state therefore has the power, one might even say the right (though the government of course does not have rights, at least not domestically), to decide what corporations are licensed to do.

The government, therefore, could be choosy about what businesses corporations are allowed to get into. If that would be a bad idea, then at least, ahead of that, the government could decide how to define the duties and obligations of corporate managers, as conditions to the grant of that corporate license. That's a lot of what corporate law does. But corporate law might be reformed to better handle that basic definitional task.

In basing market regulation on transparency, we should again credit American genius. The creation of the SEC and the system of American securities regulation in the 1930s is one of the things that have made our investment markets the envy of world finance. But we need not rehearse the tale of 2006 to 2009 yet again to conclude that our capital markets may have reached a point at which oodles of mandated disclosure does not translate into public knowledge and understanding, and therefore good decisions about risk. Market regulation founded on disclosure has interacted badly in recent years with limited liability, as the largest financial firms have turned themselves from owner-operated partnerships into shareholder-owned public companies.

Law has many potential instruments for increasing the level of management responsibility without resort to criminal punishment. An obvious first move would be to do a better job of sanctioning individual managers for corporate actions that produce public harms. Managers as well as directors can be fined in their own pockets and can be ejected temporarily or permanently from industries, companies, or lines of business. Existing law contains many such tools.

Perhaps we need to raise the price on corporate managers for the consequences of taking overly harmful risks—if not comprehensively then at least extending into additional industries, and corners of industry, that aren't covered by present legal regimes. More important, we need institutions of enforcement with the powers and personnel to pursue such regulatory sanctions at a higher rate than at present.

More fundamentally, law could arrange the corporation in a way that rebuts the tired mantra of corporate management that "my responsibility is to my shareholders and therefore to profits." The major American corporation is too big and too influential to say anymore that its responsibility—as a matter of fact—does not run to the whole public. We talk about "public" companies as ones anyone can invest in. Perhaps we should mean ones in which the general public has an interest.

We could make that matter of fact a matter of law. The legal duties of corporate managers could be redefined to include more robust duties to the public. This would open up a new body of corporate law that would require hard work and a great deal of refinement. But there's no reason we must be stuck forever with the current regime that imposes a light, and even more lightly enforced, "duty of care" on managers that extends only to the firm's investors.

The major impediment to such change is practical: the odd American system of federalism in corporate law that allows the states to compete for incorporations on the dimension of law. Delaware is the perennial winner of this game because it offers companies a favorable legal climate that, in theory, is rigorous enough to satisfy shareholders. But if the noninvesting public has an important stake in the contest over corporate law, a legal competition that plays to corporations and their owners is not optimal. An alternative would be to federalize corporate law, an idea that has been discussed but not pursued at several junctures in American debates about corporate regulation.

Then there is the higher plane of regulating the economy as a whole. Perhaps there will come a time when we'll look back at the reform discussions of 2009 and say that it was the roads not taken in Dodd-Frank to which we ultimately had to return. Maybe we can't protect ourselves—and the long-term viability of our capital system—

without a more intrusive role for government in markets. No one wants this but maybe it's unavoidable. Without real constraints on both firm scale and product safety, we may lose all control of the amazing growth engine we've created.

Break up the banks. Ban dangerous financial products. Rethink antitrust law and enforcement. Get the scale of the risks and problems down to a size, and slow them to a pace, at which it's actually reasonable to think that individual human beings can handle them. And—here it gets enormously harder, as with today's environmental problems—do so on a global scale, since the political and technological boundaries that used to hem in corporate activity are so quickly falling away.

In the present American political environment, such reform ideas are off the table, if not delusional. Until American ideas about the corporation change fundamentally, and thereby change politics, there are no good prospects for regulatory changes on a scale that matches the scale of our problems. That is why it will be imperative to have deeper conversations about the nature of our problems first.

Those problems appear only to be scaling up further and spilling out across the boundaries of national legal systems. Exxon is under investigation for the truth of what it has been saying about climate change. Volkswagen is in a legal thicket due to its gaming of automobile emissions rules in, at least, Europe and the United States. Bankers are being prosecuted in both London and New York for rigging global trading markets. Pharmaceutical companies are facing the legal consequences of corruption in sales processes, from both American and Chinese authorities.

As the conversation about the modern corporation continues, I plan to keep watching this fascinating story of business crime and its prosecution. A little of the old prosecutor in me will be rooting for the government when it has a really good case. Meanwhile, I won't be expecting the game of prosecutors chasing businesses to change much, about either the game or the industries where it's played. That may be good for me. Without it, I might be out of teaching and writing material. But we should all aspire to more.

ACKNOWLEDGMENTS

My gratitude for what I know and can say about business crime extends to every person with whom I've discussed the subjects of criminal law and corporate crime, most especially my hundreds of amazing students.

Some of these people must be thanked by name. Those who taught me how to be a lawyer, among them: Bruce Baird, Lanny Breuer, Leslie Caldwell, Ben Campbell, Valerie Caproni, John Curran, Margaret Giordano, John Gleeson, Kelly Moore, James Orenstein, Sean O'Shea, Cathy Palmer, Alan Vinegrad, Andrew Weissmann, Fred Wyshak, and above all the Honorable and legendary Jack B. Weinstein of the United States District Court for the Eastern District of New York.

Those who extended the essential helping hand into the academy and scholarship, among them: Susan Appleton, Jennifer Arlen, Sam Bagenstos, Rachel Barkow, Sara Beale, Mitch Berman, Kathy Brickey, Jane Cohen, Barry Friedman, John Goldberg, Lisa Griffin, Jim Jacobs, Susan Klein, Bill Powers, Larry Sager, Deborah Schenck, Kent Syverud, and Stephen Schulhofer.

All those who encouraged this book to life and supported my work on it, among them: Jamie Boyle, Rebecca Buell, Guy Charles, Brendan Curry and the staff of W. W. Norton, Deborah DeMott, Don Fehr of Trident Media, Elizabeth Knoll, David Levi, Elise O'Shaughnessy, Frank

Partnoy, Jed Purdy, and Jim Salzman. Those colleagues who always teach me about my own field, among them: Miriam Baer, Lawrence Baxter, Rick Bierschbach, Jim Cox, Harry First, Kim Ferzan, Brandon Garrett, Stuart Green, Doug Husak, Julie O'Sullivan, Dan Richman, Alex Stein, and Kate Stith. The vital financial press with whom I have long enjoyed edifying exchanges, especially Kurt Eichenwald, Jesse Eisinger, Greg Farrell, Mary Flood, and Patricia Hurtado. Kaitlin Karges for indispensable research assistance. My mother Janet Rogers for making me a writer (and for editing here). My father George Buell for telling me not to lose my moral compass in the law. And most of all Erika Buell, for everything at every step, not least slogging through a draft of this.

NOTES

Introduction

1. Rebecca R. Ruiz, "Woman Cleared in Death Tied to G.M.'s Faulty Ignition Switch," *N.Y. Times*, Nov. 24, 2014.
2. A. W. Jones and A. Holmgren, "Concentrations of Alprazolam in Blood from Impaired Drivers and Forensic Autopsies Were Not Much Different But Showed a High Prevalence of Co-Ingested Illicit Drugs," 3 *J. Psychopharmacology* 276 (2013).
3. Jonathan Levy, *Freaks of Fortune: The Emerging World of Capitalism and Risk in America* (2012); Lawrence E. Mitchell, *The Speculation Economy: How Finance Triumphed Over Industry* (2007).

1: America and Business Crime

1. Jeff Connaughton, *The Payoff: Why Wall Street Always Wins* (2012); Charles H. Ferguson, *Predator Nation: Corporate Criminals, Political Corruption, and the Hijacking of America* (2012); Matt Taibbi, "Why Isn't Wall Street in Jail?" *Rolling Stone*, Feb. 16, 2011; Jed S. Rakoff, "The Financial Crisis: Why Have No High-Level Executives Been Prosecuted?," *N.Y. Rev. Books*, Jan. 9, 2014; William D. Cohan, "How the Bankers Stayed Out of Jail," *The Atlantic*, Sept. 2015.
2. John Micklethwait and Adrian Woolridge, *The Company: A Short History of a Revolutionary Idea* (2003); Robert E. Wright, *Corporation Nation* (2014); John C. Coates IV, "Corporate Speech and the First Amendment: History, Data, and Implications," 30 *Constitutional Commentary* 223 (2015).
3. Thomas Piketty, *Capital in the Twenty-First Century* (2014).

4. Godfrey Hodgson, *America in Our Time: From World War II to Nixon—What Happened and Why* 489 (1976).

5. Stuart P. Green, *Lying, Cheating, and Stealing: A Moral Theory of White-Collar Crime* (2006); Stuart P. Green, "The Concept of White Collar Crime in Law and Legal Theory," 8 *Buff. Crim. L. Rev.* 1 (2004).

6. William J. Stuntz, "The Political Constitution of Criminal Justice," 119 *Harv. L. Rev.* 780 (2006); William J. Stuntz, "The Pathological Politics of Criminal Law," 100 *Mich. L. Rev.* 505 (2001).

7. John Hasnas, *Trapped: When Acting Ethically Is Against the Law* (2006); Tim Lynch, Testimony, *Over-Criminalization of Conduct/Over-Federalization of Criminal Law*, Cato Inst., July 22, 2009; Erik Luna, *Overextending the Criminal Law*, 25 Cato Policy Report 1, Nov./Dec. 2003; Harvey Silverglate and Tim Lynch, *The Criminalization of Almost Everything*, Cato Inst., Jan./Feb. 2010; Paul Larkin, *The Extent of America's Overcriminalization Problem*, Heritage Found., May 9, 2014; Michael B. Mukasey and Paul Larkin, *The Perils of Overcriminalization*, Heritage Found., Feb. 12, 2015; Paul Rosenzweig, *The Over-Criminalization of Social and Economic Conduct*, Heritage Found., Apr. 17, 2003.

8. "Visa Exposed As Massive Credit Card Scam," *The Onion*, Aug. 15, 2011.

9. Samuel W. Buell, "Is the White Collar Offender Privileged?" 63 *Duke L. J.* 823 (2014); Samuel W. Buell, "What Is Securities Fraud?" 61 *Duke L. J.* 511 (2011).

10. James B. Stewart, "Defying Convention and Maybe the Law," *N.Y. Times*, May 3, 2014; Steve Stecklow and Nick Wingfield, "Jobs Is Subpoenaed In SEC Options Suit," *Wall St. J.*, Sept. 27, 2007; Randall Stross, "So the iPhone Has Problems. What About the Stock Options?" *N.Y. Times*, July 13, 2008; Nick Wingfield and Justin Scheck, "Jobs, Apple Executives Settle Suit," *Wall St. J.*, Sept.11, 2008.

11. https://jenner.com/lehman.

12. Final Report of Neal Batson, Court-Appointed Examiner, *In re* Enron Corp, No. 01-16034 (Bankr. S.D.N.Y. 2003); Third Interim Report of Neal Batson, Court-Appointed Examiner, *In re* Enron Corp, No. 01-16034 (Bankr. S.D.N.Y. 2003); Rosalind Z. Wiggins and Andrew Metrick, "The Lehman Brothers Bankruptcy C: Managing the Balance Sheet through the Use of Repo 105," 1 *Yale Program on Financial Stability* Case Study 3C.

13. Samuel W. Buell, "Good Faith and Law Evasion," 58 *UCLA L. Rev.* 611 (2011).

14. ABA Criminal Justice Section, *Standards for the Prosecution Function*, 4th ed., Standard 3-4.3; U.S. Dept. of Justice, *U.S. Attorney's Manual* § 9-28 (2008).

15. Samuel W. Buell, "What Is Securities Fraud?" 61 *Duke L. J.* 511 (2011); Samuel W. Buell, "Novel Criminal Fraud," 81 *N.Y.U. L. Rev.* 1971 (2006).

16. Samuel W. Buell and Lisa Kern Griffin, "On the Mental State of Consciousness of Wrongdoing," 75 *Law and Contemp. Probs.* 133 (2012).

17. Morissette v. United States, 342 U.S. 246, 250 (1952) ("The contention that an injury can amount to a crime only when inflicted by intention is no provincial or transient notion. It is as universal and persistent in mature systems of law as belief in freedom of the human will and a consequent ability and duty of the normal individual to choose between good and evil.")

18. H. L. A. Hart, *The Concept of Law*, 3d ed. (2012).

19. John C. Coffee, Jr., "Does 'Unlawful' Mean 'Criminal'? Reflections on the Disappearing Tort/Crime Distinction in American Law," 71 *B.U. L. Rev.* 193 (1991); Henry M. Hart, Jr., "The Aims of the Criminal Law," 23 *Law and Contemp. Probs.* 401 (1958); Sanford H. Kadish, "Some Observations on the Use of Criminal Sanctions in Enforcing Economic Regulations," 30 *U. Chi. L. Rev.* 423 (1962).

20. Richard D. Freer and Douglas K. Moll, *Principles of Business Organizations* (2013).

21. Henry Hansmann, Reinier Kraakman, and Richard Squire, "Law and the Rise of the Firm," 119 *Harv. L. Rev.* 1335 (2006); Henry Hansmann and Reinier H. Kraakman, "Organizational Law as Asset Partitioning," 44 *European Econ. Rev.* 807 (2000).

22. Armen A. Alchian and Harold Demsetz, "Production, Information Costs, and Economic Organization," 5 *Amer. Econ. Rev.* 777 (1972).

23. *Collapse of the Enron Corporation: Hearing Before the S. Committee on Commerce, Science, and Transportation*, 107th Cong. (2002) (statement of Jeffrey Skilling, former Chief Executive Officer, Enron Corporation); U.S. Secs. and Exch. Comm'n, *In the Matter of File No. HO-9350 Enron Corporation* (Testimony of Jeffrey Skilling, Dec. 5, 2001).

24. Lee Ross, Richard Nisbett, and Malcolm Gladwell, *The Person and the Situation: Perspectives of Social Psychology* (2011); Daniel T. Gilbert and Patrick S. Malone, "The Correspondence Bias," 117 *Psych. Bul.* 21 (1995); Fritz Heider, *The Psychology of Interpersonal Relations* (1958); E. E. Jones and V. A. Harris, "The Attribution of Attitudes," 3 *J. Experimental Psychol.* 1 (1967).

25. John M. Darley and C. Daniel Batson, "'From Jerusalem to Jericho': A Study of Situational and Dispositional Variables in Helping Behavior," 27 *J. of Personality and Social Psychol.* 100 (1973).

26. Z. Kunda and R. E. Nisbett, "The Psychometrics of Everyday Life," 18 *Cognitive Psychol.* 195 (1986).

27. Samuel W. Buell, "The Blaming Function of Entity Criminal Liability," 81 *Ind. L. J.* 473 (2006).

28. Jennifer Arlen, "The Potentially Perverse Effects of Corporate Criminal Liability," 23 *J. Legal Stud.* 833 (1994); Jennifer Arlen and Reinier Kraakman, "Controlling Corporate Misconduct: An Analysis of Corporate Liability Regimes," 72 *N.Y.U. L. Rev.* 687 (1997); John S. Baker, Jr., "Corporations Aren't Criminals," *Wall St. J.*, Apr. 22, 2002, at A18; Pamela H. Bucy, "Corporate Ethos: A Standard for Corporate Criminal Liability," 75 *Minn. L. Rev.* 1095 (1991); Donald R. Cressey, "The Poverty of Theory in Corporate Crime Research," in 1 *Advances in Criminological Theory*, ed. William S. Laufer and Freda Adler, 31, 36 (1989); John C. Coffee, Jr., "'No Soul to Damn: No Body to Kick': An Unscandalized Inquiry into the Problem of Corporate Punishment," 79 *Mich. L. Rev.* 386 (1981); Daniel R. Fischel and Alan O. Sykes, "Corporate Crime," 25 *J. Legal Stud.* 319 (1996); V. S. Khanna, "Is the Notion of Corporate Fault a Faulty Notion?: The Case of Corporate Mens Rea," 79 *B. U. L. Rev.* 355 (1999).

29. William S. Laufer, *Corporate Bodies and Guilty Minds: The Failure of Corporate Criminal Liability* (2008); William S. Laufer, "Corporate Culpability and the Limits of Law," 6 *Business Ethics Q.* 311 (1996).

30. Guilty Plea Agreement, United States v. BP Exploration & Production, Inc. (E.D. La 2012); Information for Seaman's Manslaughter, Clean Water Act, Migratory Bird Treaty Act and Obstruction of Congress, United States v. BP Exploration & Production, Inc. (E.D. La 2012).

31. Washington Legal Foundation, *Timeline: Federal Erosion of Business Civil Liberties*, 3d ed. (2015).

2: Fraud

1. George P. Fletcher, *Rethinking Criminal Law* 90–113 (1978); George P. Fletcher, "Manifest Criminality, Criminal Intent, and the Metamorphosis of Lloyd Weinreb," 90 *Yale L. J.* 319 (1980); Stuart P. Green, *Lying, Cheating, and Stealing: A Moral Theory of White-Collar Crime* 76–79 (2006).

2. Allen D. Boyer, *Sir Edward Coke and the Elizabethan Age* (2011); Hastings Lyon and Herman Block, *Edward Coke: Oracle of the Law* (1992).

3. Twyne's Case (1601), 3 Co. Rep. 80b, 82a, 76 Eng. Rep. 809, 815–16 (K.B.) (reporting as Queen's Attorney General).

4. Letter from Lord Hardwicke to Lord Kames (June 30, 1759), in Joseph Parkes, *A History of the Court of Chancery* 501, 508 (1828).

5. McAleer v. Horsey, 35 Md. 439, 452 (1872).

6. Gregory v. United States, 253 F.2d 104, 109 (5th Cir. 1958) (quoting Weiss v. United States, 122 F.2d 675, 681 (5th Cir. 1941)).

7. 18 U.S.C. §§ 1341, 1346; Edward Balleisen, "Private Cops on the Fraud Beat: The Limits of American Business Self-Regulation, 1895–1932," 83 *Bus. Hist. Rev.* 113 (2009); Anuj C. Desai, "Wiretapping Before the Wires: The Post Office and the Birth of Communications Privacy," 60 *Stan. L. Rev.* 553 (2007); Jed S. Rakoff, "The Federal Mail Fraud Statute (Part I)," 18 *Duq. L. Rev.* 771, 772 (1980).

8. 18 U.S.C. §§ 1343, 1348, 1350; 17 C.F.R. § 240.10b-5; 15 U.S.C. § 78j; 15 U.S.C. § 78ff.

9. Samuel W. Buell, "Novel Criminal Fraud," 81 *N.Y.U. L. Rev.* 1971, 1972 (2006).

10. Frank Partnoy, *The Match King: Ivar Kreuger, The Financial Genius Behind a Century of Wall Street Scandals* (2010); Mitchell Zuckoff, *Ponzi's Scheme: The True Story of a Financial Legend* (2006).

11. Diana B. Henriques, *The Wizard of Lies: Bernie Madoff and the Death of Trust* (2011); "The Madoff Affair" (*Frontline*, broadcast May 12, 2009); William P. Barrett, "Madoff Mess Is Nothing New," *Forbes*, Jan. 12, 2012; Steve Fishman, "The Madoff Tapes," *N.Y. Mag.*, Mar. 7, 2011; Diana B. Henriques, "Letters From A Sociopath," *Forbes*, Apr. 9, 2012.

12. "Dennis Kozlowski: Prisoner 05A4820" (*60 Minutes*, broadcast July 23, 2007); Catherine S. Neal, *Taking Down the Lion: The Triumphant Rise and Tragic Fall of Tyco's Dennis Kozlowski* (2014); Clyde Haberman, "Greed, It Turns Out, Isn't

So Good," *N.Y. Times*, Sept. 20, 2005; David A. Kaplan, "Tyco's 'Piggy,' Out of the Pen and Living Small," *N.Y. Times*, Mar. 2, 2015; Andrew Ross Sorkin, "Ex-Tyco Officers Get 8 To 25 Years," *N.Y. Times*, Sept. 20, 2005.

13. Walter Isaacson, *Steve Jobs* (2011); James B. Stewart, "Defying Convention and Maybe the Law," *N.Y. Times*, May 3, 2014; Steve Stecklow and Nick Wingfield, "Jobs Is Subpoenaed In SEC Options Suit," *Wall St. J.*, Sept. 27, 2007; Randall Stross, "So the iPhone Has Problems. What About the Stock Options?" *N.Y. Times*, July 13, 2008; Nick Wingfield and Justin Scheck, "Jobs, Apple Executives Settle Suit," *Wall St. J.*, Sept. 11, 2008.

14. United States v. Black, 625 F.3d 386 (7th Cir. 2010); Conrad Black, *A Matter of Principle* (2012); Ameet Sachdev, "Appeals Court Upholds 2 of Black's Convictions," *Chi. Trib.*, Oct. 30, 2010; Ameet Sachdev, David Greising, and Susan Chandler, "Dark Day for Lord Black," *Chi. Trib.*, July 14, 2007.

15. United States v. Ebbers, 458 F.3d 110 (2d Cir. 2006); Ken Belson, "World-Com Head Is Given 25 Years For Huge Fraud," *N.Y. Times*, July 14, 2005; Ken Belson, "Bernard Ebbers: Victim Himself Or Mastermind?" *N.Y. Times*, Jan. 26, 2005; Rebecca Blumenstein and Susan Pulliam, "Report Says Ebbers and Others Conspired in WorldCom Fraud," *Wall St. J.*, June 10, 2003.

16. Kurt Eichenwald, *Conspiracy of Fools: A True Story* (2005); Peter C. Fusaro and Ross M. Miller, *What Went Wrong at Enron: Everyone's Guide to the Largest Bankruptcy in U.S. History* (2002); Bethany McLean and Peter Elkind, *The Smartest Guys in the Room* (2004); Kurt Eichenwald, "Verdict on an Era: Enron in the 90's: Arrogant and Reckless," *N.Y. Times*, May 26, 2006; Tom Fowler, "Enron's Implosion Was Anything But Sudden," *Houston Chron.*, June 30, 2004; Laura Goldberg and Mary Flood, "The Rise of Ken Lay as Dramatic as His Fall," *Houston Chron.*, Feb. 3, 2002.

17. Bethany McLean and Peter Elkind, *The Smartest Guys in the Room* (2004).

18. Final Report of Neal Batson, Court-Appointed Examiner, *In re* Enron Corp, No. 01-16034 (Bankr. S.D.N.Y. 2003).

19. Report of Anton R. Valukas, Examiner, *In re* Lehman Brothers Holdings, Inc., No. 08-13555 (Bankr. S.D.N.Y. 2010).

20. United States v. Simon, 425 F.2d 796 (2d Cir. 1969).

21. For a more complete version of the story, see Michael Lewis, *The Big Short: Inside the Doomsday Machine* (2010).

22. Matt Taibbi, *The Divide: American Injustice in the Age of the Wealth Gap* (2014); Jeff Connaughton, *The Payoff: Why Wall Street Always Wins* (2012); Jed S. Rakoff, "The Financial Crisis: Why Have No High-Level Executives Been Prosecuted?" *N.Y. Rev. Books*, Jan. 9, 2014; "The Untouchables" (*Frontline*, broadcast Jan. 22, 2013); "Prosecuting Wall Street" (*60 Minutes*, broadcast Dec. 4, 2011); Editorial, "Going Soft on Corporate Crime," *N.Y. Times*, Apr. 10, 2008; Government Accountability Institute, *Justice Inaction: The Department of Justice's Unprecedented Failure to Prosecute Big Finance*, www.g-a-i.org; William D. Cohan, "How the Bankers Stayed Out of Jail," *The Atlantic*, Sept. 2015.

23. Bethany McLean and Joe Nocera, *All the Devils Are Here: The Hidden History of the Financial Crisis* (2011); Yves Smith, *ECONNED: How Unenlightened Self Inter-*

est Undermined Democracy and Corrupted Capitalism (2010); Richard A. Posner, *A Failure of Capitalism: The Crisis of '08 and the Descent into Depression* (2011); Alan S. Blinder, *After the Music Stopped: The Financial Crisis, the Response and the Work Ahead* (2013); Hilary J. Allen, "The Pathologies of Banking Business as Usual," 17 *U. Pa. J. Bus. L.* 861 (2015).

24. Jeff Madrick and Frank Partnoy, "Should Some Bankers Be Prosecuted?" *N.Y. Rev. Books,* Nov. 10, 2011; Complaint, Securities and Exchange Commission v. Fabrice Tourre, No. 10-CV-3229 (S.D.N.Y. 2010); Susanne Craig, Ben Protess, and Alexandra Stevenson, "In Complex Trading Case, Jurors Focused on Greed," *N.Y. Times,* Aug. 3, 2013.

25. U.S. Dept. of Justice, Office of the Inspector General, "Audit of the Department of Justice's Efforts to Address Mortgage Fraud," Audit Rpt. 14-12 (Mar. 2014); Danielle Douglas-Gabriel, "Bank of America and DOJ Near $17 Billion Settlement over Mortgage Securities," *Wash. Post,* Aug. 20, 2014; Danielle Douglas-Gabriel, "Citigroup to Pay $7 Billion to Resolve Mortgage Securities Investigation," *Wash. Post,* July 14, 2014; Peter J. Henning, "Blurred Lines in Big Bank Mortgage Settlements," *N.Y. Times,* Aug. 22, 2014.

26. Aruna Viswanatha, Devlin Barrett, and Christopher M. Matthews, "U.S. Targets RBS, J.P. Morgan Executives in Criminal Probes," *Wall St. J.,* Nov. 17, 2015.

27. Settlement Agreement Between U.S. Dept. of Justice and Bank of America Corp., Aug. 20, 2014, www.justice.gov; Federal Housing Finance Agency v. Nomura Holding America, Inc., 2015 WL 2183875 (S.D.N.Y. May 11, 2015).

28. Letter from Denis McInerney, Chief, Criminal Div., Fraud Section, U.S. Dept. of Justice, to Steven R. Peikin, David H. Braff, Jeffrey T. Scott, and Matthew S. Fitzwater, Sullivan and Cromwell LLP (June 26, 2012), www.justice.gov; U.S. Dept. of Justice, Press Release, "Former Rabobank LIBOR Submitter Pleads Guilty for Scheme to Manipulate Yen LIBOR," Aug. 18, 2014; "The LIBOR Scandal: The Rotten Heart of Finance," *The Economist,* July 7, 2012; Dylan Matthews, "Explainer: Why the LIBOR Scandal is a Bigger Deal than JPMorgan," *Wash. Post,* July 5, 2012.

29. Bryan Burrough and John Helyar, *Barbarians at the Gate: The Fall of RJR Nabisco* (1989); Connie Bruck, *The Predators' Ball: The Inside Story of Drexel Burnham and the Rise of the Junk Bond Raiders* (1989); "U.S. Reports 18% Rise in '85 in White-Collar Convictions," *N.Y. Times,* Sept. 29, 1987.

30. Lydia DePillis, "Meet Preet Bharara, Who Just Won the Biggest Insider Trading Case Ever," *Wash. Post,* Nov. 4, 2013; "Preet Bharara: Insider Trading Is 'Rampant' On Wall Street" (*Frontline,* broadcast Jan. 7, 2014); Charles Gasparino, *Circle of Friends: The Massive Federal Crackdown on Insider Trading* (2013); Anita Raghavan, *The Billionaire's Apprentice: The Rise of the Indian-American Elite and the Fall of the Galleon Hedge Fund* (2013); George Packer, "A Dirty Business: New York City's top prosecutor takes on Wall Street crime," *New Yorker,* June 27, 2011.

31. Chiarella v. United States, 445 U.S. 222 (1980); S.E.C. v. Texas Gulf Sulphur

Co., 401 F.2d 833 (2d Cir. 1968); *In Re* Cady, Roberts & Co., 40 S.E.C. 907 (1961).

32. Carpenter v. United States, 484 U.S. 19 (1987).

33. United States v. O'Hagan, 521 U.S. 642 (1997).

34. United States v. O'Hagan, 521 U.S. 642 (1997) (Thomas, J. dissenting).

35. Stephen M. Bainbridge, *Research Handbook on Insider Trading* (2014).

36. George A. Akerlof, "The Market for 'Lemons': Quality Uncertainty and the Market Mechanism," 84 *Q. J. Econ.* 488 (1970).

37. Peter Lattman and Azam Ahmed, "Rajat Gupta Convicted of Insider Trading," *N.Y. Times*, June 15, 2015; William Alden and Azam Ahmed, "A Conflicted Jury Finds Rajat Gupta Guilty," *N.Y. Times*, June 15, 2012; Anita Raghavan, "Rajat Gupta's Lust for Zeros," *N.Y. Times*, May 17, 2013; Ben Protess and Matthew Goldstein, "Authorities Find Insider Trading Case Tied to Phil Mickelson Is Slow to Take Shape," *N.Y. Times*, May 31, 2014; Patrick Radden Keefe, "The Empire of Edge: How a doctor, a trader, and the billionaire Steven A. Cohen got entangled in a vast financial scandal," *New Yorker*, Oct. 13, 2014.

3: Loopholing

1. Kurt Eichenwald, *Conspiracy of Fools: A True Story* (2005); Peter C. Fusaro and Ross M. Miller, *What Went Wrong at Enron: Everyone's Guide to the Largest Bankruptcy in U.S. History* (2002); Bethany McLean and Peter Elkind, *The Smartest Guys in the Room* (2004).

2. Anthony Bianco, "Ken Lay's Audacious Ignorance," *Bloomberg Bus.*, Feb. 5, 2006; Kurt Eichenwald, "Company Man to the End, After All," *N.Y. Times*, Feb. 9, 2003; Laura Goldberg and Mary Flood, "The Rise of Ken Lay as Dramatic as His Fall," *Houston Chron.*, Feb. 3, 2002; Richard A. Oppel Jr., "Enron's Collapse: Transactions At Issue," *N.Y. Times*, Jan. 21, 2002; Julie Rawe, "The Case Against Ken Lay," *Time*, July 12, 2004; Susan Pulliam, Deborah Solomon, and Carrick Mollenkamp, "Former WorldCom CEO Built An Empire on Mountain of Debt," *Wall St. J.*, Dec. 31, 2002; Jerry Knight, "Tracking the Trouble Caused By WorldCom's Bernie Ebbers," *Wash. Post*, Mar. 18, 2002.

3. Kathleen F. Brickey, "From Enron to Worldcom and Beyond: Life and Crime after Sarbanes-Oxley," 81 *Wash. U. L. Q.* 357 (2003); Lawrence A. Cunningham, "The Sarbanes-Oxley Yawn: Heavy Rhetoric, Light Reform (And It Just Might Work)," 35 *Conn. L. Rev.* 915 (2003); Roberta S. Karmel, "Realizing the Dream of William O. Douglas—The Securities and Exchange Commission Takes Charge of Corporate Governance," 30 *Del. J. Corp. L.* 79 (2005); Roberta Romano, "The Sarbanes-Oxley Act and the Making of Quack Corporate Governance," 114 *Yale L. J.* 1521 (2005).

4. Committee on Capital Markets Regulation, *The Competitive Position of the U.S. Public Equity Market*, Dec. 4, 2007, http://capmktsreg.org; Committee on Capital Markets Regulation, *Interim Report of the Committee on Capital Markets*

Regulation, 2006, http://capmktsreg.org; H. N. Butler and L. E. Ribstein, *The Sarbanes–Oxley Debacle: How to Fix It and What We've Learned* (2006); P. Hostak, E. Karaoglu, T. Lys, and G. Yang, "An Examination of the Impact of the Sarbanes-Oxley Act on the Attractiveness of US Capital Markets for Foreign Firms," 18 *Rev. Acct. Stud.* 522 (2009); Hal S. Scott, "What is the United States Doing About the Competitiveness of its Capital Markets?" 22 *J. Int'l Banking L. & Reg.* 487 (2007).

5. Bethany McLean and Joe Nocera, *All the Devils Are Here: The Hidden History of the Financial Crisis* (2011); Yves Smith, *ECONNED: How Unenlightened Self Interest Undermined Democracy and Corrupted Capitalism* (2010).

6. Edward F. Greene, "Dodd-Frank and the Future of Financial Regulation," *Harv. Bus. L. Rev.* Online, http://www.hblr.org; Hal S. Scott, "A General Evaluation of the Dodd-Frank U.S. Financial Reform Legislation," 25 *J. Int'l Banking L. & Reg.* 477 (2010); Heath P. Tarbert, "The Dodd-Frank Act—Two Years Later," 66 *Consumer Fin. L. Q. Rep.* 373 (2012).

7. Michael Lewis, *Flash Boys* (2014); Jenny Anderson, "S.E.C. Moves to Ban Edge Held by Fast Traders," *N.Y. Times*, Sept. 17, 2009; Matthew O'Brien, "Everything You Need to Know About High-Frequency Trading," *The Atlantic*, Apr. 11, 2014; Jerry Adler, "Raging Bulls: How Wall Street Got Addicted to Light-Speed Trading," *Wired*, Aug. 8, 2012.

8. "The LIBOR Scandal: The Rotten Heart of Finance," *The Economist*, July 7, 2012.

9. David Kocieniewski, "A Shuffle of Aluminum, But to Banks, Pure Gold," *N.Y. Times*, July 20, 2013; Matt Levine, "The Goldman Sachs Aluminum Conspiracy Was Pretty Silly," *BloombergView*, Nov. 21, 2014.

10. Samuel W. Buell, "Novel Criminal Fraud," 81 *N.Y.U. L. Rev.* 1971 (2006); Samuel W. Buell, "Reforming Punishment of Financial Reporting Fraud," 28 *Cardozo L. Rev.* 1611 (2007).

11. United States v. Quattrone, 441 F.3d 153 (2d Cir. 2006); Andrew Ross Sorkin, "Wall St. Banker Is Found Guilty of Obstruction," *N.Y. Times*, May 4, 2004; Andrew Ross Sorkin, "Appeals Court Overturns Conviction of Ex-Banking Star," *N.Y. Times*, Mar. 20, 2006; Andrew Ross Sorkin, "Quattrone May Avoid 3rd Trial," *N.Y. Times*, Aug. 19, 2006.

12. Arthur Andersen LLP v. United States, 544 U.S. 696 (2005); Arthur Andersen LLP v. United States, 374 F.3d 281 (5th Cir. 2004).

13. Anton B. Valukas, *Report to Board of Directors of General Motors Company Regarding Ignition Switch Recalls*, May 29, 2014.

14. U.S. Dept. of Justice, Office of Legal Counsel, *Memorandum for Alberto R. Gonzales, Counsel to the President, Re: Standards of Conduct for Interrogation under 18 U.S.C. §§ 2340-2340A*, Aug. 1, 2002; U.S. Dept. of Justice, Office of Legal Counsel, *Memorandum for John Rizzo Acting General Counsel of the Central Intelligence Agency, Re: Interrogation of al Qaeda Operative*, Aug. 1, 2002; Andrew Cohen, "The Torture Memos, 10 Years Later," *The Atlantic*, Feb. 6, 2012.

15. Tanina Rostain and Milton C. Regan, Jr., *Confidence Games: Lawyers, Accountants, and the Tax Shelter Industry* (2014); Howard Gleckman, Amy Borrus, and Mike McNamee, "Inside the KPMG Mess," *Bloomberg Bus.*, Aug. 31, 2005.

16. Cheek v. United States, 498 U.S. 192 (1991).

17. James A. Strazzella, "The Federalization of Criminal Law" (Am. Bar Ass'n. 1998); Sara Sun Beale, "Too Many and Yet Too Few: New Principles To Define the Proper Limits for Federal Criminal Jurisdiction," 46 *Hastings L. J.* 979 (1995); Sara Sun Beale, "What's Law Got To Do with It? The Political, Social, Psychological and Other Non-Legal Factors Influencing the Development of (Federal) Criminal Law," 1 *Buff. Crim. L. Rev.* 23 (1997); Kathleen F. Brickey, "Criminal Mischief: The Federalization of American Criminal Law," 46 *Hastings L. J.* 1135 (1995); Steven D. Clymer, "Unequal Justice: The Federalization of Criminal Law," 70 *S. Cal. L. Rev.* 643 (1997); Erik Luna, "The Overcriminalization Phenomenon," 54 *Am. U. L. Rev.* 703 (2005); Paul H. Robinson and Michael T. Cahill, "The Accelerating Degradation of American Criminal Codes," 56 *Hastings L. J.* 633 (2005); William J. Stuntz, "The Pathological Politics of Criminal Law," 100 *Mich. L. Rev.* 505 (2001).

18. Susan R. Klein and Ingrid B. Grobey, "Debunking Claims of Over-Federalization of Criminal Law," 62 *Emory L. J.* 1 (2012).

19. Prosecutions for September 2015, TRAC (Oct. 27, 2015), http://trac.syr.edu; Immigration Convictions Drop 20 Percent, TRAC (June 12, 2015), http://trac.syr.edu.

20. White Collar Crime Convictions for September 2015, TRAC (Oct. 27, 2015), http://trac.syr.edu.

21. Daniel I. Weiner, *Citizens United Five Years Later* (Brennan Center for Justice, Jan. 15, 2015); State of New York, Comm'n. to Investigate Public Corruption, *Preliminary Report* (Dec. 2, 2013).

22. United States v. Sun-Diamond Growers of California, 526 U.S. 398 (1999); United States v. Sun-Diamond Growers of California, 138 F.3d 961 (D.C. Cir. 1998); United States v. Sun-Diamond Growers of California, 941 F. Supp. 1262 (D.D.C. 1996).

23. United States v. Welch, 327 F.3d 1081 (10th Cir. 2003).

24. Cary O'Reilly and Karin Matussek, "Siemens to Pay $1.6 Billion to Settle Bribery Cases," *Bloomberg News*, Dec. 16, 2008; Siri Schubert and T. Christian Miller, "At Siemens, Bribery Was Just a Line Item," *N.Y. Times*, Dec. 20, 2008.

25. David Barstow, "Vast Mexico Bribery Case Hushed Up by Wal-Mart After Top-Level Struggle," *N.Y. Times*, Apr. 21, 2012; Andre Tartar, "Walmart Top Brass Implicated in Mexican Subsidiary's Bribery Scandal," *N.Y. Mag.*, Apr. 21, 2012.

26. Stichting Ter Behartiging Van De Belangen Van Oudaandeelhouders In Het Kapitaal Van Saybolt International B.V. v. Schreiber, 327 F.3d 173 (2d Cir. 2003).

27. Calvin H. Johnson, "Tales from the KPMG Skunk Works: The Basis-Shift or Defective-Redemption Shelter," *Tax Notes*, July 25, 2005; Stein v. KPMG,

LLP, 486 F.3d 753 (2d Cir. 2007); United States v. Stein, 541 F.3d 130 (2d Cir. 2008); United States v. Ruble, 2009 WL 911035 (S.D.N.Y. Apr. 2, 2009).

28. United States v. Sturm, 870 F.2d 769 (1st Cir. 1989).

4: Corporations as Criminals

1. "The Spill" (*Frontline*, broadcast Oct. 26, 2010); Raffi Khatchadourian, "The Gulf War: Were there any heroes in the BP oil disaster?" *New Yorker*, Mar. 14, 2011.

2. Joel Achenbach, "In BP Oil Spill, Two Drilling Veterans Scapegoated, Attorneys Say," *Wash. Post*, Nov. 27, 2012; Clifford Kraussnov, "In BP Indictments, U.S. Shifts to Hold Individuals Accountable," *N.Y. Times*, Nov. 15, 2012.

3. Guilty Plea Agreement, United States v. BP Exploration & Production, Inc. (E.D. La 2012); Information for Seaman's Manslaughter, Clean Water Act, Migratory Bird Treaty Act and Obstruction of Congress, United States v. BP Exploration & Production, Inc. (E.D. La 2012).

4. Anton B. Valukas, *Report to Board of Directors of General Motors Company Regarding Ignition Switch Recalls*, May 29, 2014.

5. Donald R. Cressey, "The Poverty of Theory in Corporate Crime Research," 1 *Advances In Criminological Theory*, ed. William S. Laufer and Freda Adler (1989); Daniel R. Fischel and Alan O. Sykes, "Corporate Crime," 25 *J. Legal Stud.* 319 (1996); V. S. Khanna, "Is the Notion of Corporate Fault a Faulty Notion?: The Case of Corporate Mens Rea," 79 *B.U. L. Rev.* 355 (1999).

6. Samuel W. Buell, "Criminal Procedure Within the Firm," 59 *Stan. L. Rev.* 1613 (2007); Brandon L. Garrett, "The Corporate Criminal as Scapegoat," 101 *Va. L. Rev.* 1789 (2015); Jennifer Arlen and Reinier Kraakman, "Controlling Corporate Misconduct: An Analysis of Corporate Liability Regimes," 72 *N.Y.U. L. Rev.* 687, 695 (1997); Jennifer Arlen, "Corporate Criminal Liability: Theory and Evidence," in *Research Handbook on the Economics of Criminal Law*, ed. A. Harel and K. Hylton (2012).

7. Michael Sokolove, "The Trials of Graham Spanier, Penn State's Ousted President," *N.Y. Times*, July 16, 2014; Louis Freeh, *Report of the Special Investigative Counsel Regarding the Actions of the Pennsylvania State University Related to the Child Sexual Abuse Committed by Gerald A. Sandusky*, July 12, 2012.

8. Bethany McLean and Peter Elkind, *The Smartest Guys in the Room* (2004); Kurt Eichenwald, *Conspiracy of Fools: A True Story* (2005); Ken Brown and Ianthe Jeanne Dugan, "Arthur Andersen's Fall From Grace Is a Sad Tale of Greed and Miscues," *Wall St. J.*, June 7, 2002; Delroy Alexander, Greg Burns, Robert Manor, Flynn McRoberts, and E.A. Torriero, "The Fall of Andersen," *Chicago Trib.*, Sept. 1, 2002.

9. Arthur Andersen LLP v. United States, 544 U.S. 696 (2005).

10. Bethany McLean and Joe Nocera, *All the Devils Are Here: The Hidden History of the Financial Crisis* (2011); Yves Smith, *ECONNED: How Unenlightened Self Interest Undermined Democracy and Corrupted Capitalism* (2010).

11. Andrew Ross Sorkin, *Too Big to Fail: The Inside Story of How Wall Street and Washington Fought To Save the Financial System—and Themselves* (2009); "The Origins of the Financial Crisis: Crash Course," *The Economist*, Sept. 7, 2013.

12. U.S. Dept. of Justice, Asst. Attorney General Lanny A. Breuer, Address at the New York City Bar Association, Sept. 13, 2012.

13. Stephen Grocer, "A List of the Biggest Bank Settlements," *Wall St. J.*, June 23, 2014; Nick Summers, "Banks Finally Pay for Their Sins, Five Years After the Crisis," *Bloomberg Bus.*, Oct. 31, 2013.

14. Ben Protess and Jessica Silver-Greenberg, "HSBC to Pay $1.92 Billion to Settle Charges of Money Laundering," *N.Y. Times*, Dec. 10, 2012; "HSBC Bank 'Helped Clients Dodge Millions in Tax,'" BBC, Feb. 10, 2015; Stephen Platt, *Criminal Capital: How the Finance Industry Facilitates Crime* (2015).

15. Editorial, "Too Big to Indict," *N.Y. Times*, Dec. 11, 2012; "Outrageous HSBC Settlement Proves the Drug War is a Joke," *Rolling Stone*, Dec. 13, 2012; Matt Taibbi, "Gangster Bankers: Too Big to Jail," *Rolling Stone*, Feb. 14, 2013; "Too Big to Jail: Two Big British Banks Reach Controversial Settlements," *The Economist*, Dec. 15, 2012.

16. Plea Agreement, United States v. Credit Suisse AG, No. 1:14-CR-188 (E.D. Va. May 19, 2014); Statement of Facts, United States v. Credit Suisse AG, No. 1:14-CR-188 (E.D. Va. May 19, 2014); Statement of Facts, United States v. BNP Paribas, S.A. (S.D.N.Y. July 9, 2014); David Voreacos and Tom Schoenberg, "Credit Suisse Pleads Guilty in Three-Year U.S. Tax Probe," *Bloomberg Bus.*, May 19, 2014; Andrew Grossman, John Letzing, and Devlin Barrett, "Credit Suisse Pleads Guilty in Criminal Tax Case: Agrees to Pay $2.6 Billion to Settle Probe by U.S. Justice Department," *Wall St. J.*, May 19, 2014; Jessica Silver-Greenberg and Ben Protess, "BNP Paribas Pinned Hopes on Legal Memo, in Vain," *N.Y. Times*, June 3, 2014.

17. Jed S. Rakoff, "The Financial Crisis: Why Have No High-Level Executives Been Prosecuted?" *N.Y. Rev. Books*, Jan. 9, 2014.

18. "Ex-Credit Suisse Offshore Banking Head Charged in U.S. Tax Case," *Bloomberg*, July 21, 2011; "Ex-Credit Suisse Banker Pleads Guilty to Fraud, Set to Aid Tax Inquiry," CNN.com, Mar. 11, 2014.

19. Grant McCool, "Siemens Executives Charged with Bribery," *Reuters*, Dec. 13, 2011; Edward Wyatt, "Former Siemens Executives Are Charged With Bribery," *N.Y. Times*, Dec. 13, 2011.

20. Sealed Complaint, United States v. Javier Martin-Artajo (S.D.N.Y. 2013); Letter of Immunity, United States v. Bruno Iksil (S.D.N.Y. 2013); Joe Coscarelli, "Who Is the London Whale? Meet JPMorgan's 'Humble' Trader Bruno Iksil," *N.Y. Mag.*, May 11, 2012; John Cassidy, "Will Anyone Hold Jamie Dimon Responsible for the London Whale Scandal?" *New Yorker*, Sept. 19, 2013.

21. Dan Fitzpatrick, Gregory Zuckerman, and Liz Rappaport, "J.P. Morgan's $2 Billion Blunder," *Wall St. J.*, May 11, 2012.

22. United States v. Cordoba-Hincapie, 825 F. Supp. 485 (E.D.N.Y. 1993); Joshua Dressler, *Understanding Criminal Law*, 6th ed. (2012); Wayne R. LaFave, *Criminal Law*, 5th ed. (1972).

23. Global-Tech Appliances, Inc. v. SEB S.A., 131 S. Ct. 2060, 2070-71 (2011); United States v. Goffer, 2013 WL 3285115 (2d Cir. 2013); United States v. Skilling, 554 F.3d 529, 548-549 (5th Cir. 2009); United States v. Giovannetti, 919 F.2d 1223, 1228 (7th Cir. 1990); United States v. Black, 530 F.3d 596, 604 (7th Cir. 2008).
24. UK Financial Services Act 2013; Andrew Hampton, "Positive Action, But Slow Progress," *Fin. Adviser*, Sept. 4, 2014.
25. Kenneth W. Simons, "Statistical Knowledge Deconstructed," 92 *B.U. L. Rev.* 1 (2012).
26. United States v. Park, 421 U.S. 658 (1975); Noël Wise, "Personal Liability Promotes Responsible Conduct: Extending The Responsible Corporate Officer Doctrine to Federal Civil Environmental Enforcement Cases," 21 *Stan. Envtl. L. J.* 283 (2002); Amy J. Sepinwal, "Responsible Shares And Shared Responsibility: In Defense of Responsible Corporate Officer Liability," 2014 *Colum. Bus. L. Rev.* 371 (2014).
27. In re Yamashita, 327 U.S. 1 (1946); Allan A. Ryan, *Yamashita's Ghost: War Crimes, MacArthur's Justice, and Command Accountability* (2014).
28. Jenny S. Martinez, "Understanding *Mens Rea* in Command Responsibility," 5 *J. Int'l Crim. Justice* 638 (2007).

5: The White Collar Beat

1. Samuel W. Buell, "Novel Criminal Fraud," 81 *N.Y.U. L. Rev.* 1971 (2006).
2. Fourth Superseding Indictment, United States v. Salemme et al. No. 94-10287 0 MLW (D. Mass.); United States v. Salemme, 91 F. Supp. 2d 141 (D. Mass. 1999), *rev'd*, United States v. Flemmi, 225 F.3d 78 (1st Cir. 2000).
3. *The Departed* (Warner Bros. 2006); *Whitey: United States of America v. James J. Bulger* (CNN Films 2014); *Black Mass* (Warner Bros. 2015); Kevin Cullen, *Whitey Bulger: America's Most Wanted Gangster and the Manhunt That Brought Him to Justice* (2013); Dick Lehr and Gerard O'Neill, *Black Mass: Whitey Bulger, the FBI, and a Devil's Deal* (2012); Dick Lehr and Gerard O'Neill, *Whitey: The Life of America's Most Notorious Mob Boss* (2013).
4. Samuel W. Buell, "Criminal Procedure Within the Firm," 59 *Stan. L. Rev.* 1613 (2007).
5. David Barstow and Alejandra Xanic von Bertrab, "The Bribery Aisle: How Walmart Used Payoffs To Get Its Way in Mexico," *N.Y. Times*, Dec. 18, 2012; David Barstow, "Vast Mexican Bribery Case Hushed Up by Wal-Mart After Top-Level Struggle," *N.Y. Times*, Apr. 21, 2012; Elizabeth A. Harris, "Walking Away, Quietly," *N.Y. Times*, June 5, 2014; Davis Voreacos and Renee Dudley, "Wal-Mart Says Bribe Probe Cost $439 Million in Two Years," *Bloomberg Bus.*, Mar. 26, 2014.
6. Kurt Eichenwald, *The Informant: A True Story* (2001).
7. Richard Milne, "Volkswagen Says 'Mindset' Tolerated Rule Breaking," *Fin. Times*, Dec. 10, 2015.
8. Anita Raghavan, *The Billionaire's Apprentice: The Rise of the Indian-American*

Elite and the Fall of the Galleon Hedge Fund (2013); Patrick Radden Keefe, "The Empire of Edge: How a doctor, a trader, and the billionaire Steven A. Cohen got entangled in a vast financial scandal," *New Yorker*, Oct. 13, 2014; George Packer, "A Dirty Business: New York City's top prosecutor takes on Wall Street crime," *New Yorker*, June 27, 2011.

9. Jennifer Arlen, "Corporate Criminal Liability: Theory and Evidence," in *Research Handbook on the Economics of Criminal Law*, ed. A. Harel and K. Hylton (2012); Jennifer Arlen and Reinier Kraakman, "Controlling Corporate Misconduct: An Analysis of Corporate Liability Regimes," 72 *N.Y.U. L. Rev.* 687, 695 (1997).

10. Lisa Kern Griffin, "Criminal Lying, Prosecutorial Power, and Social Meaning," 97 *Cal. L. Rev.* 1515 (2009); Julie R. O'Sullivan, "The Federal Criminal 'Code' Is a Disgrace: Obstruction Statutes As Case Study," 96 *J. Crim. L. & Criminology* 643 (2006).

11. United States v. Sun-Diamond Growers of California, 526 U.S. 398 (1999); New York Central & Hudson River R.R. v. United States (1909); United States v. Hilton Hotels Corp., 467 F.2d 1000 (9th Cir. 1972).

12. Gerald G. Ashdown, "Federalism, Federalization, and the Politics of Crime," 98 *W. Va. L. Rev.* 789 (1996); Sara Sun Beale, "Too Many and Yet Too Few: New Principles to Define the Proper Limits for Federal Criminal Jurisdiction," 46 *Hastings L. J.* 979 (1995); Kathleen F. Brickey, "Criminal Mischief: The Federalization of American Criminal Law," 46 *Hastings L. J.* 1135 (1995); Sanford Kadish, "The Folly of Overfederalization," 46 *Hastings L. J.* 1247 (1995); Susan R. Klein and Ingrid B. Grobey, "Debunking Claims of Over-Federalization of Criminal Law," 62 *Emory L. J.* 1 (2012); Rory K. Little, "Myths and Principles of Federalization," 46 *Hastings L. J.* 1029 (1995); William P. Marshall, "Federalization: A Critical Overview," 44 *DePaul L. Rev.* 719 (1995); Michael A. Simons, "Prosecutorial Discretion and Prosecution Guidelines: A Case Study in Controlling Federalization," 75 *N.Y.U. L. Rev.* 893 (2000).

13. United States v. Hubbell, 530 U.S. 27 (2000); Braswell v. United States, 487 U.S. 99 (1988); Fisher v. United States, 425 U.S. 391 (1976); Bellis v. United States, 417 U.S. 85 (1974); Wilson v. United States, 221 U.S. 361 (1911); Hale v. Henkel, 201 U.S. 43 (1906).

14. Fisher v. United States, 425 U.S. 391 (1976).

15. "The Criminalization of American Business," *The Economist*, Aug. 30, 2014; "A Mammoth Guilt Trip," *The Economist*, Aug. 30, 2014; Richard Epstein, "The Deferred Prosecution Racket," *Wall St. J.*, Nov. 28, 2006.

16. U.S. Dept. of Justice, *U.S. Attorneys' Manual*, § 9-28.

17. Jed S. Rakoff, "The Financial Crisis: Why Have No High-Level Executives Been Prosecuted?" *N.Y. Rev. Books*, Jan. 9, 2014.

18. Guilty Plea Agreement, United States v. BP Exploration & Production, Inc. (E.D. La 2012); Information for Seaman's Manslaughter, Clean Water Act, Migratory Bird Treaty Act and Obstruction of Congress, United States v. BP Exploration & Production, Inc. (E.D. La 2012); Corporate Integrity Agreement, United States v. GlaxoSmithKline (D. Mass. 2012).

19. James R. Copland, "Bring These Agreements Out of the Shadows," *N.Y. Times,* Nov. 11, 2014.

20. Kathleen M. Boozang and Simone Handler-Hutchinson, "'Monitoring' Corporate Corruption: DOJ's Use of Deferred Prosecution Agreements in Health Care," 35 *Am. J. L. & Med.* 89 (2009); Lawrence A. Cunningham, "Prosecutors in the Governance Business: Improving the Quality of Deferred Prosecution Agreements," 33 *Banking & Fin. Servcs. Policy Rpt.* 1 (2014); Brandon L. Garrett, "Rehabilitating Corporations," 66 *Fla. L. Rev. F.* 1 (2014); Jennifer H. Arlen, "Removing Prosecutors from the Boardroom: Deterring Crime without Prosecutor Interference in Corporate Governance," in *Prosecutors in the Boardroom: Using Criminal Law to Regulate Corporate Conduct,* ed. A. Barkow and R. Barkow (2011).

21. Peter Lattman, "Ashcroft Expects to Earn Huge Dollars as Corporate Monitor," *Wall St. J.,* Nov. 28, 2007; Carol Morello and Carol D. Leonnig, "Chris Christie's Long Record of Pushing Boundaries, Sparking Controversy," *Wash. Post,* Feb. 10, 2014; Philip Shenon, "Ashcroft Deal Brings Scrutiny in Justice Dept.," *N.Y. Times,* Jan. 10, 2008.

22. Paul Larkin, *Overcriminalization: The Legislative Side of the Problem,* Heritage Found., Dec. 13, 2011; Erik Luna, "Overextending the Criminal Law," 25 *Cato Policy Report* 6 (2003); Michael B. Mukasey and Paul Larkin, *The Perils of Overcriminalization,* Heritage Found., Feb. 12, 2015.

23. Upjohn Co. v. United States, 449 U.S. 383 (1981); Weatherford v. Bursey, 429 U.S. 545 (1977); United States v. Irwin, 612 F.2d 1182 (9th Cir. 1980); 8 *J. Wigmore, Evidence* § 2290 (McNaughton rev. 1961); John E. Sexton, "A Post-Upjohn Consideration of the Corporate Attorney-Client Privilege," 57 *N.Y.U. L. Rev.* 443 (1982).

24. United States v. Locascio, 6 F.3d 924 (1993).

25. United States v. Stein, 435 F.Supp.2d 330 (S.D.N.Y. 2006); Andrew Gilman, "The Attorney-Client Privilege Protection Act: The Prospect of Congressional Intervention into the Department of Justice's Corporate Charging Policy," 35 *Fordham Urb. L. J.* 1075 (2008); Liesa L. Richter, "The Power of Privilege and the Attorney-Client Privilege Protection Act: How Corporate America Has Everyone Excited About the Emperor's New Clothes," 43 *Wake Forest L. Rev.* 979 (2008).

26. Tanina Rostain and Milton C. Regan, Jr., *Confidence Games: Lawyers, Accountants, and the Tax Shelter Industry* (2014).

27. United States v. Stein, 541 F.3d 130 (2d Cir. 2008); United States v. Stein, 435 F. Supp. 2d 330 (S.D.N.Y. 2006); Lynnley Browning, "U.S. Improperly Pressured KPMG, Judge Rules," *N.Y. Times,* June 27, 2007; Peter Lattman, "Judge Kaplan's Stunning KPMG Ruling," *Wall St. J.,* June 27, 2006.

28. Wilson R. Huhn, "The State Action Doctrine and the Principle of Democratic Choice," 34 *Hofstra L. Rev.* 1379 (2006).

29. Kaley v. United States, 134 S.Ct. 1090 (2014); Caplin & Drysdale, Ctd. v. United States, 491 U.S. 617 (1989); Wheat v. United States, 486 U.S. 153

(1988); United States v. Stein, 541 F.3d 130 (2d Cir. 2008); United States v. Locascio, 6 F.3d 924 (2d Cir. 1993).

30. Del. Gen. Corp. Law § 145.

31. The judge relied on a case about police officers, *Garrity v. New Jersey*, 385 U.S. 493 (1967), that is not controlling because the officers in that case were public employees.

32. United States v. Poindexter, 951 F.2d 369 (D.C. Cir. 1991).

33. John F. Pfaff, "Escaping from the Standard Story," 26 *Fed. Sent. Rptr.* 265 (2014); John F. Pfaff, "The Micro and Macro Causes of Prison Growth," 28 *Ga. St. U. L. Rev.* 1239 (2012); John F. Pfaff, "The Empirics of Prison Growth: A Critical Review and Path Forward," 98 *J. Crim. L. & Criminology* 547 (2008); Leon Neyfakh, "Why Are So Many Americans in Prison?" *Slate*, Feb. 6, 2015.

34. E. Ann Carson, U.S. Dept. of Justice, *Prisoners in 2014*, www.bjs.gov. Of the 1,325,305 prisoners under state jurisdiction in 2014, 27,831 (2.1%) were charged with fraud offenses. Of the 192,663 prisoners under federal jurisdiction in 2014, 9,055 (4.7%) were charged with fraud offenses.

35. Matt Taibbi, "The $9 Billion Witness: Meet JPMorgan Chase's Worst Nightmare," *Rolling Stone*, Nov. 6, 2014; Matt Taibbi, "Another Batch of Wall Street Villains Freed on Technicality," *Rolling Stone*, Dec. 4, 2013; Matt Taibbi, "Gangster Bankers: Too Big to Jail," *Rolling Stone*, Feb. 14, 2013.

36. William C. Powers, Jr., et al., *Report of Investigation by the Special Investigative Committee of the Board of Directors of Enron Corp.* (2002); Landon Thomas, Jr., "Call It the Deal of a Lifetime," *N.Y. Times*, Jan. 8, 2006; Kathryn Kranhold and Alexei Barrionuevo, "Complaint Says Fastow, Kopper Worked Closely To Defraud Firm," *Wall St. J.*, Aug. 23, 2002.

37. Alice Goffman, *On the Run: Fugitive Life in an American City* (2014).

38. Darryl K. Brown, "Street Crime, Corporate Crime, and the Contingency of Criminal Liability," 149 *U. Pa. L. Rev.* 1295 (2001).

6: Criminal Defense That Pays

1. Brandon L. Garrett, *Convicting the Innocent: Where Criminal Prosecutions Go Wrong* (2011).

2. Brandon L. Garrett, "The Substance of False Confessions," 62 *Stan. L. Rev.* 1051 (2010).

3. Samuel W. Buell, "What Is Securities Fraud?" 61 *Duke L. J.* 511 (2011); Samuel W. Buell, "Reforming Punishment of Financial Reporting Fraud," 28 *Cardozo L. Rev.* 1611 (2007); Samuel W. Buell, "Novel Criminal Fraud," 81 *N.Y.U. L. Rev.* 1971 (2006); Dan M. Kahan, "Lenity and Federal Common Law Crime," 1994 *Sup. Ct. Rev.* 345.

4. Jeff Connaughton, *The Payoff: Why Wall Street Always Wins* (2012); Charles H. Ferguson, *Predator Nation: Corporate Criminals, Political Corruption, and the Hijacking of America* (2012); Jed S. Rakoff, "The Financial Crisis: Why Have No

High-Level Executives Been Prosecuted?" *N.Y. Rev. Books*, Jan. 9, 2014; Matt Taibbi, "Why Isn't Wall Street in Jail?" *Rolling Stone*, Feb. 16, 2011.

5. Rachel E. Barkow, "Prosecutorial Administration: Prosecutor Bias and the Department of Justice," 99 *Va. L. Rev.* 271 (2013); Rachel E. Barkow, "Separation of Powers and the Criminal Law," 58 *Stan. L. Rev.* 989 (2006); Ronald F. Wright, "Trial Distortion and the End of Innocence in Federal Criminal Justice," 154 *U. Pa. L. Rev.* 79 (2005).

6. Samuel W. Buell, "Criminal Procedure Within the Firm," 59 *Stan. L. Rev.* 1613 (2007).

7. Peter Lattman, "For White-Collar Defense Bar, It's Happening in Vegas," *N.Y. Times*, Mar. 7, 2013.

8. Charles D. Weisselberg and Su Li, "Big Law's Sixth Amendment: The Rise of Corporate White-Collar Practices in Large U.S. Law Firms," 53 *Ariz. L. Rev.* 1221 (2011).

9. U.S. Dept. of Justice, *Department's Sentencing Memorandum*, United States v. Siemens (D.D.C. Dec. 12, 2008); Brandon L. Garrett, *Too Big to Jail: How Prosecutors Compromise with Corporations* (2014).

10. David Barstow, "Vast Mexican Bribery Case Hushed Up by Wal-Mart After Top-Level Struggle," *N.Y. Times*, Apr. 21, 2012.

11. Tom Bawden, "BP's Legal Bill for the Gulf Oil Spill Disaster Soars to $1bn," *The Independent*, Feb. 5, 2014.

12. Guilty Plea Agreement, United States v. BP Exploration & Production, Inc. (E.D. La. 2012); Information for Seaman's Manslaughter, Clean Water Act, Migratory Bird Treaty Act, and Obstruction of Congress, United States v. BP Exploration & Production, Inc. (E.D. La 2012).

13. James B. Jacobs and Kerry T. Cooperman, *Breaking the Devil's Pact: The Struggle to Free the Teamsters From the Mob* (2011); James B. Jacobs, *Mobsters, Unions, and Feds: The Mafia and the American Labor Movement* (2006); John Kroger, *Convictions: A Prosecutor's Battles Against Mafia Killers, Drug Kingpins, and Enron Thieves* (2009).

14. Dick Lehr and Gerard O'Neill, *Black Mass: Whitey Bulger, the FBI, and a Devil's Deal* (2012).

15. Matt Taibbi, "Jon Corzine Is the Original George Zimmerman," *Rolling Stone*, Apr. 24, 2012; Matt Taibbi, "The S.E.C.'s Revolving Door: From Wall Street Lawyers to Wall Street Watchdogs," *Rolling Stone*, Mar. 30, 2011; Matt Taibbi, "Revolving Door: From Top Futures Regulator to Top Futures Lobbyist," *Rolling Stone*, Jan. 11, 2012.

16. Edward L. Glaeser, Daniel P. Kessler, and Anne Morrison Piehl, "What Do Prosecutors Maximize? An Analysis of Drug Offenders and Concurrent Jurisdiction," 2 *Am. Law and Econ. Rev.* 259 (2000).

17. United States v. Newman, 773 F.3d 438 (2d Cir. 2014); Matthew Goldstein, "U.S. Prosecutor To Drop Insider Trading Cases Against Seven," *N.Y. Times*, Oct. 22, 2015; David Ingram and Nate Raymond, "U.S. Abandons Insider Trading Case against SAC's Steinberg," *Reuters*, Oct. 22, 2015.

18. Patrick Radden Keefe, "The Empire of Edge: How a doctor, a trader, and the

billionaire Steven A. Cohen got entangled in a vast financial scandal," *New Yorker*, Oct. 13, 2014; George Packer, "A Dirty Business: New York City's top prosecutor takes on Wall Street crime," *New Yorker*, June 27, 2011.

19. Kaley v. United States, 134 S. Ct. 1090 (2014); United States v. Williams, 504 U.S. 36 (1992); Costello v. United States, 350 U.S. 359 (1956).

20. Gideon v. Wainwright, 372 U.S. 335 (1963).

21. Strickland v. Washington, 466 U.S. 668 (1984); Eve Brensike Primus, "Effective Trial Counsel After Martinez v. Ryan: Focusing on the Adequacy of State Procedures," 122 *Yale L. J.* 2604 (2013); Eve Brensike Primus, "The Illusory Right to Counsel," 37 *Ohio N. U. L. Rev.* 597 (2011); Eve Brensike Primus, "Structural Reform in Criminal Defense: Relocating Ineffective Assistance of Counsel Claims," 92 *Cornell L. Rev.* 679 (2007).

22. Brandon L. Garrett, *Convicting the Innocent: Where Criminal Prosecutions Go Wrong* (2011).

23. Christopher Palmeri, "The Sky-High Cost of Skilling's Defense," *Bloomberg Bus.*, Oct. 19, 2006.

24. Michael Rothfeld and Chad Bray, "Loss Raises Question over Defense Strategy," *Wall St. J.*, May 12, 2011.

25. Samuel W. Buell, "Criminal Procedure Within the Firm," 59 *Stan. L. Rev.* 1613 (2007).

26. William M. Bulkeley, "CA Sues Ex-CEO To Recoup Legal Fee," *Wall St. J.*, Nov. 17, 2006; Phred Dvorak and Serena Ng, "Check, Please: Reclaiming Pay from Executives Is Tough To Do," *Wall St. J.*, Nov. 20, 2006; Peter Lattman, "Stuck with a Defense Tab, and Awaiting a Payback," *N.Y. Times*, June 19, 2012; Gretchen Morgenson, "Legal Fees Mount at Fannie and Freddie," *N.Y. Times*, Feb. 22, 2012.

27. United States v. Stein, 435 F.Supp.2d 330 (S.D.N.Y. 2006).

28. Kaley v. United States, 134 S. Ct. 1090 (2014); Caplin and Drysdale, Ctd. v. United States, 491 U.S. 617 (1989).

29. Wheat v. United States, 486 U.S. 153 (1988); United States v. Locascio, 6 F.3d 924 (2d Cir. 1993).

30. Christopher Shortell, *Rights, Remedies, and the Impact of State Sovereign Immunity* (2008).

31. Michael Lewis, "Eight Things I Wish for Wall Street," *BloombergView*, Dec. 15, 2014.

32. Samuel W. Buell, "Is the White Collar Offender Privileged?" 63 *Duke L. J.* 823 (2014).

33. Between 2005 and 2014, the 0.59 percent acquittal rate in federal white collar cases (embezzlement, fraud, and forgery) was close to the 0.47 percent acquittal rate across all federal criminal prosecutions. Over the same period, 7.5 percent of federal white collar cases and 9.1 percent of all federal cases resulted in a disposition other than conviction. Admin. Office of the U.S. Courts, *Statistical Tables for the Federal Judiciary: June 30, 2006 through June 30, 2014*, tbl. D-4.

34. United States v. Newman, 773 F.3d 438 (2d Cir. 2014); United States v. Ferguson, 676 F.3d 260 (2d Cir. 2011).

35. Data from only 2002 to 2004 are publicly available. Bureau of Justice Statistics, U.S. Dept. of Justice, *Compendium of Federal Justice Statistics, 2002*, at 84 tbl. 6.4 (2004); Bureau of Justice Statistics, U.S. Dept. of Justice, *Compendium of Federal Justice Statistics, 2003*, at 88 tbl. 6.4 (2005); Bureau of Justice Statistics, U.S. Dept. of Justice, *Compendium of Federal Justice Statistics, 2004*, at 86 tbl. 6.4 (2006).

36. Mark Motivans, *Federal Justice Statistics, 2005—Statistical Tables*, tbl. 4.2, Bureau of Justice Statistics (Sept. 1, 2008); Mark Motivans, *Federal Justice Statistics, 2006—Statistical Tables*, tbl. 4.2, Bureau of Justice Statistics (May 1, 2009); Mark Motivans, *Federal Justice Statistics, 2007—Statistical Tables*, tbl. 4.2, Bureau of Justice Statistics (Aug. 31, 2010); Mark Motivans, *Federal Justice Statistics, 2008—Statistical Tables*, tbl. 4.2, Bureau of Justice Statistics (Nov. 3, 2010); Mark Motivans, *Federal Justice Statistics, 2009—Statistical Tables*, tbl. 4.2, Bureau of Justice Statistics (Dec. 21, 2011); Mark Motivans, *Federal Justice Statistics, 2010—Statistical Tables*, tbl. 4.2, Bureau of Justice Statistics (Dec. 30, 2013); Mark Motivans, *Federal Justice Statistics, 2011—Statistical Tables*, tbl. 4.2, Bureau of Justice Statistics (Jan. 22, 2015); Mark Motivans, *Federal Justice Statistics, 2012—Statistical Tables*, tbl. 4.2, Bureau of Justice Statistics (Jan. 22, 2015).

37. U.S. Sentencing Comm'n., *2014 Sourcebook of Federal Sentencing Statistics*, tbl.13; U.S. Sentencing Comm'n., *1996 Sourcebook of Federal Sentencing Statistics*, tbl.13.

38. United States v. Booker, 543 U.S. 220 (2005); Charles R. Breyer, "Keynote Address: Federal Sentencing Reform Ten Years After United States v. Booker," 66 *Hastings L. J.* 1527 (2015); Amy Farrell and Geoff Ward, "Examining District Variation in Sentencing in the Post-Booker Period," 23 *Fed. Sent. Rptr.* 318 (2011).

39. Ron Wright and Marc Miller, "The Black Box," 94 *Iowa L. Rev.* 125 (2008).

40. Gerard E. Lynch, "The Role of Criminal Law in Policing Corporate Misconduct," 60 *Law & Contemp. Probs.* 23 (1997).

41. United States v. Stevens, 771 F. Supp. 2d 556 (D. Md. 2011); Jennifer Smith, "Ex-Glaxo VP on 'The Criminalization of the Practice of Law,'" *Wall St. J.*, Oct. 1, 2012.

42. United States v. Goyal, 629 F.3d 912 (9th Cir. 2010).

7: Judges and Their Sentences

1. Anita Raghavan, *The Billionaire's Apprentice: The Rise of the Indian-American Elite and the Fall of the Galleon Hedge Fund* (2013); Patrick Radden Keefe, "The Empire of Edge: How a doctor, a trader, and the billionaire Steven A. Cohen got entangled in a vast financial scandal," *New Yorker*, Oct. 13, 2014; George Packer, "A Dirty Business: New York City's top prosecutor takes on Wall Street crime," *New Yorker*, June 27, 2011.

2. Sentencing Memorandum of Rajat K. Gupta, United States v. Gupta, No. S1-11-Cr 907 (S.D.N.Y. Oct. 17, 2012).

3. United States v. Gupta, 747 F.3d 111 (2d Cir. 2014).
4. William Alden and Azam Ahmed, "A Conflicted Jury Finds Rajat Gupta Guilty," *N.Y. Times*, June 15, 2014.
5. United States v. Gupta, 904 F. Supp.2d 348 (S.D.N.Y. 2012).
6. Jed S. Rakoff, "The Financial Crisis: Why Have No High-Level Executives Been Prosecuted?" *N.Y. Rev. Books*, Jan. 9, 2014.
7. Government's Sentencing Memorandum, United States v. Gupta, No. S1-11-Cr.-907, 2012 WL 5183715 (Oct. 17, 2012).
8. United States v. Tomko, 562 F.3d 558 (3d Cir. 2009) (en banc).
9. United States v. Gementera, 379 F.3d 596 (9th Cir. 2004).
10. Mitchell N. Berman, "Punishment and Justification," 118 *Ethics* 258 (2008).
11. Gary S. Becker, "Crime and Punishment: An Economic Approach," 76 *J. Pol. Econ.* 169 (1968).
12. Richard A. Posner, "An Economic Theory of the Criminal Law," 85 *Colum. L. Rev.* 1193 (1985); Richard A. Posner, "Optimal Sentences for White-Collar Criminals," 17 *Am. Crim. L. Rev.* 409 (1980).
13. Jennifer H. Arlen, "Should Defendants' Wealth Matter?" 21 *J. Legal Stud.* 413 (1992); David D. Friedman, "Reflections on Optimal Punishment, or: Should the Rich Pay Higher Fines," 3 *Rev. L. & Econ.* 185 (1981); A. Mitchell Polinsky, Steven Shavell, and Joe Pinsker, "A Note on Optimal Fines When Wealth Varies Among Individuals," 81 *Am. Econ. Rev.* 618 (1991); "Finland, Home of the $103,000 Speeding Ticket," *The Atlantic*, Mar. 12, 2015.
14. K. M. Carlsmith, J. M. Darley, and P. H. Robinson, "Why Do We Punish? Deterrence and Just Deserts as Motives for Punishment," 83 *J. Pers. & Social Psych.* 1 (2002); P. Robinson and J. M. Darley, "The Role of Deterrence in the Formulation of Criminal Law Rules," 91 *Geo. L. J.* 949 (2003).
15. John Mikhail, *Elements of Moral Cognition: Rawls' Linguistic Analogy and the Cognitive Science of Moral and Legal Judgment* (2011); Michael Moore, *Placing Blame: A General Theory of the Criminal Law* (1997); Paul H. Robinson, *Intuitions of Justice and the Utility of Desert* (2013).
16. Midgett v. Arkansas, 729 S.W. 2d 410 (Ark. 1987); State v. Forrest, 362 S.E. 2d 252 (N.C. 1987).
17. *Why People Pay Taxes: Tax Compliance and Enforcement*, ed. Joel Slemrod (1992); Dan M. Kahan, "The Logic of Reciprocity: Trust, Collective Action, and Law," 102 *Mich. L. Rev.* 71 (2003).
18. Kathleen DeLaney Thomas, "The Psychic Cost of Tax Evasion," 56 *B.C. L. Rev.* 617 (2015); Leandra Lederman, "The Interplay Between Norms and Enforcement in Tax Compliance," 64 *Ohio St. L. J.* 1453 (2003); Richard C. Stark, "A Principled Approach to Collection and Accuracy-Related Penalties," 91 *Tax Notes* 115 (2001).
19. United States v. Stewart, 433 F.3d 273 (2d Cir. 2006).
20. Kate Stith and A. José Cabranes, *Fear of Judging: The Sentencing Guidelines in the Federal Courts* (1998); Sandor Frankel, "The Sentencing Morass, and a Suggestion for Reform," 3 *Crim. L. Bull.* 365 (1967); Susan R. Klein and Jordan M.

Steiker, "The Search for Equality in Criminal Sentencing," 2002 *Sup. Ct. Rev.* 223; Ilene H. Nagel, "Structuring Sentencing Discretion: The New Federal Sentencing Guidelines," 80 *J. Crim. L. & Criminology* 883 (1990).

21. Marvin Frankel, *Criminal Sentences: Law Without Order* (1973); Stephen Breyer, "The Federal Sentencing Guidelines and the Key Compromises Upon Which They Rest," 17 *Hofstra L. Rev.* 1 (1988).

22. Stanton Wheeler et al., *Sitting in Judgment: The Sentencing of White-Collar Criminals* (1988); Casey C. Kannenberg, "From Booker to Gall: The Evolution of the Reasonableness Doctrine As Applied to White-Collar Criminals and Sentencing Variances," 34 *J. Corp. L.* 349 (2008); Daniel Richman, "Federal White Collar Sentencing in the United States: A Work in Progress," 76 *Law & Contemp. Probs.* (2013); Stanton Wheeler et al., "Sentencing the White Collar Offender: Rhetoric and Reality," 47 *Am. Soc. Rev.* 641 (1982).

23. Kate Stith and Steve Y. Koh, "The Politics of Sentencing Reform: The Legislative History of the Federal Sentencing Guidelines," 28 *Wake Forest L. Rev.* 223 (1993); Kate Stith, "The Arc of the Pendulum: Judges, Prosecutors, and the Exercise of Discretion," 117 *Yale L. J.* 1420 (2008).

24. Frank O. Bowman III, "The Failure of the Federal Sentencing Guidelines: A Structural Analysis," 105 *Colum. L. Rev.* 1315 (2005); Gerald W. Heaney, "The Reality of Sentencing Guidelines: No End to Disparity," 28 *Am. Crim. L. Rev.* 161 (1991); Paul J. Hofer, Kevin R. Blackwell, and Barry Rubach, "The Effect of the Federal Sentencing Guidelines on Inter-Judge Sentencing Disparity," 90 *J. Crim. L. & Criminology* 239 (1999); A. Abigail Payne, "Does Inter-Judge Disparity Really Matter? An Analysis of the Effects of Sentencing Reforms in Three Federal District Courts," 17 *Int'l Rev. L. & Econ.* 337 (1997)

25. Samuel W. Buell, "Is the White Collar Offender Privileged?" 63 *Duke L. J.* 823 (2014).

26. Frank O. Bowman, "Pour Encourager les Autres? The Curious History and Distressing Implications of the Criminal Provisions of the Sarbanes-Oxley Act and the Sentencing Guidelines Amendments That Followed," 1 *Ohio St. J. Crim. L.* 373 (2004); Daniel Richman, "Federal White Collar Sentencing in the United States: A Work in Progress," 76 *Law & Contemp. Probs.* 53 (2013).

27. United States v. Olis, 429 F.3d 540 (5th Cir. 2005); Adam Liptak, "Sentencing Decision's Reach Is Far and Wide," *N.Y. Times*, June 27, 2004; Simon Romero, "Revision of 24-Year Prison Term Ordered in Accounting Fraud," *N.Y. Times*, Nov. 2, 2005; Simon Romero, "Ex-Executive of Dynegy Is Sentenced to 24 Years," *N.Y. Times*, Mar. 26, 2004.

28. Samuel W. Buell, "Reforming Punishment of Financial Reporting Fraud," 28 *Cardozo L. Rev.* 1611 (2007).

29. Jack B. Weinstein, "A Trial Judge's Second Impression of the Federal Sentencing Guidelines," 66 *S. Cal. L. Rev.* 357, 358–59 (1992); Jack B. Weinstein, "A Trial Judge's First Impression of the Sentencing Guidelines," 52 *Alb. L. Rev.* 1 (1988); Joseph B. Treaster, "2 Judges Decline Drug Cases, Protesting Sentencing Rules," *N.Y. Times*, Apr. 17, 1993.

30. Kate Stith, Marin Levy, and José A. Cabranes, "The Cost of Judging Judges by the Numbers," 28 *Yale Law and Policy Rev.* 313 (2010).

31. United States v. Booker, 543 U.S. 220 (2005); Blakely v. Washington, 542 U.S. 296 (2004); Apprendi v. New Jersey, 530 U.S. 466 (2000).

32. Samuel W. Buell, "What Is Securities Fraud?" 61 *Duke L. J.* 511 (2011).

33. United States v. Adelson, 441 F. Supp.2d 506 (S.D.N.Y. 2006).

34. United States v. Ovid, 2012 WL 2087084 (E.D.N.Y. June 8, 2012).

35. U.S. Sentencing Comm'n., *Amendments to the Sentencing Guidelines for United States Courts, Economic Crimes* (Apr. 30, 2015), www.ussc.gov.

36. James E. Felman, "A Report on Behalf of the American Bar Association Task Force on the Reform of Federal Sentencing for Economic Crimes," 28 *WTR Crim. Just.* 31 (2014).

37. James Q. Whitman, *Harsh Justice: Criminal Punishment and the Widening Divide Between America and Europe* (2003).

38. Michelle Alexander, *The New Jim Crow: Mass Incarceration in the Age of Color-blindness* (2010); David Garland, *The Culture of Control: Crime and Social Order in Contemporary Society* (2001); Marie Gottschalk, *The Prison and the Gallows: The Politics of Mass Incarceration in America* (2006); Bernard E. Harcourt, *The Illusion of Free Markets: Punishment and the Myth of Natural Order* (2011); Nicola Lacey, *The Prisoners' Dilemma: Political Economy and Punishment in Contemporary Democracies* (2008); Jonathan Simon, *Governing Through Crime: How the War on Crime Transformed American Democracy and Created a Culture of Fear* (2007); William J. Stuntz, *The Collapse of American Criminal Justice* (2011); Michael Tonry, *Thinking About Crime: Sense and Sensibility in American Penal Culture* (2004); Bruce Western, *Punishment and Inequality in America* (2006); Franklin E. Zimring and Gordon Hawkins, *The Scale of Imprisonment* (1991).

8: Washington and Wall Street

1. *Enron Fast Facts*, CNN.com, Apr. 26, 2015.

2. Mark Follman, "The U.S. Attorneys Scandal Gets Dirty," *Salon*, Apr. 19, 2007; Adam Zagorin, "Why Were These U.S. Attorneys Fired?" *Time*, Mar. 7, 2007.

3. Matt Taibbi, *The Divide: American Injustice in the Age of the Wealth Gap* (2014); Jeff Connaughton, *The Payoff: Why Wall Street Always Wins* (2012); Editorial, "Going Soft on Corporate Crime," *N.Y. Times*, Apr. 10, 2008; Government Accountability Institute, *Justice Inaction: The Department of Justice's Unprecedented Failure to Prosecute Big Finance*, www.g-a-i.org; Jed S. Rakoff, "The Financial Crisis: Why Have No High-Level Executives Been Prosecuted?" *N.Y. Rev. Books*, Jan. 9, 2014; "The Untouchables" (*Frontline*, broadcast Jan. 22, 2013); "Prosecuting Wall Street" (*60 Minutes*, broadcast Dec. 4, 2011).

4. Ted Kaufman, "Lopsided Approach to Wall Street Fraud Undermines the Law," *N.Y. Times*, May 8, 2014; Ted Kaufman, "Wall Street Prosecutions Never Made a Priority" (*Frontline*, broadcast Jan. 22, 2013).

5. Committee on Capital Markets Regulation, *The Competitive Position of the U.S. Public Equity Markets* (Dec. 4, 2007); Committee on Capital Markets Regulation, *Interim Report of the Committee on Capital Markets Regulation* (Nov. 30, 2006); H. N. Butler and L. E. Ribstein, *The Sarbanes–Oxley Debacle: How to Fix It and What We've Learned* (2006); P. Hostak, E. Karaoglu, T. Lys, and G. Yang, "An Examination of the Impact of the Sarbanes-Oxley Act on the Attractiveness of US Capital Markets for Foreign Firms," 18 *Rev. of Acct. Stud.* 522 (2009); Roberta Romano, "The Sarbanes–Oxley Act and the Making of Quack Corporate Governance," 114 *Yale L. J.* 1521 (2005); Hal S. Scott, "What is the United States Doing About the Competitiveness of its Capital Markets?" 22 *J. Int'l Banking Law & Reg.* 487 (2007).

6. Kitty Calavita and Henry N. Pontell, "The State and White Collar Crime: Saving the Savings and Loans," 28 *Law and Society Rev.* 297 (1994).

7. Brandon L. Garrett, "The Corporate Criminal as Scapegoat," 101 *Va. L. Rev.* 1789 (2015).

8. Lawrence A. Cunningham, "The Sarbanes-Oxley Yawn: Heavy Rhetoric, Light Reform (And It Just Might Work)," 35 *Conn. L. Rev.* 915 (2003); John M. Holcomb, "Corporate Governance: Sarbanes-Oxley Act, Related Legal Issues, and Global Comparisons," 32 *Denv. J. Int'l L. & Pol'y* 175 (2004).

9. *Mark to Market Accounting Standards: A Study by the SEC*, ed. Brian N. Brinker (2009).

10. William W. Bratton, "Enron, Sarbanes-Oxley and Accounting: Rules Versus Principles Versus Rents," 48 *Vill. L. Rev.* 1023, 1040 (2003); William W. Bratton and Adam J. Levitin, "A Transactional Genealogy of Scandal: From Michael Milken to Enron to Goldman Sachs," 86 *S. Cal. L. Rev.* 783 (2013); Statement of Financial Accounting Standards No. 140, FAS 140 (Sept. 2000).

11. Third Interim Report of Neal Batson, Court-Appointed Examiner, *In re* Enron Corp, No. 01-16034 (Bankr. S.D.N.Y. 2003).

12. Frank Partnoy, *Infectious Greed: How Deceit and Risk Corrupted the Financial Markets* (2009).

13. Andrew Ross Sorkin, *Too Big to Fail: The Inside Story of How Wall Street and Washington Fought to Save the Financial System—and Themselves* (2009); Adam J. Levitin, "The Politics of Financial Regulation and the Regulation of Financial Politics: A Review Essay," 127 *Harv. L. Rev.* 1991 (2014); Charles W. Calomris and Allan H. Meltzer, "How Dodd-Frank Doubles Down on 'Too Big to Fail,'" *Wall St. J.*, Feb. 12, 2014; Charles W. Murdock, "The Dodd-Frank Wall Street Reform and Consumer Protection Act: What Caused the Financial Crisis and Will Dodd-Frank Prevent Future Crises?" 64 *SMU L. Rev.* 1243 (2011); Gary H. Stern, "Too-Big-to-Fail and the Dodd-Frank Legislation," 35 *Hamline L. Rev.* 339 (2012); Arthur E. Wilmarth, Jr., "The Dodd-Frank Act: A Flawed and Inadequate Response to the Too-Big-to-Fail Problem," 89 *Or. L. Rev.* 951 (2011).

14. Jeb Hansarling, "After Five years, Dodd-Frank Is a Failure," *Wall St. J.*, July 19, 2015; Norbert J. Michel and Diane Katz, *Dodd-Frank an Unfinished Failure*, Heritage Found. (July 2014).

15. David Garland, *The Culture of Control: Crime and Social Order in Contemporary Society* (2001); Jonathan Simon, *Governing Through Crime: How the War on Crime Transformed American Democracy and Created a Culture of Fear* (2007); William J. Stuntz, *The Collapse of American Criminal Justice* (2011); James Q. Whitman, *Harsh Justice: Criminal Punishment and the Widening Divide Between America and Europe* (2003).

16. Nathan James, *The Federal Prison Population Buildup: Overview, Policy Changes, Issues, and Options* (Cong. Research Serv. R42937 2014).

17. Syracuse University, Transaction Records Access Clearinghouse, www.trac.syr.edu.

18. Vic Khanna, "Corporate Crime Legislation: A Political Economy Analysis," 82 *Wash. U. L. Q.* 95 (2004).

19. Julie Rose O'Sullivan, "Does DOJ's Privilege Waiver Policy Threaten the Rationales Underlying the Attorney-Client Privilege and Work Product Doctrine? A Preliminary 'No,'" 45 *Am. Crim. L. Rev.* 1237 (2008).

20. Lawrence Lessig, *Republic, Lost: How Money Corrupts Congress—and a Plan to Stop It* (2012); Zephyr Teachout, *Corruption in America: From Benjamin Franklin's Snuff Box to Citizens United* (2014).

21. Citizens United v. Federal Election Comm'n., 558 U.S. 310 (2010); Burwell v. Hobby Lobby, 134 S.Ct. 2751 (2014); Sorrell v. IMS Health Inc., 131 S.Ct. 2653 (2011); United States v. Caronia, 703 F.3d 149 (2d Cir. 2012).

22. Hale v. Henkel, 201 U.S. 43 (1906).

23. Adolf A. Berle and Gardiner Means, *The Modern Corporation and Private Property* (1932).

24. Louis Brandeis, *Other People's Money and How the Bankers Use It* (1914).

25. John C. Coffee, Jr., *Gatekeepers: The Professions and Corporate Governance* (2006); John C. Coffee, Jr., "What Caused Enron? A Capsule Social and Economic History of the 1990s," 89 *Cornell L. Rev.* 269 (2004).

26. John Akser, Joan Farre-Mensa, and Alexander Ljungqvist, "Corporate Investment and Stock Market Listing: A Puzzle?" 28 *Rev. Fin. Studies* 342 (2015).

INDEX